A Normal Life

A Sister's Odyssey
Through Brain Injury

A Normal Life

A Sister's Odyssey
Through Brain Injury

By

Lyrysa Smith

First Edition – 2013

Cover design by Susanne Murtha, http://www.aproposds.com.
Book interior design by CreateSpace Project Team 2.

Back cover photos:
(upper left) Molly, 6, and me, 4, in our backyard in Phoenix, AZ.
(upper right) Our annual portrait, clockwise from top,
me, 11, Molly, 13, Mary K., 5, and Sara, 9.
(lower left) Molly visiting me at my house in Copake, NY,
around 1994, ages 34 and 36. She would stop by on her
way to Houghton Mifflin headquarters in Boston.

To order additional copies of this book, please go to:
https://www.createspace.com/4227185

or http://www.lyrysasmith.com.

ISBN: 1483996875
ISBN 13: 9781483996875

Acknowledgements

I am deeply thankful to my wonderful friends for their ongoing support and encouragement.

I am indebted to my excellent editor, Marc Jaffe of Editorial Direction, Inc., for his careful work, keen eye, and enthusiasm—onward and upward!

And I am especially grateful to my amazing family for their sharing, patience, and understanding, and for believing in me and this project. Thank you.

Author Notes

This narrative was compiled from my journal and calendar notes and descriptions, and from my own recollections and memories.

It was greatly enhanced and made more complete through conversations with my family and discussions with friends and others connected to the story who generously offered their thoughts and memories.
In particular, my family's voices are heard and represented throughout this book.

I was also helped through interviews with doctors, therapists, nurses, scientists, experts, acquaintances, and many others along the way.
Each contact helped to bring the pieces together.

This book is my telling of this story, my version of the truth as I know it.

For my family – for all of your sharing and discovery with me and for believing.

For Mom – You make all things possible— opportunities, dreams, life itself—and that's the gift you give to your daughters and the world. With endless gratitude and all my love.

And for Molly – for inspiration and reminding me how to see life.

Table of Contents

❀❀

O n e

MOLLY Smith Weber sits at a table with a hammer, a hairbrush, and an orange set in a line before her. An occupational therapist seated across from her says, "Molly, which thing would you use to brush your hair?"

Molly's eyes drop to the items on the table, scanning them urgently as if one would explode if she didn't stop it. Straightening her back and with a sudden look of resolve, she scoops up the hammer. "This one?"

On that day in February 1995, my only big sister was almost unrecognizable to me. Thirty-seven years old, with degrees from Yale and Stanford, an extraordinary athlete with a six-figure salary as a regional vice president with publishing company Houghton Mifflin, Molly gently laid the hammer down as if it were a wounded song bird. Her eyes floated away from the table top in soft retreat.

I sat nearby, gripping the sides of my chair and trying to calm the queasy feeling rising inside. It was the first time I dared to wonder if I was right to have wanted so badly for Molly to live. It would not be the last.

After awakening from nine days in a coma, Molly had difficulty identifying objects. She didn't know her right hand from her left—but she could read and type. It took a team of experts and weeks of therapy before she learned to swallow, and to walk again. And yet, she would crack jokes and could recall the name of every kid in her third grade class and every lyric to any Elton John song. She knew her family members, but didn't know where she lived or what this place called ICU was, or where her husband Walt was, no matter how many times we told her.

Molly's severe brain injury was a result of carbon monoxide poisoning. Her husband, Walt Weber, died as he lay next to her in their hotel bed.

The last thing Molly remembered was having her hair cut. About three weeks later, once she could speak again and was able to ask questions, my mom, my dad, my two younger sisters, her best friend, and I slowly started teaching her the rest. At least as much as we had been able to piece together.

We learned that Molly got a short, layered cut that first Friday in February. Her brown hair glimmered with honey highlights and she made sure it always looked great. It also grew fast, which suited her ever-shifting moods. Cropped one day, but in a few months it could drape down her back.

Only 5 ft. 6 in. tall, Molly was slim and very fit, and many underestimated her strength. With her angular face, long legs, and year-round tan, Molly had more of my father's build and dark coloring than I did, and she made the most of it. She wore beautiful Ann Taylor outfits to work, and usually zipped around town on weekends in shorts or flirty skirts.

But despite her winning appearance, it was her energy that got to people first. It radiated from her confident, sometimes mischievous, smile and flashed from her striking blue eyes. Teasing eyes when she joked around with friends, sexy eyes when she snuggled with Walt. Yet, her immediate warmth was laced with toughness and pride. She was intense, competitive, and powerful and could catch you off guard—a boisterous laugh, then a fierce sharpness. Sometimes a stinging remark, sometimes an indifferent silence. I had been stunned and baffled many times in 30-plus years by her changeability—and it could really hurt.

Molly was all sunny anticipation, however, with Cindy her hairdresser that day. She said she was psyched to get to the mountains with Walt that evening to ski for the weekend. She had also told a few publishing colleagues earlier in the day that she was excited about her ski weekend and eager to get going.

Cindy remembered teasing Molly about how she and Walt could water ski in the morning and snow ski in the afternoon—thanks to living in north L.A. and being experts on both surfaces. Molly laughed and said Walt actually had gone water skiing that morning and that he had wanted to leave earlier—he had the whole day off because he'd worked the weekend before, but she'd said, "No way!" She had some work she needed to do and she wasn't giving up her 3 o'clock at the hair salon. Appointments with Cindy were hard to get.

On that Friday morning, Walt had called the North Village Inn, a family-owned lodge in Mammoth Lakes, to ask if they had a room available for the weekend. He knew Molly didn't like the Inn too much, she preferred fancier places. But they loved the snowy slopes of the Sierras in

Mammoth County, and other places were already booked. Walt was told that the only room left had a broken heater, but it would be repaired before they arrived that night.

Molly and Walt checked in around 11:30 p.m. and paid for two nights with a credit card. The desk clerk remembered they said they were tired from the workweek and the five-hour drive, and remarked how nice they were.

Nerves were short, however. The people next door heard Molly griping at Walt about the small, basic room through its thin walls. But after the few minutes it took for them to brush their teeth and collapse into bed, the room fell quiet.

Molly and Walt didn't respond to the 7 o'clock wake-up call on Saturday morning. The desk clerk thought maybe they'd decided to sleep in. They didn't respond to the 7 o'clock wake-up call on Sunday morning either, and they didn't check out by noon.

After knocking repeatedly, a maid discovered that their door was chained from the inside. She went around to the side of the building and peered in the window through a gap in the curtains. She saw a man and a woman lying in the bed, but they looked strange—uncomfortable, with distorted faces. She ran to the office.

The firemen cut the door chain to get into the room and quickly discovered that the dead man was an FBI agent. In a matter of hours, the FBI launched a full-scale investigation into the death of their 11-year veteran, Walt Weber, age 42. With a slow, baseline pulse, only Molly was immediately removed from the room.

The fire department chief scooped her up in her pretty nightie and went outside into the cold mountain air. Firemen are well acquainted with carbon monoxide poisoning, and the chief knew what she needed.

He set her on the snowy ground, kept his arm behind her shoulders and prayed she'd take another breath. Suddenly, she stirred and looked up at him with total dismay and terror. Her short breaths were labored and coarse. He explained who he was and that he was trying to help her, and said if she understood him to blink her eyes. Molly stared hard at him, gave him a deliberate blink and closed her eyes.

Molly was airlifted from Mammoth Hospital to Loma Linda University Medical Center in L.A. even though she was in a coma, on a ventilator, had no brain activity, and her heart, lungs, and other organs were barely functioning, if at all. The nurse on the flight knew Mammoth had a contract with Loma Linda for hyperbaric oxygen treatments for carbon monoxide victims, but what good would that do? My sister had been declared clinically brain dead by the attending physician at Mammoth Hospital. The nurse wondered why they were even bothering to transport her. Maybe, she figured, because her organs had been evaluated for transplant. This initial assessment was a standard procedure for any patient like Molly with healthy organs.

Sunday night of that same weekend, my mother, father, two younger sisters and I, scattered all over the country, got either a phone call or two FBI agents in dark suits at the door. Each of us heard the deeply dreaded words that, like most folks, we had only ever reluctantly speculated about.

There's been an accident. A loved one is dead. A loved one is barely alive. Get on a plane. Now.

We did. It was one of the few clear-headed, decisive, and rational things we would do for some time. We tore through airports, jobs, bank accounts, and relationships to be there for what we thought might be days, and ended up being months. Now, all these years later, we are, in a way, still there, still wrapped up in Molly and continuing to feel the strain from an injury that occurred so long ago.

Back then, as I waited to board the plane at Albany International, about 60 miles north of my home in Columbia County, New York, my mind clamored to recall snippets of the last time I had been with Molly, just a few weeks earlier. The two of us, Walt, and his 14-year old daughter, Kristen, from his first marriage, were together in Colorado visiting my mom for the holidays. Lacking any type of sled, we used plastic shower curtains to toboggan down an irresistible hill.

I recalled playing in the Arizona desert when Molly and I were little. She taught me how to catch lizards in a coffee can. Before we'd let them go, we'd lay them on our bare arms and feel the tickle of their odd, shuffling feet. I remembered taking turns on my mom's sewing machine as we made our own peasant-style blouses when we were teenagers. I thought about us pogo punk dancing to Joe Jackson and The Ramones at Stanford when I returned from my junior year in Europe and she was working on her master's degree. I thought about the long conversations and laughter shared over frozen margaritas on Columbus Avenue when I lived in New York City and she'd come to town on business. We'd walk all the way uptown, arm in arm, just like women I'd seen in Madrid.

Now, I waited to get on a plane and fly out of New York—fast. I wanted to be with my big sister before it was too late.

The doctor who usually covered the Sunday night shift at the Intensive Care Unit at Loma Linda was on vacation. Dr. Takkin Lo, head of the ICU and medical director of hyperbaric oxygen, was filling in.

He surveyed the airlifted comatose adult female on the stretcher attached to the full array of life support equipment. Nice face. Trim. Defined biceps. Muscled legs. There was a pressure bruise on her thigh where her blood had pooled over the past two days, but there wasn't as much as a scratch on her body.

Calling her "very buff," Dr. Lo announced that he would not declare her clinically dead yet and sign off on the organ transplants. A neurologist at Loma Linda had already signed the organ donation form. Two physician signatures are required to declare a patient brain dead and activate the organ donation process.

Instead, Dr. Lo wanted to put this patient through treatment in his hyperbaric oxygen chamber, just to see what would happen. He told his bewildered staff, "Why not? We have nothing to lose."

Takkin Lo was born in Hong Kong and raised in Bangkok, Thailand, from the age of six when his father became the manager of a Sears & Roebuck store in the capital. Takkin had been a mischievous and intelligent boy. He had collected thousands of crickets in crates to hustle money from the street gamblers by hosting cricket fights, and he spoke three languages by the time he was 10. His parents, devout Buddhists who spoke Cantonese, enrolled him in a Seventh-day Adventist (SDA) school filled with students from around the world. His parents knew Takkin, who learned Thai from his friends, would receive an excellent education and learn English.

Takkin became very religious and was being groomed to become an SDA minister, but instead decided to put his leadership skills and passion for interacting with people to use as a doctor. He earned his undergraduate, master's, and finally, his medical degree from Loma Linda, the only SDA medical school in the United States. He specialized in hematology and internal medicine through his residency.

Dr. Lo, the same age as his new patient, was already one of the nation's leading researchers on hyperbaric oxygen and was vigorously investigating new uses for the technology, including how it might promote the healing of internal injuries.

He recalls that despite Molly's condition, or maybe because of it, he had a strong gut feeling that she could survive. Dr. Lo was never uncomfortable blending his instincts with his medical and scientific knowledge. He even encouraged his students to do the same.

Tall and agile, Dr. Lo moves like an orchestra conductor, in swift, precise gestures. He always uses both hands to explain the potential of hyperbaric oxygen. His enthusiasm for it pours from him like a Mozart symphony.

He explained: The air we breathe is about 21 percent oxygen. Hyperbaric oxygen treatment provides 100 percent oxygen in a pressurized chamber, which greatly increases the amount of oxygen delivered to body tissues by the blood. Molly's first three-hour treatment reached a pressure that was like being 70 feet underwater; it would force out any carbon monoxide still clinging to her red blood cells and push oxygen into her hemoglobin. That's all a typical oxygen-deprived victim would need: a deep-sea diver with the bends, a firefighter suffering from excess smoke inhalation, a homeowner with a leaky gas clothes dryer who sidesteps becoming a carbon monoxide casualty.

Hyperbaric oxygen chambers have been in use since the 1930s, and have been recommended to treat poisoning by carbon monoxide, or CO, since the 1960s, along with about a dozen other accepted, standard uses. However, Dr. Lo was among the first to experiment with hyperbaric oxygen, or HBO, as it is frequently called, for healing other types of injuries, such as diabetic foot ulcers and deep tissue lacerations. It was groundbreaking work, but also unconventional and sometimes controversial. There were no prospective studies or scientific research to back him up. But he was encouraging such studies and helping to organize them, while also documenting and reporting his own anecdotal cases.

Several hours after the first, Dr. Lo gave Molly a second HBO treatment, saturating her body's tissues with pure oxygen. This round would start to eliminate toxic substances created by over-stimulated white blood cells during her long exposure to carbon monoxide, and begin to create new vessel and capillary networks so more red blood cells could get into her brain and the rest of her body. HBO helps the healing process by stimulating blood vessel growth and enhancing the immune system's ability to fight infection.

Almost imperceptibly, Molly's pulse pumped a little stronger, but her brain remained silent.

Dr. Lo was intrigued. Through his careful observations that night, like a one-sided conversation, he learned a lot about who his new patient was. He had treated hundreds of people with CO poisoning, but no one like Molly. Usually people with that much CO in their blood had rigged gas ovens or car tailpipes to deliver plenty of CO to die from. And, so far, in Dr. Lo's experience, they had.

But Molly was a rarity. Dr. Lo couldn't compare her to anyone. She was alive despite all the CO in her body, and she was fighting to live.

A perfect opportunity for his research had landed from the heavens at the hospital that night. As her attending physician, he was to decide her program of care, track her progress, and look for any signs of improvement or, finally, declare she was clinically brain dead. She was fair game for the organ harvesters, but he told them: Not this donor, not tonight. Not yet.

My mother, Sally Shuler, arrived at the hospital from Denver in the pre-dawn hours of Monday, and one by one my other family members and I made our way to Molly. When I first saw her that day, I fainted into my mother's arms.

I'd run out of the elevator and into Molly's room. I stood at the foot of her bed and tried to digest the scene. Mom in a chair near Molly. My beautiful, older sister suspended, clinging. Mom rose to greet me. "Hey, Honey..." Mom's voice faded, my ears rang loudly, I passed out.

A few minutes later I stood at Molly's bedside again. I could see that she was both dead and alive. Her body seemed to possess exaggerated gravity—too dense, too laden, too still. Her chest did not rise and fall. Her skin was chalky. Her eyebrows strained toward the center of her forehead as though she was trying to think of something she once knew. With the exception of her heart—a beep sound at each peak on a small monitor screen near her bed—she wasn't functioning on her own. She had assistance from what seemed to be dozens of machines, clicking and churning away. But somewhere in the tangle of wires, tubes and emotions, Molly was there. I could feel her pull.

With my mother's wholehearted agreement, Dr. Lo would keep up his aggressive schedule of HBO treatments. Molly would spend six to nine hours a day, in two or three separate sessions, inside an HBO chamber, a long, clear acrylic cylinder. By day three, I thought Dr. Lo had a remarkably clear picture of Molly. He told a nurse to write "highly motivated" in her chart. My mom had told him about her fine education, her successful career, her loving relationships, her sense of humor. Dr. Lo, an avid skier himself, knew that if she skied the tough terrain at Mammoth Lakes, she was an ardent and powerful athlete. He recognized Molly as stubborn, smart, and strong; an uncommon fighter. He told my mom he, too, was tenacious; he didn't give up easily.

Dr. Lo believed HBO would revitalize Molly's organs. He hoped it would spark the signal-sending, information-receiving connector part of nerve cells—or dendrites—in her brain. He wanted to see how far she might go. When he spoke about it, his delicate Asian eyes, set on the edges of his face, would glint his excitement.

In a hospital gown, lying inside the HBO enclosure, her head on a white pillow, Molly looked like Sleeping Beauty—despite the respirator tube in her mouth. We all took turns accompanying her to her HBO treatments. I couldn't hold her limp hand, but via microphone and speaker, I could talk to her.

"Hey, Smith, you OK in there?" We've called each other "Smith" since we were teenagers. "You look beautiful, really."

The HBO technician offered a small smile and finished checking the dials.

As the pressure slowly increased inside the sealed tube, Molly's face would become flushed and she'd breathe rapidly, as if she were running a race. It shocked me the first couple of times. She was in a coma, but looked like she was sprinting, hard.

After a couple days of HBO treatments and high doses of medicines, Molly's kidney infection, pneumonia, and a blood clot in her calf acquired during the accident were all a little better. Each day her heart beat more steadily, too. But it was Molly's lack of brain activity on EEG tests that distressed Dr. Lo. His conviction about what was possible with HBO kept him persistent, even with several neurologists telling him Molly had no chance of recovery and he'd done enough already.

"But I reminded them that they are consulting on the patient and I'm her primary doctor, so I make the decisions," Dr. Lo said.

My family and I, and Molly's best friend, were all staying in a nearby hotel and, from the beginning, were allowed, without ever formally asking permission, to be with Molly almost around the clock. We arranged shifts and didn't leave her alone, except from about midnight to 6 a.m. This would let her brain sleep, we reasoned. Being in a coma, her body seemed asleep all the time. But per Dr. Lo's directive, we were to try to stimulate her brain constantly in every way we could—talking, questions, reading aloud, music, singing—even while she was in the HBO chamber.

Typically, I would put down the *Los Angeles Times* after an hour or so of reading the news to her and read one of her favorite books to her instead. A couple of years before, she had read *The Phantom Tollbooth* for the first time to her step-daughter, Kristen, during her annual summer visit. Molly loved it and sent a copy to me in New York and said I had to stop everything and read it. I did and sent her, *Time and Again,* which I had just finished. We would often exchange books and music. I liked knowing what she was thinking about and what her mood was.

Hour after hour, my mom sat next to Molly's bed, held her hand, and told her stories about her childhood. How, at about 2½, she'd created a 24-inch high "mural" in purple crayon along the full length of a wall that led downstairs to the basement. How, at age 5, she refused to be Mary in the Christmas nativity play and insisted instead on being the lamb—all in white, with tall, furry ears, crawling around on all fours. And how, as an 8-year-old, she strapped evergreen branches to her arms and ran through the backyard and jumped off chairs, convinced she could take to the air.

"Molly, you always wanted to fly. You would watch the birds and you wanted to fly, too," said Mom wistfully, to my sister's marble-still face.

The memories my mother shared helped other people who came to visit Molly learn more about who she was. The ICU nurses and staff all enjoyed listening to Mom's stories.

Molly's closest friend and publishing colleague, Amy, would update her about work and tell her jokes. Day after day, my younger sister, Sara would sing Indigo Girls songs to Molly or put headphones on Molly's ears and play her favorite tapes, like Tom Petty's *Wildflowers,* which she had given to Molly and Walt for Christmas and knew they'd really liked. My youngest sister, Mary K., read her books, like *The Secret Garden,* a family favorite. My niece, Abigail, Mary K.'s 3-year-old daughter, would listen to the story while she did her "very, very best coloring." We helped Abi snip the pages from her Disney coloring book and Abi helped us hang Mickey Mouse, Goofy, Donald Duck, and Grumpy, Doc, and Sleepy around Molly's room.

I would brush Molly's hair, massage her head, hands, feet, and her knotted brow, and, because I almost always took the night shift, I whispered to her.

Molly, you'd be amazed at how much Brian and I have gotten done on the house. The new roof we put on hasn't leaked at all this winter, and we're almost done with the upstairs bedrooms. He's refinishing the old wood floors, which is a huge mess, but it'll be worth it. You'll have to come and visit us again this summer. By then, I should have new plaster on the ceilings. You can help me in the vegetable garden, and we can make tabouli again with all the parsley and tomatoes.

Brian is here, too, remember Molly? He visited you earlier today. He's asleep at the hotel right now. He has to fly home in a couple of days and go back to work. Then he's going to Florida for 10 days to visit his family. It'll be hard—I'll miss him a lot. But I'm staying here with you until you wake up and get better.

"I've got to get in here, dear, and take vitals and check her fluids," a nurse would say, and I'd let go of Molly's hand and move away from her bed. Never having spent any time in a hospital, much less an ICU, I learned that even when a patient is on life-support and in a coma, nurses still appear every few hours through the night to do their rounds. They never told us to leave, and, in fact, often jotted in Molly's chart that her supportive family was at her side.

So, you know what, Smith? You know what a workaholic I am? Well, I'm not doing any of my writing jobs right now. I put all my deadlines on hold and told my editors and bosses I'd check in with them later.

I love you so much, Smith. You're my only big sister. Don't worry—we'll have you back on your feet soon. Can you hear me? Squeeze my hand, OK? Try again, just squeeze. I really miss you. I miss you so much.

From day one, an FBI agent had always been present at the hospital, even overnight. We had not requested this, but like quiet guards for Molly— and for us—one agent after another would appear and simply wait outside her room, sitting in a chair at the door. We got to know their names and how they liked their coffee. We didn't know the FBI before the accident. Walt was always tight-lipped about his work or he'd make jokes about "just another day at the office." Now, the FBI had become family.

Five or six days after the accident, Mom suggested to two FBI supervisors who had come to visit that the agents should go home to their families, they didn't need to stand vigil outside Molly's room. One supervisor matter-of-factly explained that this is the FBI, and Walt Weber was part of it. And whether the agents knew him personally or not, they *did* know if it were one of them or their family members in a coma, barely alive, Walt would do the same thing.

Mom knew this was true. It's what family does.

In addition to the agents who stood sentinel, Walt's supervisor on the tech squad and close friend, Nancy, organized the FBI agents and their duties. She stopped by the hospital almost every day to check on Molly and ask us how we were and what we needed. She was the liaison for our family and for Walt's to the FBI. This caring, smart agent was a lifeline.

From the start, Nancy had worked with FBI agents all over the country to help Walt's family and ours. FBI agents had delivered the bad news to our family and Walt's, professionally and gently. They picked each of us up at the airports in Los Angeles and brought us directly to the hospital to be with Molly. They found us a hotel nearby where we could have rooms together on the same hallway. They helped our two families make funeral arrangements.

My mother, who lives in Denver, was packing for a business trip when the FBI agents came to her door late that Sunday afternoon. She was vice president of strategic marketing for U.S. Computer Services and ran the Denver office for this California-based company.

She got a late flight to L.A. and asked her husband, Harold Shuler, a fine arts painter, to organize their house and prepare to join her in a few days. Harold made phone calls to my sisters and me and notified their neighbors, his two daughters, and their cat-sitter. Mom winces when she recalls how she spent more than $200 making calls from the plane's telephone, leaving messages for everyone she needed to reach to cancel her business meetings for the next day and briefly explaining why.

My dad, Ralph Smith, a former Methodist minister and retired high school math teacher, and his wife for almost 20 years, Martha, had FBI agents knock on the porch door of their lakeside log home in rural Virginia that Sunday evening. The snow was deep, it was 10:30, and my dad figured it was someone who needed car help. The agents came in and sat by the woodstove so my dad and Martha would sit down, too. Dad flew to L.A. early the next morning, while Martha stayed behind a day to cancel their numerous volunteer obligations and line up the neighbors to care for their dogs and cats. Dad says he doesn't remember the flight; he didn't talk or sleep, he only felt desperation. None of it seemed real.

My parents separated in March 1973, when I was 13 years old. Molly was 15, Sara was 11, and Mary K. was only 7. My dad moved to an apartment about an hour away. Mom and Dad had worked for years to pull their marriage together, which I believe helped them to be cordial with each other after they split up and in the years that followed—for the weekend handoffs, at our swim meets, school graduations, and all three of my sisters' weddings. There was still anger and they weren't friends, but they could manage to be friendly.

My sister Sara was at home when she got the phone call about Walt and Molly. She was a graduate teaching assistant in the Romance and Classical languages department at Michigan State University in East Lansing and was working on her PhD in Spanish. Divorced several years earlier from a husband who physically abused her, Sara had a steady and very sweet boyfriend, also named Walter. We always called him by his full name, which he preferred, and to avoid confusion with Molly's Walt. He was an entomologist at Michigan State whose specialty was honeybees. He had shared custody of his two young sons from his first marriage. Sara loved spending time with Walter at his house with his boys.

My youngest sister, Mary K., and her husband, Stephen, and daughter, Abigail, were living in Castle Rock, just south of Denver. Stephen was a senior Navy lieutenant and worked in intelligence. He and Walt would often seem to have conversations in code about their jobs; it was something only the brothers-in-law could share. Stephen took the phone call Sunday night. He told Mary K. that Walt was dead and Molly was in critical condition and "it didn't look too good." She "wound up very quickly," Stephen recalled, and knowing Abi was upstairs asleep, Mary K. ran out the front door. She cried in the front yard and then ran across the street to seek comfort at a close friend's house. Stephen didn't follow once he'd seen where she'd gone. He wanted to be home in case Abi awoke in the commotion. About 20 minutes later, Mary K. returned and apologized to Stephen for leaving, but said she had been overwhelmed and had to let it out without Abi potentially witnessing her shock.

The weekend before Molly and Walt's accident, Mary K. had learned she was pregnant again. She'd mailed Molly a note announcing her good news, but wasn't sure when she arrived in L.A. with Abi on Monday, if Molly had received it before she and Walt had left home for their ski weekend.

Although all of us sisters were close, Molly and I were especially so—maybe because we were the first two daughters, or because we'd always shared a room, our shoes, and most of our secrets, or because Molly enjoyed looking out for me and appreciated how much I looked up to her. I always wanted to be with her. I've never been to a homecoming or reunion of mine at Stanford, but at Molly's request, I have accompanied her to many homecomings and reunions at her alma mater, Yale. She would fly to New York City where I was living, rent a car, and we'd drive to New Haven. She would wear her Yale cheerleader sweater with jeans, and she looked great, like a senior with her whole life ahead of her.

I was in New York City about to begin a week of work filming an educational TV production I'd written when I got the news. I always tried to find a cheap place to stay in Manhattan when I was there working. The YMCA on West 23rd Street had bunk beds, shared bathrooms down the hall, and no telephones in the rooms. On Monday at 6 a.m., I was up and dressed when there was a knock on the door. I peered through the peephole and saw my boyfriend, Brian. This was bizarre, since he was supposed to be 130 miles north at our home in Copake, in upstate New York. Instead, he was standing in front of me, his face full of urgency.

He'd gotten the phone call late Sunday night and had no way to reach me by telephone. He'd driven four hours in a snowstorm to the YMCA to tell me about Walt and Molly and get me to an airport.

In the ICU, I would gaze at Molly's motionless face and think about our family photo albums: Molly, age 7, standing next to me, age 5, her hand on my shoulder. A group shot when we were teenagers with everyone else looking at the camera, but with me looking at Molly. Consistent through the years; we only grew taller.

A group of neurologists examined Molly a couple of times a day, and checked up on her family, too. During the daily meetings with others on the medical staff, the neurologists would warn us not to be "overly optimistic."

Why the hell not? I thought. How annoying. As if it were somehow dangerous to be extra hopeful. I wanted the boldness of it. It suited us.

On day five, the neurology team appeared en masse, like a Greek chorus, saying Molly might remain in a vegetative state forever. They asked if we had discussed as a family when to stop the life support systems.

"In fact, we were just figuring out what book to read to her next," said Sara, "and I was asking if someone had found the Jackson Browne tape."

I held up a spiral notebook. "Look, we're jotting down everything that happens and our thoughts about it all in this notebook we keep by her bed, so we can share them with her later."

"We haven't chatted even once about pulling the plug," said Mom. "And now it's time to take her for her HBO treatment."

We'd only become more resolute every day in our attempts to stimulate a response from Molly. She gave us reasons.

Mary K. piped up and said Molly had definitely squeezed her fingers one time the day before when she asked her to. Mom said just that morning she and Amy both caught a twitch of Molly's lips when they said something funny and were laughing.

The chief neurologist listened and then glanced at his cadre of medical students. He lowered his chin, and looked over the top of his narrow eyeglasses at my mother. His left eyebrow edged up. Then he sighed, pressed his lips together tightly, and turned and walked down the hallway with the white wave following after him.

We appreciated that the chief neurologist was evaluating Molly using his considerable skills and years of experience. We understood he had only her occasional, very weak brain waves on EEG. But we also knew he was assessing her without knowing one important fact: Molly's determined and competitive spirit was like no other.

At age 2, Molly began wearing corrective shoes because her right foot turned in. At first, she had been evaluated for a brain tumor because she would fall down every time she tried to stand up. She wore the special shoes until first grade. By fourth grade she was a faster runner and better baseball player than most of the boys her age.

In 1970, Mom got all four of us to join a swim team and we became serious competitive swimmers. Although Molly only started swimming competitively at age 12, about the time most female swimmers' abilities begin to peak, she became a national champion while she was at Yale.

Years later, an ultimate challenge to her strong will and toughness left her with an almost mysterious fortitude—the very attribute, I believe, that helped her cling to life at Loma Linda.

While in the midst of being raped, with a knife at her throat for two and a half hours in the middle of a sunny Wednesday morning in August 1982,

Molly memorized the tattoos on her rapist's arms. Later, she drew them in detail for the police. Molly had been an excellent artist since she was a child.

She had been out running a familiar route, twice around a lake near my mother's house in suburban Maryland. She was living at home with Mom and Mary K., who was in high school, trying to save a little money before she started her first job in publishing.

In a lovely, but remote, swampy corner of the lake, a man wielding a large knife stepped into her path. He said he would kill her if she didn't do what he said, and ordered her to take off her clothes. She began to pull off her shorts, but, in a burst, she turned and ran desperately, screaming, fully aware the man's knife could, at any moment, end up deep in her back. He overtook her, threw her to the ground, seized her neck with one hand and with the other pressed his knife against her throat. She grabbed at it, trying to wrest it away, but his chokehold had her gasping. She thought she would pass out. Suddenly, life, and whatever she had to do to preserve it, was her only objective. Endure anything.

She withdrew her bloodied palm and he let her breathe. He told her not to scream again. For 150 minutes, she turned inward to exist only in her brain, the place you land when reality goes beyond the limits of tolerance. She didn't cry, she merely waited, and studied his coarse tattoos.

After he left her, she got dressed and began searching for her jewelry, which had scattered in the struggle. It was her first impulse: to put all the pieces back, to put things right, like they were before.

At home that evening, after the extensive hospital examination and the excruciating, highly detailed report she gave at the police station, she told Mom and Mary K. that she'd severely handicapped herself by categorically denying that such a thing could ever happen to her. After all, she said, she was smart and self-assured. But her pluck had been wrecked. How could she have been so smug, so stupid, she asked me on the telephone the next day. My mom had called and given me the details. I might as well have been on the moon instead of in Manhattan, I felt so helpless. I rearranged my waitressing schedule for the week and took the Amtrak home.

Molly needed to talk and did so, willingly. She plowed through the incident again and again, sometimes scrutinizing each step, sometimes in huge, thrashing strokes as if she were swinging a sickle. It seemed she was trying to find a comfortable place in her mind to stash the memory. I wanted to help her not feel shame. Molly quickly came to acknowledge her limitations, and soon accepted that she wasn't to blame. But she didn't imagine the bitterness that would follow.

Molly revisited the site several times with Mom and with a police detective, scraping through the mud and grass, looking for one missing little diamond earring, and for answers, she said, about her vulnerability that morning. The earring was never found.

For weeks, for months, she replayed the day in her mind. She told me she felt she'd never know again what it was to be carefree. Nearly a year later, she said, "The only time you really aren't safe, is when you think you are." That statement seemed like progress to me.

They never found the man, but Molly's grit, her steely edge, grew ever sharper.

For a couple of years, Molly would tell her unhappy secret to anyone she'd even begin to get close to, especially men. It was as if the rape was who she was and people had to deal with it, like she had to. She'd break her news and watch them squirm. She wanted them to share her burden, but it was a cruel test, she admitted. She drove men away, even if they truly cared about her. She'd just shrug it off as an encounter with a guy who couldn't cope. And she never pursued someone, even a friend, who would withdraw from her and her story. She didn't like being abandoned, but she couldn't keep herself from the pain either.

Two and a half years later, she met Walt, and he responded differently than all the others had when she gave him her "treatment." He said he was surprised at the hostility in her explanation and said he wasn't sure if she was trying to push him away or not. She said she didn't know either. And somehow, in their honesty, an opening appeared.

When she told me about Walt's response, she pondered out loud for the first time I'd heard, what she would have been like if the rape had never happened: More gentle? Less careful? Less hostile towards men? Less concerned with control?

"I know I lost the ability to assume bad things wouldn't happen to me," Molly said. "I used to say that I'd rather die than be raped. Now I acknowledge my vulnerabilities and limitations, even my own mortality. I can work to protect myself without any denial."

"Don't get too carried away, Smith. You're alive and you're safe, and smarter than ever," I said. I wished I could see her face.

"Yes, but I'm awake to the fact that troubles and dangers are very real and always present—that's life. I'm on this earth for a finite period, so I'm going to live life to the fullest."

"Well, that's a great life philosophy. It's the right choice—for all of us," I said. "So maybe Walt understands this stuff about you."

"Maybe," she said, thoughtfully. "Maybe he does."

That was his chance. Walt didn't trigger Molly's defenses. Instead, he seemed to melt away her resentment. This release was scary to her, but wonderful, too.

To make sure she stayed grounded and didn't "mess it up," Molly invited my sister, Sara, to come along on her first dinner date with Walt. Sara had moved back to the area to attend George Washington University and loved living near Molly again. Sara always had profound admiration for her oldest sister and they were very close.

Sara recalled that they went to a casual pizza place and Walt was sort of quiet, but very sweet. "When he looked at Molly, he'd smile and it changed his face completely," Sara said. "I could tell they were falling in love." Over pepperoni pies, Walt charmed Sara and wooed Molly.

Walt seemed to know intuitively to give Molly plenty of room—to explore her career, go out with her sisters and friends, and even dance with other men. And wisely, he let her wonder about his feelings for her. He stood by and she drew ever closer to his quiet confidence, calm manner, and gentle assurances. Walt became her sanctuary. He made her feel safe.

At their wedding, a close friend commented to me how steady Walt was and how the two of them seemed in perfect balance. Molly would glide around the room, laughing and talking with friends, while constantly staying connected to Walt. He was gravity and she could orbit freely around him. Even at a distance, they were joined.

As the days of Molly in a coma slowly passed—with whirring machines, HBO treatments, beeping monitors, her hushed face—each of us dug into our own coping mechanisms. We were all documenting in the spiral notebook what happened during each of our shifts with Molly—what therapy she had, how it went, what the medical staff said and did—and how we felt. Not only was it useful to know what was going on with Molly, reading each other's thoughts helped us feel connected as we received and then passed the baton for the next shift.

I was also journaling, the way I always have, splaying my fears and hopes into the privacy of a blank book. And I was the family's secretary at the daily meetings with the medical staff, taking notes in my journalist shorthand of everything that was said.

Mary K., a pregnant mom and the most religious among us, prayed. Sara was reading novels in Spanish, and when she could focus on something other than Molly, she would study for her upcoming comprehensive exams. My dad and Martha would take walks and watch birds.

My mother, the organizer, made phone calls to work colleagues, insurance companies, Molly's employer, the bank—trying to make arrangements to be with Molly for however long she needed to be and also keep her work and home afloat.

Midweek, Harold, Mom's husband, and Stephen, Mary K.'s, drove from Denver to L.A. in Mom's car. Harold brought Mom some clothes, the mail, and her computer. Stephen delivered clothes and books for Mary K. and a few toys for Abi.

My partner, Brian, a carpenter and an aspiring photographer, had his camera with him, as usual. I had also packed my camera, but none of us took photos of Molly in a coma. It simply didn't occur to me. It would have felt macabre, like taking photos at a wake.

Harold, the artist, however, sat in a corner of Molly's room and made line drawings of her. It was his way of processing, he said. His were true depictions—with all the needles, IV bags, machines, wires, and tubes. Like painting a beautiful tree and including the telephone poles, electric lines, and roadside litter cluttered around it. His drawings captured her in the days of suspension. And they are priceless artifacts to me, more painfully accurate and startling than any photograph or memory could be.

The question of how you capture the essence of someone you know so well became critically important to us in those early days. How do you sense her presence? For me, it was like instinct, it was there without me even realizing it. It's how I began to feel Molly surfacing. Just an inkling, an impression, like the way a great artist can project his subject's deepest mood in a portrait, so you feel her there on the canvas. It's not a likeness only.

We knew Molly beyond a cellular, scientific level. We understood her. We could take into account her personality, her character, and see her with all of our senses, our heads, and our hearts.

The chief neurologist and the neurology residents remained dubious that any amount of Molly was there at all. They said that even in a miraculous best-case scenario, it was unlikely Molly would ever be able to talk, walk, or think on her own again, and her "probability of a meaningful life was zero." But we weren't doing that math.

While Molly showed us fleeting moments of wakefulness, she still refused to perform for the neurologists. Mom told the neurology team that even as a child Molly had never taken commands very well, and suggested they might try a calm request to her to move her toes or fingers. The neurologists often spoke to Molly in loud voices; the way some people do with others who speak a foreign language.

Molly would tell us later the neurologists had pissed her off. Always yelling at her to wiggle her fingers. Couldn't they see she was moving her whole hand? What idiots. So she'd stopped trying for them, she said.

In truth, the neurologists didn't see her do anything at all that first week. Despite daily HBO and our round-the-clock stimulation efforts, Molly's EEG tests were still mostly flat lines, meaning no brain activity. It was around that time that a gentle psychologist, who frequently worked with families of brain-injured people, gathered my family together.

"It's been studied and it's widely accepted." Tony Benjamin said, pausing, looking at Mom and each of us. "When one family member gets a brain injury, the whole family gets a brain injury."

None of us said a word. We had no idea what he was talking about.

It was, quite possibly, the truest statement and best forewarning we got from anyone during our many days at Loma Linda, but we couldn't realize it then and didn't for a long time. Our collective and individual brain damage was already seeping in, affecting our thinking, planning, communication skills, and judgment. We didn't know.

The days of disorientation were nearby. Discussions filled with hurtful assumptions and intense agitation were looming. I didn't recognize my growing sense of helplessness and simmering anxiety as symptoms.

T w o

ON day four of Molly's coma, Kristen Weber, Walt's daughter, flew in to Los Angeles from Hawaii where she lived with her mother, her step-dad, and several new step-siblings. It was two days before her father's funeral. Kristen was an experienced flier for a 14-year-old, having made the long overnight flight many times to spend the Christmas holidays and summers with Molly and her dad. When she was a little girl, Walt used to accompany her to and from Hawaii, but now she flew solo. We'd all known Kristen since she was a toddler, having met her before her dad and Molly were married 10 years earlier. We had watched her grow up in six-month chunks of time.

Walt's sisters and mother were arriving later that day, and Kristen was looking forward to staying at the hotel with her grandmother. I arranged with my family and the FBI to meet Kristen's plane at 5:30 a.m., make contact with the agent who'd be waiting there, and bring her directly to the hospital to see Molly.

"Why is Molly alive and my dad's dead?" asked Kristen, before we were even out of the airport parking lot. Her voice was blank as she squinted at the sun, which had just cleared the horizon, a glowing disk in an unwholesome gray-orange color through the L.A. haze.

"Well..." I stalled, "it's a good question. We don't really know, and the doctors don't know either. I'll warn you, Kristen, Molly doesn't look very alive right now. It's kind of scary. But we're really hoping she'll come around."

"How does carbon dioxide kill you?" Kristen stared at the early morning commuters on the freeway. Her thin frame looked like a collapsed marionette as she slumped in the passenger seat. Her long black hair hung like a curtain around her face. Kristen's eyes were rounder than her father's, who was half-Chinese, but hers had enough of the Asian shape to give her young face an exotic beauty.

"Carbon MON-oxide," I said. "When you breathe it in, it robs your body of oxygen. And if you don't have oxygen, your heart and lungs and your other organs just shut down. Even your brain stops working."

"So, is Molly brain damaged? My mom says Molly is like a vegetable."

"Well, we really don't know about her brain right now. She's in a coma. We don't believe she'll be in a vegetative state. We don't even know if she's going to live yet. But we're big believers in her, Kristen." I tried to muster a confident smile.

I had never thought much about carbon monoxide poisoning myself until a few days before, and I had some of the same questions Kristen had. On my long flight to California, I tossed dozens of scenarios about Molly and Walt around in my head. Did they have bad headaches as they crawled into bed? Did they talk to each other in the middle of the night about feeling really nauseous all of a sudden? Did they try to get up and move on Saturday?

I had thought, wasn't it carbon monoxide poisoning that killed that professional tennis player in a cabin on Long Island last year? Vitas Gerulaitis? A malfunctioning heater was at fault there. Could that be what happened to Walt and Molly? Gerulaitis was the first well-known celebrity to die of carbon monoxide poisoning, and his death at age 40 made many of us aware of this lethal hazard for the first time.

But I really knew nothing about carbon monoxide—where it comes from, what causes it, the effects, symptoms, dangers. Nothing. I didn't have a CO detector in my house. Neither did my mother or father, or any of my sisters. No one had one to put in a backpack or suitcase to take on trips away from home either.

Now we do. I never sleep without a CO detector nearby. My family and I pass out CO detectors to friends and mere acquaintances like some people hand out business cards at a conference. We all became quick studies on carbon monoxide while Molly was in a coma. We dug through books at the Loma Linda library and learned about it as if we were immersed in an intensive language course in a foreign land.

The fact is, once you become aware of something, you find it everywhere. Our friends mailed us dozens of articles, too. A single mom in Minneapolis trying to heat her small house with the gas oven. Four dead. A couple running a generator in the basement after losing electricity during a hurricane in Florida. Two dead. A father and infant child sleeping in a rocking chair in front of a wood-burning fireplace on the first cold day of autumn in Colorado; the chimney blocked by a squirrel's nest. Two dead. A college student in Nebraska who started her car in the attached garage to warm it up while she finished getting dressed and reviewed her assignment one last time. She never made it to class.

I learned from the *Journal of the American Medical Association* that carbon monoxide causes more unintentional deaths than any other poison in America. A pamphlet from the Centers for Disease Control and Prevention stated that, on average, 500 to 600 people accidentally lose their lives each year to this silent, invisible killer. You can't see, smell, taste, or feel carbon monoxide gas. It's not irritating in any way. You don't know it's slithered into the air you're breathing and that the threat of lethal poisoning is coiling around you. You just feel sick—a bad headache, dizziness, nausea, like you're coming down with the flu. Most folks just go to bed.

Annually, more than 15,000 people in the U.S. seek medical attention for their symptoms, discover they've been exposed to carbon monoxide, and get treatment. They're the lucky ones. Like the whole family of five coming down with the flu all at once. Or the two couples in a rented beach bungalow all feeling like they have food poisoning even though they hadn't eaten the same seafood. Fortunately, such circumstances strike these folks as peculiar, too coincidental, and they get help before the disorientation stage of the venomous carbon monoxide sets in.

Ironically, if carbon monoxide is present, simple inhalation causes asphyxiation in the body. By cruel bio-chemical hijinks, carbon monoxide binds to red blood cells up to 250 times more readily than oxygen does. In other words, if carbon monoxide is around, oxygen doesn't stand a chance. Carbon monoxide easily replaces oxygen in the blood stream and prevents oxygen from being carried throughout the body. Victims' tissues are smothered. Their organs and brain are choked off and they suffocate from oxygen deprivation.

When I walked Kristen into Molly's room, she staggered at the sight of her stepmother. I guided her away, and the FBI agent outside the room folded Kristen into his chair. I rubbed her back and found myself, strangely, pondering the smoke detector over our heads on the ceiling. Thanks to state laws and building codes, smoke detectors have been installed in nearly every home, office, hotel, and hospital room for decades. I had just read the day before that in 1994, Chicago became the first municipality to mandate the installation of CO detectors in new residences. It would be 2004 before New York City would require by law that all homes and apartments have CO detectors. To this day, our human inclination to take precautions after the fact is still disturbing.

A few minutes later, I stood nearby and watched Kristen lean over Molly's bed, her bewildered face studying the motionless mask stuffed with tubes and wires. I was horrified to realize how unconscious we all had been about carbon monoxide—this totally preventable, but particularly stealthy assassin. It had murdered Kristen's father and had tortured my sister's body into a barely living shell.

Fewer people die from accidental carbon monoxide poisoning than die in car crashes annually. It's even fewer than those who die in fires or by falling. But it's a lot more than those who die by lightning strikes. Walt and Molly were not just bearers of bad luck. They were casualties of ignorance and neglect.

This is piercing irony to those of us who knew Walt. He was the ultimate protector. It was his job every day and his life with Molly. He worked to get criminals and assailants off the streets. He skied back up a steep mountain to rescue Molly when she blew her knee out on their first ski vacation together. It was that moment, while lying in the snow, waiting for Walt to ski down the mountain again and return with the medics, that she decided she would marry him, if he asked. He did and he kept his promise to be with her always—till death did them part.

Walt, a self-trained and expert locksmith since he was a teenager, always had the best safety gear and gadgets. Complicated alarms on the doors, windows, and running under all the floors in their house. Bottled water, canned food, a battery-operated radio, and counter-poison medications to last for days stacked in a corner of the garage. Emergency supplies and tool boxes, like mini-hardware stores, in their cars' trunks. Complete lightweight repair kits on each bicycle. A two-way radio, GPS device, and top-of-the-line life preservers onboard their boat.

Walt also always slept on the side of the bed closest to the sliding glass door in their bedroom because that's where an intruder would most likely enter. His FBI-issued gun was never more than an arm's reach away.

It's possible that because Walt was sleeping closest to the door in their hotel room and Molly was near the drafty window, he may have received

slightly less fresh air. But Molly's constant guardian must have sensed something was wrong. Walt was found with a phone book open across his body,
as if he'd wanted to cry out for help, but in his deeply poisoned state wasn't
able to reason or make even the simplest three-digit phone call.

After a few minutes, Kristen moved away from Molly's bed and pushed
back her hair. She began to look around the hospital room and giggled to
see herself in so many of the photographs we had taped to the walls. The
ICU nurses had suggested that we display photos of Molly to remind us
what we were fighting for and to help them get to know her better, too.
Sometimes, I think they doubted our hope, but the photos gave Molly a
presence. The nurses saw a stylish, vibrant woman—tan and fit, confident in
her various sports, sophisticated with her business colleagues, laughing with
friends, kissing her husband, and hugging her stepdaughter.

Kristen and Molly's relationship had become rocky over the past year.
Kristen had grown into a moody teenager, and Molly was sometimes snippy
and impatient with her. Over the recent Christmas holiday when the family
was together in Winter Park, Colorado, Molly and Kristen had bickered
over how much of Molly's expensive hair conditioner Kristen had used when
she showered. Their squabbles seemed absurd to Walt and broke his heart.
As he and I walked back, a little ahead of the rest of the group after our
afternoon of sledding on shower curtains, Walt had asked me how his wonderful wife and precious daughter could be so hard on each other. I told
him Kristen would grow out of it and that I'd never understood Molly's
harsh side.

But now, as Kristen looked at the snapshots covering the decade she
and Molly had known each other, she could see Molly teaching her to swim
at the community pool, reading to her on the couch, and gently braiding
her hair.

After the FBI's investigation of Walt's death was completed at the ski lodge,
his partner, Don, was to drive Walt's SUV down to us in Loma Linda. Don
had told Nancy, his and Walt's supervisor, that he wanted to do it. "It was a
little weird to drive Walt's truck, though," Don admitted. "Really... it was
very, very difficult."

Don and a few other FBI colleagues also helped us get into Walt and
Molly's locked and alarm-protected house in Saugus, about an hour and
forty-five minutes drive from Loma Linda. They had left home Friday

thinking they'd be back home Sunday night. The next Thursday afternoon, my mother, Kristen, and I walked through their front door and stepped back in time.

Their two Siamese cats, Sugar and Pepper, meowed nonstop and padded in circles around us, more confused and lonely than hungry, it seemed, since they had food and water. We doled out extra large doses of petting and gave them fresh food and water. On the refrigerator under a ceramic cat magnet, I found the phone number of their cat-sitter, the teenage daughter of the Hotts, a family in the neighborhood who were close friends of Walt and Molly's. I called and she said she was happy to take care of Sugar and Pepper, until Molly could come home.

I packed up fresh fruit, a bag of bread, and a box of crackers that had been left on the kitchen counter. The Moosewood cookbook I gave Molly was next to the stove with a bookmark in the page for split pea soup. A nearly full pot of the soup was in the refrigerator. I decided to take it with us. We could heat it in the hotel lobby microwave. I left condiments, pepperoni, beer, and Walt's Dr. Pepper in the refrigerator. I put the lettuce, tomatoes, sliced turkey breast, yogurt, and cheese in a grocery bag to take with us, too. I poured a half-full carton of milk down the drain, even though it was still good. I didn't know when or under what circumstances anyone would be back. I washed the few dishes that had been left in the sink and watered the plants.

Kristen had come with us to collect a few of her things and to point out what she wanted to be shipped to Hawaii. I made a list: bicycle, electronic keyboard, art supplies, water skis, snow skis. We said we'd do our best.

Mom found some comfortable clothes Molly could wear at the hospital if she became conscious. Then she started digging through the file cabinets in the office. Kristen and I soon joined the search. We hunted all over the house for a will for Walt or Molly and for a living will or health proxy for Molly. The FBI was not aware of any documents and we never found any either. One big clue was the software package for creating a will, still in the shrink-wrap, on top of Walt's computer monitor.

Before we left, we chatted in the driveway with a few neighbors who stopped by. They were planning to attend Walt's wake that night, and we told them we didn't know yet about Molly.

At the hospital on Friday morning, day six, for just a minute or two, Molly opened her eyes—not pop-up, wide open, like in TV soap operas, but tiny blue beams through barely-there slits. She looked around the room as my mom and sisters prepared to leave for the day to attend Walt's funeral. Molly's energy felt urgent, like a bird in a paper bag wanting to burst out. Then her eyes closed and I noticed the space between her eyebrows was more deeply creased than before. As I rubbed her forehead, Mom said she was certain she'd seen a tear on Molly's cheek the afternoon before when she'd spoken to her about Walt.

Around 10:30 a.m., several tears rolled down Molly's temples and almost into her ears before I smoothed them into her hair with my fingers. At the time, I was doing my best to explain to her again what had happened to her and Walt the weekend before, and that she and I would be alone together for many hours because Brian had flown home, and our family, Kristen, and Walt's family were all at Walt's funeral.

Despite having made Molly cry, I was excited to tell everyone later that I'd seen a few more tears. And I wished, once again, as I had all week, that Walt could be there to help Molly, to help me reach her.

Tucked in close to her bedside, I read just a few chapters of *The Phantom Tollbooth* and played only Side A of the Indigo Girls tape. I wanted to give her some quiet time to be with Walt on that breezy, sunny Friday. That notion felt totally realistic to me, very normal. I noticed the nurses, HBO technicians, and neurologists were slightly subdued around us, knowing about the event that was taking place. We all spoke in hushed voices as if we, too, were in the chapel.

Like zealous cheerleaders who pay no attention to the score, we had urged Molly on nonstop all week. I knew she might need a chance to rest, but it wasn't easy to step back and wait quietly on the sidelines. Instead, I was thinking, OK, what can I do now to stimulate her, get a reaction from her limp body and pull her back to life? Then I stopped. That cliché survival instruction from the airline attendant on my Monday flight echoed in my head: "Please put on your own oxygen mask first before assisting others."

I, too, was aching and disoriented for the loss of Walt. I, too, had shed many tears. Settling back in my chair, I held Molly's heavy hand and gazed out the window at the palm tree fronds lifting and falling in the wind like waves. I began to realize what Molly had lost. She went away for the weekend with her husband. She went to sleep one night. Whole lives seeped away in a hotel room. I looked back at her still face and it dawned on me. "Smith, you're a widow," I said out loud. She didn't react, not even a flicker, but the words hung like thick smoke in the air and burned my eyes.

Throughout the day, nurses came through and checked Molly's machines. When the afternoon shift began, one nurse observed our reflective mood and asked Molly's roommate if she would lower the volume on her TV. She put on a headset and I was grateful.

After picking at a salad for a late lunch, I brushed my teeth with a toothbrush from the hospital's toiletry items in the bathroom that were waiting for Molly. As teenagers, we used to walk around the house and do other stuff while brushing our teeth—make our beds, put on our shoes, pack our lunch. It's a habit I still have. Molly was used to brushing her teeth three or four times a day and I imagined somewhere in her coma, she yearned to brush her teeth now.

I cleaned her quiet face with a damp washcloth, patting cautiously around her mouth so I didn't bump the respirator tube. I told her as I had a thousand times before, how I wish I had unblemished skin like hers and that it wasn't fair she got most of the good-skin genes. Then I brushed her hair, styling it as best I could the way she would, and lifted her head just a little to smooth the back. I rubbed the nape of her neck for a moment and recalled the times when we were kids how we would lay on our backs in the grass, arms folded behind our heads, and call out the animals we found in the clouds. I would say, "Look, that's a bird, see the wings?"

She would point elsewhere and say, "That's a mountain lion hunched down on a rock waiting to pounce, and just above it, right there, that's a bald eagle."

My family members described Walt's funeral to me over the next day, reliving the images and emotions. One of Walt's supervisors, Charlie, delivered the eulogy to the crowd packed into the small chapel. He'd spoken with Walt's family members and colleagues, gathering the pieces of Walt's life. My dad got a copy of the eulogy so he could share it with me, and with Molly, one day.

Walt's four sisters said that because Walt was the youngest and the only boy, he got away with more than they ever could, even though with a working mother, they were often in charge of taking care of him. Walt liked to play with toy trucks, didn't like to take baths, and would go down to the creek with his buddies and play for hours to get away from the girls. His idea of getting into mischief was to tell his mom he was going to his room to study, but instead sneak canned peaches into his room. She'd find the empty cans the next day.

After high school, Walt started college to become a geologist and worked in highway construction, which appealed to his love of mechanics and of being outside. He used a variety of tools, operated cranes, and drove big trucks. After his father, a retired career army man, was shot and killed in a parking lot, Walt dropped out of college and enlisted in the Navy. He was stationed in Hawaii, his birth state, became a Sea Bee, the Navy's engineering division, and was trained in photography. Over time, Walt married, left the Navy, returned to Maryland with his wife to live near his mother, had his daughter, Kristen, got divorced, and finished his degree in geology. Walt got a job driving a truck and began training for the FBI.

At his first FBI assignment in Kansas City, Charlie said Walt was a very independent individual who didn't like to sit behind a desk. He much preferred to be out scoping locations, planting wiretaps, and investigating interstate thefts. Agent Weber helped bring down Mafia families, capture bank robbers, and track down fugitives.

In the Los Angeles office, Walt worked on the bank robbery squad, then in foreign counter intelligence, and then on the "Tech Squad," a job he was perfectly suited for with his organized and meticulous nature. Most of all, Walt kept a cool head, even under intense pressure. His partner, Don, said he trusted him completely, in any situation.

Walt was always an outdoorsy, active person, and once he met Molly, they shared that passion. Almost every weekend, their neighbors would see them up early to go camping, cycling, fishing, skiing, or something. One neighbor, Mrs. O'Sullivan, shared how Walt and Molly went house to house down their street moments after the deadly Northridge earthquake, in 1989, checking on people, helping them turn off their gas lines, and looking to see if the cracks in the walls were imminently dangerous.

Charlie said it was clear to everyone in his life that Walt was dedicated to Molly, she was his soul mate, and that Kristen was the other member of Walt's triad. Then Charlie spoke directly to Kristen seated in the second row, and said, "I want you to know your father loved you so very, very much."

Charlie said Walt worked hard and played hard. He was doing what he loved and lived his life to the fullest. He finished his eulogy with a saying, which I knew to be somewhat overused, but I felt it applied to Walt. "'It's not the years in a life that counts; it's the life in the years.' Walt Weber lived," Charlie said. "We will miss him."

Many people were standing outside listening because the chapel was full, but everyone walked up the hill to the gravesite following a bagpiper. Ravens swooped overhead in the breeze, sharp black against the powder blue sky.

My brother-in-law Stephen brought his camera to the funeral. "It was odd to take pictures, but I was feeling loyal to Molly and wanted to give her a memory," he said. "It was so ethereal that Molly was alive, but not able to attend her husband's funeral. I felt heartbroken as I took the pictures, but I believed she would see them one day."

Mom had arranged that Molly's presence at the funeral be represented by yellow roses, which Walt had always given her, and daisies, a longtime favorite among Mom and all her daughters, from the movie, *Harold and Maude*. The casket was covered in an American flag and surrounded by a ring of Hawaiian flowers.

At the gravesite, Mom stood next to Walt's mother, a petite Chinese woman. "Ah Mee was amazing," Mom said, "stoic and dignified." At one point, Ah Mee laid her head on and reached her arms around the casket, giving one last hug. Then she stood up, restrained and quiet.

Mom flinched at each of the three volleys as a 21-gun salute shattered the air and scattered birds from the trees. Then FBI agents lifted the flag from Walt's casket, folded it into a crisp triangle, and presented it to Mom for Molly. A bugler sounded "Taps."

Walt was buried that afternoon on the grassy hillside north of L.A., near where he and Molly had lived. A small stone was set flat on the ground with his name.

My sister, Mary K., was very moved by the number of people who came and soothed by their presence in the chapel. Standing at the gravesite, she wondered what it would be like for Molly to wake up and discover Walt not only gone but also buried.

My sister, Sara, felt overwhelmed by sadness and found it hard to pay attention, taking care, however, to watch over Kristen, who was shaky—in shock, really. Sara wasn't sure Kristen could really comprehend what was happening before her very eyes.

As the sun slid down behind the horizon and Molly's hospital room grew dark, I studied the creases between my sister's eyebrows. A look of real determination had formed on her face. These tiny muscle movements seemed to project her mood or reflect an emotion going on inside her that could only be revealed in a minute twitch or a subtle resetting of her features.

I massaged her temples and wondered if, like other near-death experiences I'd read about, she had been in a tunnel six days ago and seen a bright, white light at the end. Clearly, she'd turned around. Or maybe even ran like hell in the other direction. Soon, her face relaxed, like a long sigh, and I decided that one day, I would get to ask her about the light in the tunnel.

In the early evening, Dr. Lo came in to speak to his patient before he left for the weekend. He always talks to his comatose patients, he said, because he knows they can hear him. I had been with Molly at her HBO treatments that day and Dr. Lo knew the rest of the family was at Walt's funeral. I told Dr. Lo about Molly's eyes opening a tiny bit and the few tears she'd shed earlier. Then I stood just outside the room and leaned against the doorway, listening.

Dr. Lo told Molly that her vital signs were getting better, but after doing HBO all week there wasn't improvement in her EEG, and he was getting pressure from the neurologists. He had passed the standard protocol 10 HBO treatments for CO poisoning. He needed her to give him a signal like she had to her family—to wake up, open her eyes, something, very soon, he pleaded, otherwise it would be difficult to continue the HBO treatments.

He paused, watching Molly's face. Then he noticed tears at the edges of her closed eyes, a couple of tears spilled onto her cheeks. A chill went down his spine.

"The chamber is working!" he shouted, his face beaming like a spotlight. "Thank you, Molly!"

He ran out the door and down the hallway, yelling to the startled nurses at the desk, "The chamber is working!" He went on to tell the HBO staff to keep working with her daily. He came back to the room a half-hour later to tell me that Molly was the first comatose patient to give him reinforcement that she could hear and understand him. He said he knew right then, in that moment, that she would make it.

"She gave me a sign—a tear. I thought maybe I would get a blink one day," he said, breathlessly. "But it was her way of telling me. And any sign of a chance is enough to keep me going." Molly's determination would be a big factor in her recovery, he said. "But we just don't know what the extent of that recovery will be. She's showing emotion now, and she's strong and smart—she's motivated," Dr. Lo said, adding, "She is no average Jane Doe."

Over the weekend, Walt's sisters, Ah Mee, and Kristen visited Molly again and then returned home. FBI agents drove them to the airport and other agents continued to take up their around-the-clock post outside Molly's room. It had been a long, long week, but we carried on with our stimulation efforts.

On February 13th, eight days after she arrived at the hospital, Molly's eyes were still closed. But she had begun over the past 24 hours to move her hand in a slow gesture, grasping, like a claw, toward her throat—ready to yank the respirator hose out of her throat herself if she had to. A nurse told me that having a respirator tube in place is excruciating, and that one of the first signs of consciousness and self-breathing for many comatose patients was an attempt to get rid of the horrible pain.

I was elated—Molly was feeling pain! Brain response. And moving appropriately in an effort to do something about it. Brain activity.

The day before, Molly had opened her eyes a little for a couple of minutes without focusing on anything. I thought it was wonderful to see even a sliver of her blue eyes. Sara, however, got a very different treatment during her late afternoon shift.

The nurses had just put restraints on Molly's arms to keep her from reaching up and pulling on her respirator tube. Sara was reading in the chair next to Molly's bed. She wrote in our spiral notebook that at one point Molly tilted her head and looked at her with fury. "It was a look of horror, as if she couldn't breathe, but also with intense anger, like she wanted to kill me," wrote Sara. "Her eyes were barely open, but her stare was so powerful. It was scary to be in the same room with her."

Sara spoke gently to Molly for a few moments, reassuring her that she was OK, and tried to comfort her, but she didn't register Sara's soothing words. She looked panicked. Sara, unable to calm Molly, was afraid to leave her alone for fear she might suffocate or that something else might go wrong. But she was also afraid to look at her. Sara tried to distract herself by writing in the spiral notebook.

The irony struck Sara like a cold slap. After days of urging Molly to open her eyes, Sara hoped she would just close them and go to sleep. Sara couldn't imagine how she would survive the next couple of hours in the same room with her sister. Finally, Molly did fall asleep, a few minutes before my dad arrived for his shift. Sara went into the hallway, leaned on her father, and cried her eyes out.

"It was pure hell," Sara said. "It was clear Molly was getting better and trying to connect, but I didn't know why it had to be so awful." The image of Molly's frenzied, desperate eyes haunts Sara to this day.

On the morning of February 14, after nine days and 15 HBO sessions, Molly's respirator was removed. Her urgent trauma had passed. Once the respirator was gone, she kept her eyes closed and had the relaxed look of a sunbather. The lines of distress on her forehead melted away as she took steady deep breaths, in and out, on her own, for the first time.

Molly was sleeping quietly when the chief neurologist came in. He said he would review the MRI/EEG they'd done earlier that morning, but anticipated that Molly would have a slow, incomplete recovery. He said she might do better or worse than we expected, and her being a quadriplegic for life was possible. As he left, I looked over at my resting sister. Her mouth, finally tubeless, wore a tiny smile. I'd swear she heard every word he said.

That afternoon, Molly defied medical science and sent the perfect Valentine, purring her first words to her dear friend Amy, who was in the room, "Hi-i-i-i-i Aim, How are you-u-u-u?"

Amy nearly choked. In a burst of laughter and tears, she replied, "I should be asking *you* that question."

Three

WITNESSING Molly's slow emergence from her coma was like watching a butterfly shedding its sticky cocoon. She'd rub her face and scratch her head. She'd flex her leg out straight, stretching, then release it. During my shift late one night, she opened her eyes, turned her head to look at me sitting in a chair nearby, reached out her hand to mine, and smiled.

It felt wonderfully familiar. When I was 12, I was hit by a car while riding Sara's bicycle through our L.A. suburb's streets. The driver raced through a stop sign and hit me on the other side of the intersection. I went up and over the car, banged off the trunk and onto the ground. The firefighters sitting outside at the firehouse across the street called an ambulance and I was whisked away to the emergency room.

Sara's bike was destroyed, and she got a new one, but it wasn't as cool as the one I'd been riding, she always said, and she was right. I had a concussion, broken collarbone, and other injuries and bruises, which knocked me out of an important national championship swim meet I'd just qualified for. I spent the whole summer in a bulky brace, not swimming at all.

The day after the accident, I remember Molly came and sat on the edge of my bed in our room, took my hand, and held it in her lap. I don't remember what she said, if she said anything, but I lay there, floating and feeling warm, knowing, just by the look on her face, that my big sister understood my disappointment, my frustration, and my fear.

Now, I hoped she could feel my empathy and encouragement.

Molly slept a lot over the next few days, but reassured us by being awake and alert for hours at a time. Dr. Lo was ecstatic; his lanky figure positively glided down the hallways. He told Molly the entire staff was fighting for her, especially those who were with him the night she arrived.

We were very fortunate that Molly could speak. Many brain-injured patients lose that ability entirely, the ICU nurses told us. Molly often had trouble finding words and getting the words she wanted out, but she had a voice. She also had some memory.

From the start, Molly knew all of her family members, our relationships, and our names. She might call me Lyrysa, but usually, at her instigation, we would call each other "Smith," as we'd done for so many years.

She also remembered that my real name was Barbara. She called me "Barb" when we were kids. By high school it was "Smith." When I moved to New York City after college, I had the opportunity to join the Actor's Equity Union but I needed a unique name to do so. After trying every variation of my birth name I could come up with, all of which were already in use by another actor, I created my own new first name by connecting the names of my sisters: LY from Molly, RY from Mary K., and SA from Sara—Lyrysa. I wanted to honor my family with my new name. It was one-of-a-kind, and it fit me.

Molly also recognized friends who came to visit—from work, her kick-boxing class, neighbors, some FBI agents—and she amazed us as she called each one by name. However, she usually wouldn't remember for even a few hours, much less the next day, that someone had visited. Often we'd tell her that Bucky or Suzanne and Jeannine or the Bogans had visited the day before and she couldn't believe it, but she knew them when they were in her room.

On day 10, the chief neurologist and his team stopped by. "So, Molly, here you are," he said. "How are you doing?"

"Oh, I'm 50/50," Molly replied, with a sly smile.

He smiled back and then told us that her capacity to reacquire speech right away was very good evidence of brain function at a fairly high level. He said he could not do anything further and would no longer need to follow her case, unless requested. "On to rehab—very soon," he said, and they left. Honestly, I think they were all stunned.

After they'd gone, Sara and Mary K. and I giggled about how we wanted to say, "Nyaaaa, Nya, Nya, Nyaaaa, Nya. You were wrong, we were right." But everybody was so happy. The neurologists simply had their own way of showing it, we decided, giggling again.

Dr. Lo poked his head in. "Hello, Molly. You've got everyone laughing!" He beamed proudly and said he would keep going with her HBO treatments.

We were all riding high, like victorious soldiers after a grueling battle. Sara told Molly's boss at Houghton Mifflin the good news of Molly coming out of her coma and said, "We expect her to be walking out of this hospital very soon." This was so typically Sara, especially, but such were all of our expectations and determination. We were winning and she was our champion. We saw no possibility for setbacks or losing ground.

Disconnected from all the intravenous bags, we fed Molly liquid nutrition through a tube in her nose four times a day and kept a log for the nurses. Each family member was trained in how to attach the bottle to the end of the feeding tube taped to her arm and continuing into her right nostril and down to her stomach. One time, as I was setting up the bottle, I accidentally yanked the feeding tube at Molly's nose.

"Ouch! Smith! God, that really hurts," she yelled.

"I'm so sorry, Smith, it slipped! I'm sorry, I didn't mean to hurt you."

"What are you trying to do, anyway?" she asked, "Kill me?" Molly paused, then burst into laughter at her own joke. Her wit seemed as sharp as ever.

Once Molly was completely out of her coma, "like shaking off a bad dream," she said, she progressed at a speed not usually associated with humans, but instead with sunflowers or baby birds.

Along with remembering names right from the beginning, Molly used small words appropriately, the automatics—Hi, How are you, OK, That's good, Thank you, Good bye. She quickly advanced to complete sentences, could read several paragraphs at a time, sing Jackson Browne or Elton John lyrics, and learned to lean on her cleverness. When she couldn't find the words for a typical response or couldn't remember something she was just told, she would compensate by using the longest word she could think of, sometimes to comic effect.

Noticing the college banners hanging above Molly's bed, a nurse asked her what she liked best about Yale.

"What an... idiosyncratic question," Molly replied. "Why, it's a megalopolis."

Molly became adept at using her vocabulary to get out of not knowing something she knew she once did. I couldn't blame my big sister. I think she remembered she had a good education and a good job. She knew she was smart. It had to have been so confounding for her—to realize or see, perhaps, the word or thought she wanted, but have it evaporate, like mist, as she reached for it. It was bizarre for me to witness the gaps in her thinking.

But there were also moments that assured us Molly was present. Each day, the medical staff would ask her the same series of questions, and she grew more and more agitated with them.

"What day is it, Molly," they'd ask, indicating with a nod the large one-day-at-a-time calendar on the wall.

"Sunday? No, maybe it's still Saturday," Molly would say, gazing out the window.

"And where are you, Molly?"

"Some place with ubiquitous doctors."

"Where do you live?"

"Really, I have absolutely no idea."

"OK, Molly. Who's the President?"

"Why the hell should I care?"

Most of the time, even if they gave her the correct responses to these questions and asked her again a few minutes later, she couldn't remember the answers.

She was doing so well, but her short-term memory loss and inability to retain anything was pronounced, and I found it unsettling. When I watched her struggle with simple tasks, panic welled up inside me. I bit my lip not to jump in and coax the answer out of her or just blurt it out myself. I wanted to cover for her and sometimes thought I could elicit the answers from her better than the medical staff could.

I was trying to bring Molly back, to speed her recovery. And for all the joy of her progress, I was often crestfallen. Perhaps the medical staff already understood this wasn't about reclaiming, but about retraining.

It was exasperating for Molly. It soon became difficult to detect from her responses whether she really didn't know an answer or if she was answering incorrectly to spite the questioner.

"So, Molly, who discovered America?" asked the neurology resident. Molly had heard this question and the answer he expected for days.

With a grin, she said, "Leif Erickson."

Molly also learned a few phrases and responses she liked and would pull them out whenever she'd feel stumped or just didn't want to be bothered.

"Good morning, Molly. Can you tell me what day it is?" asked the nurse.

"My short-term memory is really shitty right now, OK? So, eat doo doo."

Molly did a lot of bona fide, full-out cussing, too, which raised some nurses' eyebrows. I'd read it isn't at all unusual for people with brain injuries to cuss up a storm, especially early on, but Molly was extremely good at it. Before her brain injury, she was very sophisticated and polished. Using foul language casually would have been out of character for her. But now she had a brain injury and she was feeling thwarted and agitated by what, to her, was an inexplicable and confusing situation. I'd read that when the frontal lobes are damaged, the brain's filtering system and judgment fall out of whack; impulse control is gone, emotions run amok, and base language flies out unfiltered.

She gave Sara and my dad the finger. She told Mary K. to "shut the hell up," and she said to me, "Damn you, bitch. Go to hell," when I tried to adjust her leg compressor. Sara, Mary K., and I were all told to "fuck off" dozens of times. But Molly didn't swear at my mother—she somehow remembered you don't mouth off to Mom.

I didn't care about the cussing. I clung to every syllable that came out of her mouth, as if they were an infant's first words. She was thinking and expressing herself. I decided she could learn etiquette later.

Happily, Molly had a sweetness, too, which would pop up and help soothe the sting from her unpleasant behavior. She leaned up to kiss Mom when she arrived for her shift, and said, "Bye, Dad," her turquoise eyes sparkling, as she blew him a kiss as he left her room. These were large, dramatic gestures for her, and I was relieved to see her joy.

Best of all, her sense of humor surfaced right from the beginning, along with her voice, which indicated to us that our Molly was definitely coming back. Maybe in a few weeks, or a month or two. She had come so far in less than two weeks; she was already a miracle. Her terrific wit was a hallmark of her character, and she seemed right on target. And she still loved to laugh—a sweet giggle or a big guffaw—most often tinged with a bit of mischief.

A group of five neurology residents, all of whom happened to be of Asian descent, couldn't have imagined what was coming when they gathered in Molly's room and started the round of questions with her.

"Molly, where do you think you are right now?" a woman with a slight Asian accent asked, her pencil poised over her clipboard.

Molly looked from face to face and answered, "Tokyo?"

She knew it was funny, and began laughing. After a beat, my mother and I joined her.

A couple of days before, just after the breathing ventilator had been pulled out and her voice was still deep and hoarse, the entire family had crowded around her bed, all wide-eyed in amazement. Molly peered around at the group she knew was rarely, if ever, in the same place at the same time and asked, "What are you all doing here? Don't you have jobs?"

She was right to question what we were doing to our careers and our lives to be there with her, and we were wrong to believe the Molly we once knew would return to us.

By day 11, Molly was moving her arms and legs, and could stand with assistance. But she had become toothpick thin, and for the first time I could recall, she was fragile and seemed very uncertain in her body. There she was—the swimmer, cheerleader, cyclist, skier, kickboxer, triathlete— quivering to simply stay upright on her own two feet.

For more than 30 years, I'd wanted to keep up with my big sister, but I never could do it, at any age or in any sport. She was always ahead of me, and I swam in her wake. Now, I looked into her face, contorted with fright, and was very glad that she probably wouldn't remember the next day how hard it was just to stand up.

Thankfully, Molly's willpower was ever-present. Physical therapists worked with her twice a day to redevelop her muscles, especially her arms, legs and back. She would complain to George, a PT, as he stretched her limbs while she lay in bed, that he was being a wuss and he should push harder. "My muscles can take it," she said. "I know them better than you do."

Later that day, at a meeting with the medical staff and our family, George said he'd never seen anyone regain strength and agility so fast, and that he was ready to teach my 37-year-old sister how to walk again.

Molly was anxious to eat real food, now, too, but first had to be taught how to swallow again. Turns out, swallowing isn't instinctive. I found out that humans learn to swallow by suckling as infants. Molly could well remember how enchiladas, oatmeal, oranges, or pizza tasted, but she no longer knew how to swallow them.

So several times a day, a therapist would go through a series of throat and facial exercises that would help her learn to swallow. Molly called the exercises "those stupid, ridiculous faces" and she hated doing them. The therapist would simply remind her that she had to pass a swallow test before she could have solid food again. So Molly kept practicing.

Trying to chart progress in Molly's brain was trickier. A new neurologist, a young woman, checked in on Molly now, and reported that her latest MRI/EEG revealed evident and severe brain damage, but also, some improvement in certain areas and the return of some regular brain activity. Molly would follow commands. Move your feet. Look at your sister. Stick out your tongue. She performed that one with zeal. The neurologist said she thought that perhaps Molly might be able to solve analytical problems in the future.

Later that day, in the HBO room, Dr. Lo said he didn't know how much Molly would recuperate, but he believed that HBO was continuing to help her brain cells connect and regenerate.

As he slid Molly into the chamber, she asked, "Dr. Lo, are you happy to be recharging my batteries." His large smile appeared from beneath his bushy moustache, "Absolutely, Molly. It's working."

After she was sealed in, Dr. Lo would pat the top of the clear chamber where she could see him as if he was giving her an encouraging pat on the back. We had all told Molly that Dr. Lo saved her life. She might not have been able to remember who the President was day to day or even what day it was, but she never forgot Dr. Lo's name. She was told once and it stuck.

For all the fancy machines, nothing could measure Molly's yearning and determination. On the morning of day 12, after my mom detached the nutrition bottle from Molly's feeding tube and pulled her up from her wheelchair, holding her with both arms so that they could shuffle to the bathroom—Molly stopped, looked at Mom, and sighed deeply. "All I want to do is lead a normal life," she said.

Mom stood firm in front of her daughter, squeezed her forearms, and looked directly into her eyes. "I know, Molly. I know. And we are going to get you there." They gently touched foreheads as if to share strength of mind, willpower, a promise.

In that moment, Mom silently vowed to do everything in her power to help her oldest child have a normal life. Mom told Mary K., Sara, and me about the incident later that day. Such a simple, fundamental, yet mind-bogglingly difficult request, I thought. What is normal? You hear the phrase "a normal life" all the time. It's what every newspaper story or TV news report says about victims of fires or floods, tornadoes or car accidents, or people who have cancer or AIDS—they just want to lead a normal life.

It's even what family and friends say to victims or victims say themselves—
get back to a normal life.

Can Molly have a normal life? Do I? Does anyone?

Molly's wish became our family's goal. We've had family goals for as
long as I can remember. It's how I grew up. Just before my parents divorced,
Mom suggested a family goal: To put four revolutionary women into history. Even as an 11-year-old, it seemed radical and a lot to ask for, but I felt
my mom's conviction and believed. The goal was repeated regularly and I
was game. It gave me a duty and I understood what was expected.

When my sisters and I were in college or just finishing high school, and
Molly was fresh out of Yale, we all sat with Mom on her bed and Molly said
we should revise our family goal. "Each of us should make individual goals
and we should support each other in those goals," Molly proclaimed. Again,
I understood my part and how it had an impact on the whole.

Now, years later, our world was shifting and we had a new family
goal. Often it seemed unreachable, even crazy, but a normal life resolutely
remained our mutual purpose. We clung to it like a revolution song, and
sang it in good times and bad.

F o u r

CONFIDENT that Molly was out of danger and stable for the time being, the FBI agreed to disband their 24-hour vigil at the hospital, but an agent from Walt's office would come by or call every couple of days to check on her and ask what they could do for us.

On the afternoon of day 12, my extended family of parents, spouses and significant others, and Molly's best friend, Amy, and I sat on the floor at the end of a quiet wing of the ICU and together planned alternating trips. Each of us would go home for a week or two and pull our lives together as much as possible, then return to Loma Linda for however long we could manage. We had all dashed to Molly's side two weeks before; now it was time to catch our collective breath so that we could be ready for what we anticipated was the long run ahead.

Only my mother refused to leave. Instead, she arranged for her husband, Harold, to travel back and forth to Denver to bring her what she needed and take care of things at home. She took a three-month "family leave" from her job and told them, "Don't call me, I'll call you." No matter what we said to assure her, she said she could not let go of being with Molly every day and caring for her. Nothing else was important, she said.

As it worked out, I went home right away for about nine days. I contacted my employers to get "portable" freelance writing work lined up. I also spent time with Brian and tried to prepare us for my absence for an extended period of time.

Brian and I had met in New York City after I returned from a nearly two-year job in Zimbabwe, partially supported by a grant from Rotary International for professional journalists. We'd been together for four years and now shared a mortgage on a 150-year-old farmhouse in rural upstate New York. We lived in the house and were giving it a full-gut renovation ourselves, a gigantic and messy process.

Brian was a much-in-demand contractor and carpenter around the county, and I worked from home writing documentary scripts and freelance magazine and newspaper articles. We worked together on our house during every moment of free time we had. It was worthwhile and gratifying, but also a hassle-filled and stressful living situation. Mostly, we managed the difficulties with plenty of humor and love.

In a journal entry from the week I was home I wrote:

Long hard sad day. We continued putting insulation in the walls and ceiling and hanging sheetrock upstairs. We also had a difficult talk about Molly and my life. I'm scared. Scared of Molly, our house, career, money, and what's happening with Brian. He's distancing—in a self-protective mode, I think.

Many tears shed with Brian over my priorities. Right now, that's not the house, not my work, not even him. This sucks. But we're moving ahead with optimism. I take a long walk with my love. He's the best.

Meanwhile, the FBI had helped my family find a rental apartment in Loma Linda, only a short walk from the hospital. With a little juggling, it was possible to sleep all the family members and Amy as we each came and went. We made it work with two bedrooms, one foldout couch, and one or two of us in sleeping bags on the carpeted living room floor.

A couple of days after the family moved in to the apartment, my mom and Harold drove the two hours to Molly's house and collected her cats, Sugar and Pepper, to bring to live in the apartment. Mom said she hoped Molly would be able to come visit them soon. Mom also borrowed bed linens, towels, dishes, clocks, a boom box radio, and some of Walt's tools from Molly's house. Amy, who lived in northern California, brought a bunch of stuff from her place, too. These familiar things and the cats helped make the apartment feel more like a home.

On February 18, a mere 13 days after she'd arrived, Mom called to tell me that Dr. Lo wrote in Molly's chart that she was doing well and was ready to transfer to the rehab unit. Mom quoted from Dr. Lo's note: "Will wean HBO down over the next few treatments, and she can have HBO treatments as needed, per Dr. Lo."

Later that same day, Molly's organs were declared "stable" and she was moved out of the ICU on the 9th floor to the rehabilitation unit on the 6th. Mary K. said that as she pushed her sister in her wheelchair into the elevator Molly observed that a "9" is just a "6" turned upside down.

When I returned to Loma Linda, I went directly from the airport to the hospital. Molly had improved dramatically in the nine days I'd been away. I walked into her room in the rehab unit and her voice rang out from her bed, "Hey, Smith! I missed you. I love you." I was stunned. She reached out her arms and embraced me, her eyes smiling. She seemed truly glad to be alive. Such purely loving expressions from her were scarce, but utterly glorious.

Several of the ICU nurses would come down to the rehab floor on their breaks to check in on Molly. She made them laugh saying, "I got out on good behavior."

The ICU nurses commented quietly to me that it was rewarding to have an ICU patient improve, especially so dramatically. They were too used to seeing patients die. Molly gave them hope, and they felt inspired about their work when they heard her voice.

I'd brought my computer, printer, and fax machine from home. I set up a desk in one corner of the apartment. It was made from the cheapest door I could find stacked on concrete blocks—all purchased at a nearby Home Depot. This was early 1995. It would be years before anyone in my family had a cell phone or an email account, or would surf the Internet from home or a café or a public library. Instead, we all made good use of my fax and the answering machine on the apartment telephone.

We held weekly family meetings (including Amy), and I'd make a chart of our "Molly shifts" and post it on a kitchen cabinet. The schedule would ensure that for the 16 or 17 hours Molly was awake, one of us would always be with her. This wasn't too difficult to manage since we'd all become accustomed to this since her time in the ICU.

Every morning, I'd get up early to make a large plate of fresh fruit for the family, often with my niece, Abi, kneeling on a stool nearby watching me peel and chop. We'd whisper to each other and try not to giggle for fear of waking up whichever family member was sleeping on the couch or living room floor.

To deal with the growing number of phone calls we received from Molly's and our friends, wanting to know how she was doing, we put a special outgoing message on the answering machine. Mary K.'s husband, Stephen, recorded the beginning of the message in his "official" Navy lieutenant voice: "Hello. This is the Molly Smith Weber Command Center. Here's an update on Molly." One of us, usually my mom, would add a brief synopsis of Molly's recent activities and accomplishments to the outgoing message every few days.

"Molly spoke simple words yesterday, and is speaking in complete sentences today. She recognizes her family members and calls us by name. She enjoys frequent hugs. She understood the questions she was asked even if she couldn't find the right words for the answers. She's also standing with assistance and stretching her muscles so she can learn to walk again soon. Her determination is amazing."

Friends from all over the country would call in every few days just to listen to the update, as if they were checking the weather. We were setting up to be in the trenches fighting for Molly for the long haul. It's what we imagined we needed to do to prepare.

We began working on the list of what we needed to do to gather the strands of Walt and Molly's life that had been left dangling. I was anxious to set things right to quell my stomach jitters. As if somehow, keeping busy fixing things and putting life in order would make use of my revved up adrenalin so I could better cope with the uncertainties of Molly's situation.

My assignment was to look into renting Walt and Molly's house, furnished. Mom and I made a couple of trips and began compressing closets and storing things in the garage to create enough empty space for a tenant. Most of Walt's clothes became Goodwill donations, except for a few nice items we gave to Don, his FBI partner. We gave their close friends, the Hotts, most of sports equipment since they often went with Walt and Molly on their fishing, water skiing, and bicycling activities. We also paid the Hott's teenage daughter for taking wonderful care of Sugar and Pepper for almost two weeks. I couldn't have known that we'd never show the house to even one potential renter before our scenario would shift again.

Mary K. and Stephen looked into selling Walt's truck and boat. They were also focused on keeping 3-year-old Abi happy and Mary K., now two months pregnant, healthy.

Sara arranged with the FBI to collect Molly and Walt's mail at the post office near their house and have their mail forwarded to her in Loma Linda. Sara would also keep in touch with Kristen about Molly's progress.

Dad stayed in contact with Walt's mother and sisters. Amy kept Molly's boss and publishing colleagues at Houghton Mifflin informed.

Mom dealt with copious amounts of paperwork including Molly's health insurance claims and hospital bills; her disability insurance; her old electric, telephone, and credit card bills; and a myriad of financial matters. She was also working with an attorney.

Once Molly went to the rehab unit, Dr. Lo was no longer her lead physician. He did see her when she came in for her daily HBO sessions. Molly now enjoyed watching TV or a videotape movie during her treatments. The images seemed to reconnect her to familiar places. One afternoon, Molly emerged from the HBO chamber and announced that she felt like she was "floating in heaven."

Dr. Lo smiled and said, "I bet heaven is even better than this, Molly."

That set her to singing: "Almost heaven, West Virginia, Blue Ridge Mountains, Shenandoah River."

Molly received her last HBO treatment on February 20, the 20th of 20 treatments. With her new inclination for numbers, Molly noticed and enjoyed the repetitiveness of this numerical sequence. "On 2/20, the 20th of 20 treatments!" she sing-sang over and over that day.

It was all thanks to Dr. Lo, who had pressed hard to administer the extra HBO treatments. "The guidelines say 10 treatments for extreme CO poisoning," he told me, just after Molly's last treatment. "If a patient doesn't get better by then, some doctors would say it's useless to go on. Molly is a rare situation. I didn't believe she was too far gone and I was not going to give up."

Fifteen days in, I expected Molly to continue to progress, to go on healing and recovering. Even her confidence was rebounding. She'd respond, "I'm fine," to a "How are you?" greeting, and if anyone responded to her "How are you?" by saying, "I'm good," she'd correct the grammar with glee, "You mean, 'I'm *well*.'" She'd nab me every time, and I never bothered to explain that it's grammatically fine to say, "I'm good."

When Molly was asked to do some task in therapy, she'd say, "I can do that, piece of cake." After finally taking her first few steps with Trudy, a PT, at her side, she said, "I am at the pinnacle of achievement." I assured her that I thought she would climb mountains one day.

An occupational therapist, usually Lisa, worked with Molly every day on ADLs, or activities of daily living—which was her left foot or her right hand, where to buy milk, how to mail a letter. And although she needed assistance to stand up, Molly remembered a lot of her ADLs—how to take a shower and wash and comb her hair, how to get dressed, how to fold clothes or roll socks together, and how to write, both in print and cursive letters.

She was also thrilled to be able to brush her teeth—no review needed—that is, in the actual brushing technique. One afternoon, however, Mary K. looked up to see Molly in her wheelchair in the bathroom aligning a strip of toothpaste on the head of a shaving razor. Mary K. grabbed for the razor, but Molly fought her for it. Later, Mary K. winced as she told us how strange it was to see Molly with the razor and how impressed she was with how strong Molly's arm was. Once Mary K. wrested the razor away, she handed Molly her toothbrush, and with her motherly temperament, explained the danger of the razor. But Molly was spitting mad and yelled, "I don't need you to keep me safe, Mary K.! I can do it." She'd always hated being wrong, and I guessed being corrected by her youngest sister was especially intolerable.

More and more, Molly despised being corrected about anything by her three "little" sisters. I understood it might be humiliating for her, but her anger was confusing and wrenched my heart. But one of us was often alone with her and we decided we had to risk her wrath to help teach her and protect her. Molly didn't exhibit her intense resentment to the therapists, the nurses, Amy, or Mom. It was reserved for her sisters and it felt like being punched.

As I was showing her the heel of her sock and where it should go on her foot, she yanked the sock away from me. "You are a mean-spirited, horrible woman. Just shut up and get away from me!" she shouted. "Go stand in another part of this stupid room."

I obeyed and stepped back as if I'd been walloped by an ocean wave. Almost dizzy, I breathed in, tried steady myself, and waited out her storm of frustration.

"But don't go away… OK, Smith?" she added, after a few moments.

About once a week, members of the medical staff and our family would have a meeting to discuss Molly's treatment and progress. On day 19, at the February 24th meeting, the PT said Molly was making "significant gains in mobility and balance" and the OT chimed in that Molly's ADLs were getting better, too. The speech therapist said that Molly's progress in communication was slower, with impairments in her verbal expression and difficulty with word retrieval, but that she was very motivated. The psychologist Tony Benjamin agreed and added that her family support was "very extensive." Tony also said that the family was being "followed for emotional adaptation." I smiled; we all understood that he was almost as concerned about our mental states as he was about Molly's.

At a meeting a week later, a doctor was discussing some potential long range plans for Molly with hospitals, specialists, and rehab. And we became aware that despite our best intentions for Molly, money would be an issue. Mom knew this already. She was embroiled in the escalating costs and with the insurance companies. We would face hard decisions in terms of the finances for Molly's care, even with the excellent health insurance Molly had through her job. Still, we knew that Mom, and all of us, would do as much as possible.

Mom took on a huge load of expense to have us all in Loma Linda—the apartment and its rented furniture, groceries, the utility bills—even though we all chipped in as much as we could. Mom was very generous because she believed it was critical that we all be there as much as possible to help Molly and each other. Mom put her "I'll find a way to get it done" attitude out in front and stuck to her priorities. Eventually, she even took on heavy credit card debt. She was also trying to sort out Molly's finances. With the help of Don and other agents who helped us track down checkbooks and statements at Molly and Walt's house and their local bank, Mom was able to pay their ongoing bills, their mortgage, and sort out their financial affairs.

With two cats and eight or nine people coming and going in the two-bedroom apartment, it was always a busy place, but we squeezed in time to cook meals, exercise, and laugh together. We took turns using the one telephone to do business, send faxes, and importantly, reach out to loved ones we'd left behind all around the country. We all managed to sleep a little every night. It seemed we were functioning pretty well.

Near the end of February, Brian left from New York for our Florida vacation without me as we'd agreed he should do. I'd exchanged my ticket to fly back to Loma Linda. The next night I stayed a little later than usual and told Molly about his trip to visit his family and escape the New York winter. She wanted to hear all about it.

Then she talked about Walt, but sometimes the word "Dad" came out instead. I'd read that it's common with people with brain injuries to actually know people's names and the names of objects, but often the wrong word pops out. This happened a lot to Molly and she'd struggle to say the word or name she wanted and knew was right. She most frequently confused "Walt" and "Dad," which was somewhat revealing, I thought. But her emotions were precise.

"I feel like I shot the horse out from under Walt."

"You didn't do anything to hurt Walt, Smith. The heater in your hotel room was broken."

"Now what kind of husband wouldn't check that heater? I mean with earthquakes and Dad not coming back, and everyone knows that he's not coming back and I'm supposed to cope and keep going, and I'm not ready to cope," she said.

"I'm here to help you, Molly. Your whole family is. And you're right, Walt isn't coming back. But you're doing really great. I know you miss Walt. Believe me, we all do."

"My thinking is all jumbled up," Molly said. "I just keep trying to get married, but we're in different time zones. You take someone into your home, and you make a nice place for them, and you love them very much, and then… then they aren't there anymore."

With all that said, I felt pretty sheepish. Here I was fretting because Brian had gone on vacation without me, but Walt was really gone. It was the first time I realized that Molly might feel "abandoned." She'd often felt that Dad had left her behind when our parents split up, and now Walt had left. And he was the one who promised never to forsake her.

I found that even though the concerns of my life were real, I couldn't dwell on them for very long. My reasoning was turned inside out. I felt such urgency to help Molly; it separated me from everything else, like a thick, heavy, dusty curtain.

With our apartment, weekly family meetings, scheduled shifts, and Molly's daily routines with a parade of doctors, neurologists, and therapists, life at Loma Linda began to have a routine. But then something would hurl me back into my bad-dream reality and I'd awake to my part of my family's "collective brain injury" in the spotlight. Sure enough, bit by bit, I began to discover my distracted, disjointed thinking. Pieces that didn't come together. And worse, sometimes I didn't notice pieces were missing.

On day 21, just 12 days after Molly first began to move her legs, I wrapped up my usual late-night shift at the hospital about midnight with Molly sleeping soundly. I was tired, too. I had gone in earlier than usual and did a double shift, because Abi was sick and Mary K. needed to be with her. I gently pulled up Molly's socks and put the electric leg-compression device on her left calf. I leaned over and softly kissed her forehead, but I forgot to raise the side-rails on her bed.

Out of habit or instinct, Molly tried to get up by herself about 4 a.m. to go to the bathroom. She was continent and wore diapers only at night. On this night, however, she managed to sit up and unwrap the leg compressor and take it off. But she was still unable to walk or even stand on her own. Her legs must have buckled beneath her and she crashed to the floor. She banged her tailbone badly and bruised her knees, her hip, and a few other places. My mother, on the first shift the next day, got the details from the overnight nurse who'd found her on the floor.

When I stopped by the hospital during my run the next morning, Mom wasted no time letting me know how angry she was at my mistake and how dangerous, even deadly, a fall like that could have been. She was right and I was mortified.

I apologized to Molly, the nurse, and my mother, but Mom kept putting my mistake back in my face. Her tirade was harsh. I felt sick. My insides were convulsing. I wanted to shrivel up. I trembled as I walked back to the apartment.

That night, once I was alone with Molly, I told her it was my fault she was hurting and I said over and over again how sorry I was and how horrible I felt. I was sobbing and in moments, she was, too.

Crying on each other's shoulders is something we've done together many times in the past. When our blind cat, Lucy, got out and Dad and Sara found her drowned in the neighbor's pool. When I swam poorly and lost the relay race for our team so we didn't qualify for the national meet. When one of her college boyfriends decided he'd rather date her roommate. We'd shared tears for decades, but never had I felt so frightened and so unsure.

F i v e

MOLLY Smith Weber sat at a table with a fork, a knife, and a spoon set on a placemat with a folded napkin. An occupational therapist seated across from her said, "OK, Molly, please pick up the fork."

Molly lifted up the knife and held it in front of her face as if it were a candle lighting her way.

"Is that the fork?" asked the therapist.

"No, it's not," Molly said, staring as if into a small, flickering flame, "and I don't know why I picked it up. My arm wouldn't do anything else. It didn't obey me."

The therapist gently took the knife from Molly and put it back in the table setting.

"We're working on getting the signals firing between your brain and your arms and legs," she explained, pointing toward Molly's body parts. "Don't worry. We'll get them communicating to each other again."

"I'm so tired of this," Molly said, frowning at the floor. "I'm constantly fighting with myself. I just want to be up high."

My youngest sister, Mary K., described this scene in our spiral notebook after watching her oldest sister in the therapy room. I read her words on my shift and asked her about it later.

"Molly just being wrong would have been easier," Mary K. said. "She's still got a feeding tube. She's not even using a fork. But she *knew* she didn't get the right thing and she couldn't help herself.

"It grieved my heart," said Mary K. "I mean, how do you teach someone that? I can't fix this. I can't just love her a lot and make it all better."

Mary K. had it exactly right. It was a crushing realization that all of us were just beginning to make.

The OT commented to Mary K. that Molly was improving in her cognitive daily activities, but had some hesitancy that tended to confuse her a bit. She noted that Molly was much better at finding her "middle" and establishing equilibrium. Now, she wanted Molly to focus on doing more than one thing at a time and gaining more fluidity.

"The beauty of the therapist," wrote Mary K. in the spiral notebook, "is that she has the training to realize the fine degree of Molly's brain struggle as well as her accomplishments."

Molly's family, however, did not. Molly was improving exponentially, every day. Her physical strength, agility, and coordination were progressing extremely well. But we were looking for the complete Molly to return, and soon! As if she could just shake her head, fling the brain injury aside, and go back to being who she was. It was dawning on me that recovery was not going to be quick, or perhaps ever complete.

Molly's short-term memory was sketchy—her ability to remember specific words she wanted to use, or facts or events. She could remember our pets' names from childhood to the present, but not what she did with the physical therapist that morning. It was mysterious. The hazy look in her eyes felt to me like she wasn't sure of herself—or of us either.

It was both frightening and maddening to witness what she'd lost. Not only the gaps in her cognitive skills, but also what I was losing as a result. I was elated that Molly was alive, to have my big sister in my life. But at the same time, I felt disappointed in her, and terrified of her future. My doubts turned my stomach. I wasn't ready to think about the impact her brain injury would have on my world. I thought that part was far away, but it wasn't. It was happening now, *and* for the long term. I began to realize that I'd probably have to readjust my whole life. None of our lives would ever be the same again. Even our dreams would have to be revised—everyone's. I resisted even considering it.

I also saw my utter selfishness, my impatience. And I was overcome with guilt. I wanted to escape—get away from all of it. And I hated myself for that. When I'd stop and remember that it had been only some three weeks since Molly had landed at Loma Linda, I'd grasp again how truly miraculous it was that she was speaking or thinking at all.

Like the big sister I knew, Molly would go after the kindergarten-level exercises with utter determination. This Yale and Stanford graduate took pride in putting the orange block in the orange square, rather than the purple round hole. This adult with a wounded brain was learning to walk, swallow, and sort colorful shapes. This was both delightful and discouraging for me.

On a day-to-day basis, caring for Molly, and sometimes even being around her, was becoming difficult. I needed a tough skin because I never knew what I was going to get from her. Sometimes it was fun, sometimes it was harrowing. Most of the time, it was just exhausting.

On the afternoon of February 27, just 13 days after she began to emerge from her coma, and the day after I'd made the mistake with her bed side-rails, Molly passed her swallow test. She had failed the first attempt a few days earlier. But, of course, that only made her more determined to buckle down, practice more, and get it done right. At the next test, I watched her demonstrate that she could eat an entire graham cracker—biting off little bits, chewing, then swallowing—and slowly sip and swallow, not gulp, a cup of fruit punch.

When she'd finished, the therapist said, "You pass, Molly. You can eat real food again and tomorrow we'll get rid of that ol' feeding tube."

I jumped up and yelled, "Whooo-hoooo! Way to go, Molly!" and gave her a big hug. Without looking at me, she said, "Oh, so what, Smith. Big deal."

Later the same day, she wowed the doctors at the "gait clinic" with a short stroll around the room. I was thrilled and told her how proud of her I was, but she glared like she wanted to strangle me. With that, my giddy cheerleading suddenly felt asinine, laden with my fears and soured by my guilt.

The whole family gathered in Molly's room and held a little celebration in honor of her accomplishments that day. She enjoyed the attention from all of us as she ate a real-food lunch. She sat up straight at a small table and ate a tuna fish salad sandwich and green beans, and Jello cubes for dessert—all with her fingers. Even though the feeding tube had to stay in place until the next day, just in case, Molly maneuvered around it and was in high spirits. It was heartwarming to feel her joy. And because Mom and Dad and medical personnel were around, she didn't snap at anyone.

Over the next several days, the rapid rate of her improvement continued. Dr. Lo would stop by occasionally to check on her, but even without daily HBO treatments, Molly was busy. She was walking farther and more smoothly, and using each of her hands more successfully. She was dressing herself with only a little assistance to aid her balance, and she could recite the days of the week and the months of the year perfectly, and do simple puzzles, too.

The day of therapies was taxing, but like the competitor she'd always been, she liked to train hard and win. After reading two full pages one afternoon with the occupational therapist, she sighed and said, "God, it's like an entire semester in one day! You just don't know sometimes what you've enrolled for."

I sat nearby and beamed.

Then she looked at me across the room and smiled. "Well, don't you look like something the cat dragged in?"

Molly's therapists shared a number of techniques with us that we were to use when we were alone with her, too.

"Communication is a large deficit for Molly," said Julie, a speech therapist. "The specifics get mixed up. So we need to help her work on getting the exact, right word she wants to come out. She'll know the word, but when she tries to use it, another word pops out."

"That's a persistent problem for her. She does it all the time," I said.

Julie didn't want me to feel discouraged. "This communication work will trail behind her physical recovery, which has been very fast," she said. "It takes months of repetition to make the communication connections. But she had a high performance body *and* brain—she's doing better than most people could."

So, as Julie suggested, to help Molly use the right word and express her needs accurately, we were to work on opposites and on categories.

"OK, Smith. I'm supposed to get you thinking of words about food," I said, just after her lunch tray arrived. "So, is your food tray empty?"

"No. Duh. It's got accoutrements on it," Molly said.

"Well, how about you? Are you full?" I asked.

"No, stupid, I'm hungry," she said.

"OK, good. Is your iced tea steaming hot?"

"It's steaming cold!"

"So, you have a taco, salad, and corn. What else might go with tacos?" I asked.

"Cheese, beans and rice, and that, those… chopped tomatoes."

"You mean that spicy dip with chopped tomatoes, onions and peppers?" I prompted.

"Salsa!" she yelled.

"Right!" I chimed in.

"Olé! Ay Carumba!" she said, tossing her head back, laughing.

Despite her amazing progress, an inky mood was seeping in along the edges. The very fact that she was improving meant she was beginning to realize everyday, in new ways, her new reality. She was becoming more aware of herself and her situation. With each waking moment she remembered more and understood more about herself, and so she also felt more frustrated. The unfurling recognition of her loss, although a positive sign of her brain repairing, was bewildering to her and painful for us.

She was no longer blithely oblivious, going through motions she was asked to perform. Now she knew she was saying weird stuff and couldn't always control her body or get it to do what she was asking it to.

"I'm confused and perplexed. I can't get my brain back!" Molly said, as we returned to her room one afternoon. "I feel like I've been robbed."

"Well, in a way you were, Smith. But it's going to be OK. You're here, you're alive, and we love you very much. You're really doing great."

"What do *you* know about it anyway," she snapped.

She was right. I sounded ridiculous. I didn't know anything about it. She was beginning to know what her life once felt like. She could recall that she went to excellent colleges and read a dozen books a month. She used to bike, run, and ski on water and on snow. She used to drive a nice car and have a prestigious job. She had a house. She had a husband.

And now, here was some therapist teaching her how to go up and down stairs and how to put large-piece puzzles together. It made her more and more furious. Worst of all, it was her three "little sisters" helping her match pictures to a correct word, and tie her shoes, and get her seated on a toilet. Talk about demoralizing. No wonder she'd spit her resentment at us.

"Smith, it's noisy, you're bombarding me. I don't want to be bombed!" she yelled, after I had shared a laugh about something with Sara at our shift change.

"I'm sorry, Smith, Sara was just heading back to the apartment. Maybe you'd like to stretch out for an afternoon nap," I suggested.

"Look, I don't have time for this shit," she said. "I haven't got time for stupid-ass naps. I'm not tired, OK? Damn it, already."

I'd read recently that for Molly, and most brain-injured patients, getting better necessarily meant getting teed off. Greater realization meant greater frustration. It was unavoidable. Her angry verbal outbursts were unfiltered expressions of aggravation from damaged parts of her brain. As her losses were becoming more clear to her with her increased cognitive function, she was likely feeling scared and out of control. Her tirades likely meant she felt helpless.

The trick was she really needed help, but I didn't want to set her off or have her feel patronized. I think she felt left out sometimes, even though her family was around her nearly all the time, even though she was the core of our world. She was isolated in her situation even though she was the pivot point for her whole family.

Molly was always on her best behavior with her therapists, and she would put all of her energy into accomplishing the tasks they asked her to do. They loved working with her. She made progress daily and she was fun. One afternoon, she was with a PT in the gym. She was on all fours and she was supposed to raise one leg, then one arm as the PT asked her to. Instead, she made her arm an elephant's trunk and waved it up making impressive elephant trumpeting sounds. The PT and I laughed ourselves silly, and Molly loved it.

Usually, I would observe her with the therapist; nearby, but out of her sight. It was hard at times. But I'd learned not to interject or do anything to help Molly unless the therapist asked me to. I'd squeeze my fists on top of my thighs to shut down my urge to jump in and help Molly choose the purple block to put in the purple square to complete the pegboard exercise. Every time she'd pause, grasping for the right word, exertion on her face, I'd bite my lip.

Molly's crankiness at me and my sisters was tiresome, but as long as she ate her peas with a fork, put her right shoe on her right foot, kept reading, and walked across the therapy room with her head held high, I convinced myself I really didn't care if she hollered and cussed at me. Sara, Mary K., and I would also debrief together about Molly and whatever she'd yelled at us about, and that helped us soothe our bruised feelings and sometimes even laugh.

The psychologist, Tony Benjamin, talked with Molly regularly, and also kept an eye on her family and how we were managing. When we told him about her surliness, he said that brain injuries often accentuate to the extreme the way a person acted before the injury. So, if a person was a little shy before her brain injury, she might become a recluse. If a person was competitive or had a sharp temper, like Molly, those qualities would likely be exaggerated.

When Dr. Lo visited, he explained that for people with severe brain injuries, like Molly, the brain's frontal lobe functions—planning, compassion, self-awareness, and social behavior, were the most difficult to rehabilitate. Dr. Lo said that usually there are inhibitory pathways, a positive force and negative force, which work together in a fine balance and help us say the right things and do the right things at the right time.

"Molly lost her inhibitory pathways," said Dr. Lo. "Without those inhibitors, or limiters, appropriate behavior is missing for her. It's like driving a car without brakes and not knowing it. She can't control her social behavior and she's not aware of the problem."

This was a lot to wrap my head around, but on the days Molly got really irritable and grouchy with me, I would try to think of her behavior as raw and unfiltered. And I would repeat silently in my head—"this is brain injury, this is brain injury, this is brain injury."

Molly was usually pleasant with the hospital staff, but they'd heard her chew me out and tell off my sisters more than once or twice. By now, they were getting a pretty good idea of what we meant when we spoke about Molly's spunk and her fire.

Then there'd be the complete disjoints. A couple times a week Molly would look around and it would seem to dawn on her; she'd ask, "Where's Walt?" We all experienced versions of this question from her. No matter how simple I tried to make my explanations, it was pretty clear that certain things were going to be easier for her to forget from one day to the next than others.

Sometimes she might be reading one of the many get-well or sympathy cards sent by a friend of hers or Walt's. We would read the cards to her when they arrived, and then she'd read them, and then she'd often pick them up again from the display shelf and read them again.

"It's so strange. I don't understand all of this," Molly said to Mom one morning as she studied a card.

"Are you wondering about Walt, Molly? He died, remember?" said Mom.

"Where is he?" Molly said, surprised.

"He died from the carbon monoxide poisoning, Molly."

"Oh. I am just... trying... to get over the shock," she said, and paused. "I feel like I've been left behind."

"Do you wish you had gone with Walt?" Mom said, softly.

"Yes."

"But you're alive for a reason."

"Life isn't fair," Molly said.

"No, it's not," Mom said. "I'm so sorry Walt is dead, Molly."

"I don't know why I can't remember that."

The truth is it took her many months to remember on a consistent basis that Walt had died. I wondered if the brain, like the lungs or eyes, has its own protective response. I thought perhaps like a hacking cough or tears when there is debris blowing around, the injured brain tends to reject the most pointed, painful memories. Molly could remember negative events from her more distant past, but this most recent, most terrible sadness was just not sinking in.

Molly met Walt at a country western nightspot called Bronco Billy's near Washington, D.C. when he asked her to dance. He was a good dancer and taught her some new moves. He loved her smile and her laugh and wanted to impress her. Not long after they started dating, Walt went skiing in Wyoming for a week with his best friend. Molly got a photo in the mail that Walt had taken of himself using the self-timer on his camera: He is knee-deep in snow, with the majestic Grand Teton mountain range behind him. He is propping up a huge paper sign, the size of a mattress, that says in large block letters, "Molly, I think YOU'RE grand!!!" It melted Molly's heart.

Molly wore my Mom's wedding veil of Belgian lace and a Mexican lace wedding dress. Molly's sisters were maids of honor and she walked herself down the aisle. She didn't need Dad to "give her away," she told Mom; "Dad gave me away more than 10 years ago."

But she did ask Dad to perform their ceremony; they'd written their own vows. So Dad and Walt were waiting at the front of the church for her, smiling at each other and at Molly, who beamed at everyone.

Their wedding reception was a country western dance party and they spent their honeymoon in the Grand Teton and Yellowstone parks. Almost every year, the two of them would vacation in Jackson, Wyoming, while during the summer months and school holidays, they focused all their energy on Kristen at their home.

For all of us who knew them, Molly and Walt fit together like two puzzle pieces; enhancing and completing each other.

By the end of February, about day 24, we reduced our Molly shifts to 7 a.m. to 10 p.m., which gave each of us a little more time for ourselves. I used it to work on my freelance writing jobs, make phone calls to employers and friends, and go running. I also tried to connect every day with Brian in some way that felt at least a little intimate. Phone calls were tough with the coast-to-coast, three-hour time difference, and privacy was rare in our apartment. With no email then, I wrote letters and postcards to Brian and he wrote me, too. That was romantic.

But Brian often seemed distant to me. He had been in Florida visiting his family and was now working in New York City on an upscale renovation job and crashing at his brother's apartment. He was not in our home working on our project. He was detached from me.

My mission was to focus on Molly and I was trying to build some sort of a routine in Loma Linda. But my life back home —my boyfriend, my work, my house—was beginning to feel estranged. I missed sleeping in different rooms with Brian, waking up with a different view as we renovated the house around us. I even missed contributing regular paychecks to our finances. I missed seeing us progress on our projects together.

I know my sisters were also striving to nurture their relationships from a distance, or at least minimize wear and tear. We were all struggling with split focus. I felt normalcy slipping away in one place while I was trying to get accustomed in a new place. I felt out of sorts, as if my perspective was warped. I assumed this would be temporary.

Some days I'd think about Brian—lean and long-limbed with shoulder-length dark hair— and how he'd bound into a room like an excited black Lab. He'd scoop me up in his arms and lift me off my feet in an all-out embrace, his hazel eyes glinting. I thought, it's good to know he's busy with work, seeing friends, and getting along fine. I don't need to fret about him.

Other days, more than I needed food or water or sleep, I needed to hear Brian's voice reassuring me.

On day 25, after weeks of struggling to know what day it was, Mary K. said Molly looked up at the calendar in her room after finishing breakfast and said, "Look, it's March 1st, Mom and Dad's anniversary." Mary K. was astounded. It was a date none of us had spoken of or probably even thought about in decades. Our parents had been divorced for 20 years.

I could tell Molly was feeling pleased with her progress, and she was receiving lots of praise for her achievements. Taking notes, as I usually did, at a family and medical staff meeting a few days before, Trudy, the PT, reported that Molly had made significant gains in her functional mobility, increasing her walking distance from 40 to 80 feet in just a couple of days. She was also better with trunk alignment and planning her body movements, but still had "profoundly impaired sequencing for body parts she cannot see, like her feet or knees." Trudy added they were working on that and on Molly's balance and "motor perseveration," gestures that Molly would repeat over and over again, unable to control them or stop. "But Molly is very motivated and we're aiming to go 100 feet by the end of the week," Trudy said.

The speech therapist said that Molly's progress in communication and cognition was a bit slower, but she was now managing two-step commands about 50 percent of the time. She also said that Molly had words to use but had a difficult time with "specific word retrieval" and often had "verbal perseveration," or repeating the same syllable or word many times without being able to complete the word or phrase she wanted. Tony Benjamin told us that perseveration is often seen with brain injury and that neurologists associate it with damage or abnormal functioning in the brain's frontal lobes.

Just a few days later at the family and medical staff meeting, the therapy folks were buoyant; looking at each other and across the table at us with excitement, as if a 4th of July parade was about to come around the corner. The therapists could barely wait until their turn to read aloud to us from their notes about Molly.

"Molly has made dramatic increases in her overall functional abilities," read an OT. "With moderately complex reasoning exercises, Molly was able to follow directions and displayed good problem solving. Her attention span has also increased. She is sometimes unable, or unwilling, to ask for help, but she agrees when asked if she needs help."

George, the PT, said, "Molly expressed some fear yesterday when she was walking fast, but she didn't slow down or stop. She walked 100 feet a total of *four* times, with a short rest between walks." He looked up and smiled. "She is inconsistent in achieving a heel strike on her forward stride but we're practicing lunges and squats and abdominal crunches to build strength."

It was great for us to hear from the therapists about Molly's excellent progress. I felt relieved and encouraged. The only somber moment in the meeting came from Tony Benjamin, who commented that through separate conversations he'd been made aware of rising concerns and surfacing stresses in Molly's family members.

To be honest, I was much more interested in helping Molly with her handwriting and reading than just about anything else. Sara seemed to enjoy working through the memory and association exercises. Mary K. and Abi had fun tossing a ball to Molly so she could practice alternating her left and right hands. Mom went with Molly to nearly all of her daily therapy sessions to watch and learn. I thought, it's good to be aware of stress, but really, we're being pulled along with Molly's successes. We're doing all right.

Molly's therapists were now trying to incorporate some of her former activities and had her painting pre-printed designs with watercolors in the art room, throwing balls through hoops in the gym, and doing some floating and kicking in a pool. When they were resting at the pool edge, the PT with Molly asked what her hobbies were.

"Sports, swimming, and competing with my colleagues," Molly said. I was standing on the pool deck and said, "You're a strong girl, Molly." She shot me a look. "I am WOMAN, hear me ROAR!"

Later I reminded Molly that she was a great swimmer—a national champion—and also an excellent artist. Even as a little girl, Molly loved to draw, and demonstrated considerable talent. When handed a sheet of paper in school and asked to draw a picture, Molly would immediately divide the page into eight squares and draw a fully conceived story cartoon. When we lived in Phoenix, Mom and Dad found a woman who taught oil painting, because Molly, about age 8, wanted to take classes and Dad decided to do them with her. Eventually, after a several weeks of lessons, they each painted a canvas of a desert landscape. Both are beautiful and reveal excellent artistic skills, but you cannot tell which was painted by an adult and which was painted by a child. Molly has always hung the two paintings together wherever she lives.

Molly had continued to sketch through the years, usually on a whim, but with an expert's touch. She even began teaching Kristen how to draw using a beautiful art set, a Christmas gift from my Mom.

A few days later at the Loma Linda pool, Molly became uneasy in the water. She clung to the side, refused to try floating on her back, and didn't want to put her face in the water. The same week, Molly was asked to sketch or paint a still life in the art room. She scowled at the bowl of fruit, slapped her pencil down on the drawing pad, and folded up her arms tightly. I tried to encourage her but she ignored me. I was so disappointed in her reluctance; she'd been swimming and drawing all week. Later when I talked to Sara and Mary K. about it, I thought maybe she was remembering that she used to do these activities so very well. Her growing self-awareness gave her determination, but also, perhaps, some self-protectiveness.

I began to see that with brain injury, just like with a job, or friends, or a family, some days are better than others. Some days Molly could be charming, sail through her physical therapy, eat oatmeal with a spoon, and type on a keyboard just fine. Other days, nothing seemed to flow. She'd be cross at hello. She'd put her pants on backwards, push her toast around with a spoon, and mumble in complete distraction through her reading exercises.

On those hard days, it seemed unreal, like a bad déjà vu. I'd watch my big sister clutch her arm when she could not follow instructions to move a ball left and right or up and down. At the end of that session, Molly slumped as she listened to the therapist describe what they'd work on the next day. As I took her arm to walk back to her room, she turned to me with tears in her eyes, and said, "Why is this so hard to process? It's a disturbance in my pursuit."

I fell into my cheerleader role. "You're doing great Molly. You'll get it, don't worry." I tried to hug her but she didn't want my affection. It felt like trying to hold an agitated cat.

I told myself I was trying to reassure her, but I was also trying to square myself with myself, too. I needed her to get better. I had high expectations for both of us. This was Molly, after all. I didn't easily adjust to the two-steps-forward, one-step-back, enigmatic progress of her injured brain.

Back in her room, she was resting and voiced my thoughts. "Do you know what the missing ingredients are, Smith? I'm looking for pieces of the mystery. Do you have any clues?"

"Look Smith, I know you'll do it. All those pieces will come together. I'll help you. You just have to keep at it."

It was a flat response. Molly could hear that. And I could, too. I was also wrong.

The next day, Sara, who'd been sick and away from the hospital for a couple of days, watched Molly working with her therapists all afternoon. When I arrived for my evening shift, Sara seemed puzzled, "You know, today I saw how much recovery Molly still needs to make. I know progress takes time, but this is a lot. It's pretty scary. It's like her healing meanders, a little over there, back in, back out. I just didn't see it before."

Later that night back at the apartment, Sara and I stayed up late talking in hushed voices in the kitchen about the rising level of tension and strain we saw in Mom. She was seeing Molly's sputtering rehab the same way we were. Mom did more than anyone for Molly—spent more time, dealt with all the paperwork, logistics, and money for all of us—and it seemed to be breaking her down. We didn't have solutions; it just helped to express the concerns we had, for all of us.

Usually my evenings with Molly were mellow; she'd be tired from a full day of therapies. We could make each other laugh easily, just by cracking jokes or being silly—making slurping noises in cups with straws or remembering some embarrassing thing I did. She loved to laugh at my self-deprecating humor. Like the time I climbed up on the starting blocks at a big swim meet, cap and goggles on, very serious and intent and not looking around at all, ready to dive in. I didn't realize until I finally heard the yelling and someone pulled me away that it was the boys' race not the girls'. Molly laughed a long time and said, "Yep, you were going to swim with the boys, but they didn't want you to. They didn't want you there."

Brian would often call me in Molly's room after her dinner time. It became a welcome custom. If he didn't call for some reason, I'd use the hospital's pay phone to leave him a message on our home answering machine.

One night Molly asked, "Hey, isn't Brian supposed to call you now?" as she squeezed toothpaste on her toothbrush.

"I hope so, Smith, but I never know."

"He better so I can give him a talkin' to," Molly mumbled, as she brushed.

Brian and I often had good conversations by phone at the hospital. Molly didn't even mind if I moved towards the window in her room, dragging the phone and its cord across her bed, to talk with him. She knew her turn was coming.

I'd ask him about his work and we'd discuss house logistics. I could picture his eyes looking down at something he would be fiddling with in his hands—a camera lens, a pair of pliers—and I could picture his long eyelashes making crescent shapes on his cheeks.

He also listened to my concerns about my work or Mom not sharing some of her burden. He'd say, "Try talking to her again and tell her that you are worried about her, that you want to help. Keep trying."

And we would always exchange I miss yous and I love yous.

Finally, I'd move back towards Molly and tell Brian how much she was progressing and he'd ask to speak with her. She so enjoyed his attention and the nice things he'd say to encourage her. He was glad to talk with her for a few moments and then she'd hand the phone back to me, smiling. He'd tell me he thought she sounded great, and not to worry. He was carefree and breezy. To me, to Molly, back to me, and then he'd be gone. Good night.

I wrote him more letters, he sent fun greeting cards, and I felt like we were doing our best to stay connected. But the distractions of family, finances, and floundering careers tangled my heartstrings. My anxiety piled up being away from him for so many weeks. I felt isolated and stuck.

S i x

ON March 5th, exactly one month after she arrived at Loma Linda, clinically dead, the woman who some had predicted would remain in a vegetative state for the rest of her life made her first trip beyond the hospital grounds. She walked with a physical therapist on each side to and from the post office, several blocks away. She needed propping up only as she stepped off the curbs. Stepping up was easier. She told the PTs when they reached the first corner that she didn't want to use the curb ramps. "I'm not a wimp," she said.

By now, Molly and her story were well known to many of the Loma Linda staff, about how she beat the odds of being in a coma with a severe brain injury, the HBO treatments, and her rapid recovery. Lorna, a nurse and Trudy, the PT, remarked that even in the rehab unit where Molly was now, they had patients who might survive, but who didn't have much will to go on.

"They slowly decline and many of them will never again be as able-bodied as they once were," Lorna said.

"But not Molly," Trudy said, smiling at her. "She's determined to get better and she rewards our efforts with great results."

That day, on a mat in the gym, Molly had rolled over on to her stomach and pressed up to all fours. This time she didn't imitate an elephant. Instead, she crouched, concentrated, and then stood up with just a little assistance She also walked down a long hallway with Trudy spotting her from behind and only one hand on the rail. Then she sat down and stood up alone with a cup of water in her hand, twice, without spilling a drop.

After Trudy and the nurse left, Molly remembered with no prompting that two therapy dogs had been in the activity room.

"I want to see them every day," Molly said. "I loved those dogs."

"Really soon, Smith, you can come visit your very own kitties at the apartment. Sugar and Pepper would be so happy to see you."

"Yeah, that would be good," she said, looking at the floor.

"We'll make a plan and do it soon," I said.

"Just shut up, Smith."

As ecstatic as we were with the simple fact that Molly was becoming more stable each day, the enormity of what she'd lost was becoming more obvious. I wondered to myself, how far can she go? Will she improve enough to live on her own and be happy? Friends would always ask when Molly would be fully recovered and get back to normal again.

At first, when she was still in a coma, I celebrated every spark of life, every tiny remnant of Molly that was there. A finger twitch, a blue sliver of her eye barely open. But after she was conscious for a few weeks, I began to see the shadows, not the light; to hear the silence, not the sounds. I was looking for what was missing in Molly, not what was there. My view of the world went into reverse. I was allowing Molly's successes to be dimmed in my mind by her deficits.

A day earlier, Molly's OT had given her memory/association exercises. She was able to follow the directions and gathered the pictures correctly into groups—fruit, clothing, colors, animals. But she could not get the task of alternating her right and left hands to pick up the pictures. The image of her hesitating and staring at her jittery, confused hands stuck in my mind for the rest of the day. I wanted to feel gratitude for her improvements, but I was distracted by my own fears.

Molly was joyful, though, sometimes, especially when Abi would come with Mary K. on her shift. Abi was usually the only child around the rehab unit, and she was spirited and adorable. One morning, Molly surprised everyone by greeting Abi in her Donald Duck voice. When we were kids, Molly would do a terrific Donald Duck imitation. I hadn't heard it in years. But there she was sitting up in her hospital bed, wearing a Yale T-shirt, chirping and teasing Abi as Donald Duck. Abi hugged her and squealed and giggled in delight. Abi, a bright 3-year-old, was already a huge fan of all things Disney and couldn't believe her funny "Tia Molly" could turn into Donald Duck. Abi loved it and it meant the world to the rest of us.

Molly's friends also lifted my spirits when they'd call or leave messages on the "Command Center" answering machine or when they came to visit her. Molly would be on her best behavior and her friends would tell me how much they admired and loved Molly, and what a miracle it was she was alive. I needed those reminders.

One evening, around day 29, I tried to help Molly use silverware with her dinner and suggested she eat her soup with a spoon rather than the handle end of a table knife.

"I'll do it this way. I'm fine, I don't need you," she snipped. "You don't have to tell me what to do."

She quit the soup and began picking with her fork at the illustration of a pear on the paper placemat. I suggested she use the same technique on the broccoli pieces on her plate, and she scowled at me and bellowed, "No." I resigned and sat quietly nearby. I thought, at least she's using the tined end of the fork to stab at the pear after trying to cut her chicken breast with the spoon a few minutes earlier.

Writing in my journal as Molly drifted off to sleep, I described her as "striving for independence." She didn't want to be assisted with anything, especially by a little sister. Tony had warned us about this frustrated, sharp-tongue phase and that it was actually an excellent indication of mental recovery and progress. "She's making more and more connections in her mind, she's more aware of herself, of everything, and the harshness to you is part of the result," he said. "Try to keep perspective and a sense of humor. And don't take it personally."

Molly still bitched a lot more at me, my sisters, and now Amy, than at my mom or the medical staff. I reminded Mary K. and Sara (and myself) that this was just a phase she's going through and we had to concentrate on moving forward.

Later that night, I dropped the one grocery bag out of four that had two bottles of wine in it, in the apartment's parking lot. I'd bought the wine to share with the family, and to have a glass myself that night with anyone who might be awake. Remarkably, Dad had done the same thing, breaking two bottles of wine in the parking lot, a few days before. I wanted to laugh, but instead I cried.

I wanted to keep my energy up to push my sister through, to pull her along. But that energy was eroding, and, like driving down a road full of potholes, I dodged but could not avoid the jarring. The entire family was beginning to falter under a strain we didn't even realize. Cracks were splintering across the neat little world we'd created to revolve around Molly.

Sure, we were functioning, sticking to our daily schedules, but our lives were crumbling.

Mom developed a disturbing facial tic. One side of her face or the other would twitch like a hiccup, interrupting the smoothness of her pale fair skin. Her blue eyes lacked some of their glimmer. She found it hard to smile. Her practical side and familiar softness waned. Yet she remained determined. I asked to take over some of the paperwork with insurance people and financial stuff that she'd been handling, and she agreed to let me help. But in the end, she wouldn't let go of it and never did allow any of it to be delegated.

We'd asked Amy, who was away from her job, her home, and her fiancé, to stay as long as possible. But Amy rattled Sara, in particular, by wading into personal family issues in ways that she meant to be helpful, but that seemed simply to be meddling.

Meanwhile, Sara was concerned about putting her teaching and her PhD work aside. She was facing deadlines she wouldn't make, job pressures she couldn't resolve, and struggling to cope with uncertainty about her future with her boyfriend, Walter.

Mary K. had her own family and felt torn. Stephen was protective and he wanted her home with him in Colorado. They both wanted to return Abi to a more normal environment as soon as possible. And Mary K. was pregnant, after all. She had already suffered a miscarriage four months before and we all wanted her to have every advantage this time around.

I missed Brian and his adoring ways, but I felt confident that we were A-OK, most of the time. However, I got mired in a terrible argument with my dad; a convoluted misunderstanding that lasted weeks. It nibbled away in the background and sometimes felt like it chewed right through my chest. It was devastating to fight with him, and to my surprise, it also had me battling with his wife, Martha. She and I had become friends during the 20 years of their marriage, though my sisters did not have this closeness. Like many screw-ups, it all started by trying to do the right thing when we should have kept our noses out. Sara, Mary K., and I sat down one night at the apartment and shared our concerns about Molly and Mom, and Dad's imminent return from his home in Virginia to Loma Linda. Our priority was to do what we thought was best for Molly, and we decided to suggest to Dad that he come back on his own this time, without Martha. It all seemed logical, but it was to blow up into a major conflict.

Somehow ignoring the complicated family background, we made a dreadful misjudgment. We put Dad in our shoes. We had sent Brian, Walter, and Stephen home to their lives and to manage our home fronts in our absence. We were trying to save space at the apartment and save money at home. I was wrecking my work potential and my savings account to travel to Loma Linda and be there to help, and we had no idea how many months of rehab lay ahead. We wanted Dad to plan long term and think about conserving his financial resources just as we were. We thought, better that Dad can come and go twice, rather than using two tickets for him and Martha to fly here only once. We had no business even wondering about his time or resources. We were way out of line.

We had also learned from the doctors and through our own experiences that one-on-one time with Molly was the best way to help her learn and reconnect with each of us. We knew Mom was staying put and needed all the support she could get. We needed Dad's help with Molly, who definitely needed her father. And we wanted him to have time with her alone.

Much later, I realized how the time in Loma Linda was such an odd scenario for me and my sisters—the awkwardness of our long-ago divorced parents, who really got along OK with each other, now needing to be together a lot, even living under the same roof, for the sake of Molly, their first child.

Before her accident, Molly and Dad had begun to forge a healing process after years of being somewhat estranged. With a couple of visits and more frequent communication, they were finally beginning to mend long-standing gaps. After she came out of her coma, it was obvious how much she needed and loved her dad. The opportunity for them to have a closer relationship was of primary importance to me.

After our talk, my sisters nominated me to call Dad. I was closest to him, and something about being the middle kid or a Libra or a ridiculous optimist, I don't know—but I've always been the "United Nations negotiator" in my family. I actually always believed I was doing the right thing. (Several years earlier, Molly had described this trait, this "bad habit of mine," as she called it, to be so prevalent as to be "almost to a fault.")

For much of my youth I tried to balance my volatile sisters on either side of me. Let's all play Parcheesi together. We should all go ice-skating. We can ride our bikes to the pool together. Usually I wound up getting rejected by both Molly and Sara as they paired up and went off without me. I'd made the same mistake with my parents. As a kid, I'd get out of bed late at night to try to help resolve their late night arguments while my sisters slept. A little child unarmed in the adults' crossfire—ineffective, but persistent. Why are you crying? What's wrong? What are you fighting about? I wanted so badly to make things right.

It took years of therapy for me to finally learn that I should set aside this "peacemaker" role, to learn that I cannot fix people or their situations. But at the time, in our Loma Linda apartment, phone receiver in hand, I was chockfull of a collective brain injury I wasn't aware of, my judgment terribly awry. I blurted out our "request" to Dad and all of our misaligned, faulty logic. He was shocked and angry.

Later, after he told Martha, he called and told me she felt unfairly treated and excluded. He said he was desperate to get back to Loma Linda and Martha had decided not to come.

"I'm really hurt. Y'all have made a terrible decision and just added one more difficult thing to my plate," Dad said, after he arrived, his southern accent suddenly rigid and stern.

Once the wheels of misunderstanding were set in motion, I couldn't find a way to stop the train. Everything I did seemed to fuel the engine with more fury and grease the track with resentment.

When Dad would call Martha from the apartment on the one phone we had, he'd say aloud he didn't know why we'd done this to him. That he needed support, too, and that came from being with his wife. He told her he felt as if we were opposed to him being there for Molly. "But they can't tell me not to come—I'm her father," he said.

"Dad, our request wasn't about excluding you or Martha," I told him. "We very much want you to be with Molly." We kept on squabbling.

"You asked me and Martha to abide by your decisions—you didn't consult me, you didn't ask us."

"I was wrong. But you could have said something at the time about your concerns and your anger. You had a lot of plans you didn't tell me about."

"You seem not to have considered that I could spend time with Molly alone even if Martha were here," Dad said.

"Why didn't you say something about that when I first called?"

I didn't know Mom had offered Dad frequent-flyer miles or that he was thinking of staying in a hotel with Martha. He didn't know I was unraveling over finances, Brian, my career. We were in utterly different circumstances and I should have never tried to see his choices through my haze.

Try as I might to untangle the mess, I couldn't make it clear to him what we'd intended, what I had tried to communicate, where I went wrong. I was so sorry for my mistakes, I wanted him to hear my apologies. Instead, I felt rebuffed. He felt burned and misjudged, and he couldn't hear me through his anger.

The conflict was consuming. Weeks of wrenching arguments, most often in letters, lay ahead and fell on my shoulders alone as my sisters stepped aside. I'd always had a good relationship with my father, and now this had to happen.

I wanted to help Molly. I needed to do my writing work. I didn't have the time or energy to constantly work and rework it with Dad and Martha, but I did it anyway. I discussed it. I wrote letters. I told Dad and Martha that I loved them and was sure we could resolve our rift, but on my own, in quiet moments, as I walked to the hospital or when I would watch Molly sleep before I left her for the night, I felt disoriented. I was in disarray. Hopeless.

Only time, a lot of it, brought slow recognition of how daunting and draining the Molly ordeal was on me—on the whole family. I believe all of our emotions, reasoning abilities, and communication skills were being snarled by our collective family brain injury, just as we'd been warned. But that realization was a long time in coming.

Back then, it felt like drowning. The more I struggled, the more I sank. I couldn't pull myself up long enough to breathe, to get perspective. And even if I could have realized my part of the family's brain injury, I couldn't understand its impact. I was held under by it.

Amidst my own turmoil, there was my mother's tic, my father's resentment, and my sisters' struggles. Some days we'd pass each other like zombies, either at the hospital with Molly or at the apartment. And now, with all of our concerns and complications so big, the few rooms did not seem to contain us all.

I wore the same clothes, ate the same foods, stared into space over my coffee cup day after day. Wandering in the quest that was pulling me along. I wrote in my journal—*I am so stressed out. Everyone is. The stress here is a big deal.*

The words looked puny. As if this stress was like a bad day at the office.

I jotted a list of things to help me de-stress: *Play with Abi more. Walk with her to feed the ducks at the pond. Brush the cats. Try to get some writing work done. Stretch. Exercise. More phone calls and postcards to Brian. Meditate.*

I also tried to create a sense of normalcy and fun in our hacked-together apartment. I taped funny snapshots my friends sent me on the bathroom mirror: Gay friends dressed up in tutus and tiaras at New York's Halloween parade; a little girl's feet standing in the bathtub surrounded by a dozen floating naked Barbie dolls; a group portrait with everyone in goofy paper plate masks they'd made with magic markers, cotton balls, and dry macaroni.

I hung different inspirational quotes on the refrigerator each week, next to the new Molly Shift Schedule: From Charles Dickens ("It was the best of times, it was the worst of times...") to Abby Hoffman ("Never impose your language on people you wish to reach"). From Lily Tomlin ("The road to success is always under construction") to Eleanor Roosevelt ("The future belongs to those who believe in the beauty of their dreams") to Shakespeare ("It is not in the stars to hold our destiny but in ourselves").

These notions made me feel like I was creating a home life and doing something active about my stress, but my family members didn't react much to my efforts. Or they didn't mention it. They were coping in their own ways, which was OK. We often retreated to our own corners in the apartment when we weren't dealing with Molly issues together. This was sensible.

Nothing was really working for me though. Even though I honestly tried, I could no more meditate than I could speak Arabic. I kept exercising even though I often got cramps in my gut when I did. My hair was falling out by fistfuls in the shower. I was also having bad dreams almost nightly about Brian being with someone else and leaving me.

I told myself I didn't have good reasons for feeling edgy. During his trip to Florida, he'd sent me a touristy postcard, a packet of seashells, and even a coconut covered in postage stamps with "I'm nuts about you" scrawled on it. From his condominium renovation job in Manhattan, he wrote a sweet note on a chunk of 2x4 lumber and mailed it like a postcard to me. He was being thoughtful and creative, I thought.

I called him one night at his brother's apartment in New York City. "I just want you to know how sexy you are," I said, "and I *really* miss you," I was imagining his sinewy body, his long hair in a ponytail, and his smiling, Irish green eyes.

"Aw, I miss you, too. So how many more weeks will you be there?"

"Three more. We're getting there, babe. Then I can take a break and come home for a while."

"OK. That's really good. Wow, there are a lot of sirens out on Broadway, can you hear them?"

"Yeah. Maybe there's a fire. I hear sirens all day at the hospital."

"I'm gonna grab my camera and check it out. Let's try to catch each other tomorrow. I love you."

"Be careful. I love you, too."

I sensed interference. Like static on the radio. As soon as you step aside or take your hand off the antenna, the buzzing starts and the music fades away.

My self-doubt became intense. I wondered what a horrible person I had become to leave Dad angry, Martha bitter, Mom off-balance, and Brian wanting photos of fire trucks and strangers on city streets more than a conversation with me.

Everything in my life, except Molly, seemed to be moving backward, no matter how hard I pressed to go forward.

I looked for comfort in my routine in Loma Linda. Up early. Make fruit plate. Exercise. Run errands. Work. Go to the hospital. Be with Molly. Call Brian. Back to the apartment. Try to sleep. Just be normal and get through.

But there was nothing normal about what we were doing. We were trying to cope with Molly's severe brain injury. It was not routine at all. I ignored, or didn't allow, that fact. I was chin up, eyes ahead, march.

I should have known to approach each day with caution and careful steps; the way you might enter an unfamiliar house in the dark. I was fumbling in dim light, bumping into furniture. Getting jostled, but still going; pushing forward to the next room, glossing over the bruises.

On March 8th, (day 31, though it seemed like years since the accident) at the family and medical staff meeting, I made notes, as usual, about what was said. Dr. Scott Strum, the director of Loma Linda's brain injury and rehabilitation program, was Molly's new attending physician.

"I see that Molly's mobility and ADLs (activities of daily living) are improving, however she's struggling with apraxia," Dr. Strum said, looking up from Molly's chart.

"Right, for instance, she's not able to stack different sizes of blocks," said a PT. "But we're working on coordination and on her midline orientation, too."

I learned that apraxia is a movement planning problem, an inability to sequence motions, and it's often seen in people rehabbing brain injuries.

A speech therapist said they were working with Molly to get two-step commands with 70 to 80 percent accuracy and would focus on her listening skills to improve her attention span to two minutes. "Molly reads pretty well, but has difficulty with comprehension and concentration," the speech therapist said. "We're also practicing writing full sentences and spontaneous words and phrases."

Then Tony said, "Molly *is* dealing with the loss of her husband, although I expect her grieving process to go on given Molly's cognitive deficits. She does express her..." he paused, looking for the right word, "frustrations—at least to her family members. So I'll continue checking in with them about their stress levels and ability to cope with Molly's disabilities."

The next day, Molly only walked about 50 dinky steps with Trudy, the PT. She also had a hard time changing directions to walk around a corner in the hallway. It was strange. But I shrugged it off, called it a blip. Molly, however, was pissed off, cursing at her shoes, the wall, and at me, but I was used to her growling. It wasn't a good day, but I didn't sound a single negative note. I kept up my praise for Molly and her incredible progress so far.

After all, I thought, wasn't she alive because she'd refused to give up? Because we had never allowed a moment of doubt about her ability to pull through? I'd been conditioned my whole life to believe Molly was going to succeed. Now, just five weeks into brain injury, I was already accustomed to quelling any flickering of uncertainty I had along the way.

Later, Trudy, the PT, tried to encourage Molly to take a longer stride by having her kick a ball as she stepped forward. It helped her feet advance a little better, but without the ball Trudy had to give Molly "maximum verbal cues," as she called it. Trudy even had to physically push Molly's heel from behind with a small prod from her own toes.

In the midst of all this staggering effort, Molly stopped, looked down at Trudy and said, "Why in the world are we doing this?" Her sarcasm surprised Trudy.

"I want you to take longer steps."

"I can't see my legs. It's too intimidating to take longer steps."

"They're right here. Look. Your legs are right here," Trudy said, patting Molly's thigh. "C'mon, Molly we can do this. You can walk."

"I don't care. I just can't do it. My husband died last week," she said, her face flat.

It'd been over a month, but the comment halted me like a twisted ankle.

"I know. I'm so sorry, Molly," Trudy said, pausing. "Ready? Let's try again."

"Oh, sure, what the hell," Molly grumbled.

That day, Molly stopped being able to place one foot in front of the other in a normal walking motion. Trudy put up-arrows in her chart next to "distractibility," "irritation," and "fear." The next day, in the pool with another PT, Molly did arm and leg exercises for coordination. She said she was "very afraid" as the PT guided her to step down into the pool and when it was time to step out.

Then, Sara and I both noticed that Molly was suddenly fearful of moving backwards and turning, too. "I just don't understand what to do," she said, as we tried to have her back up and sit down. Her confidence was missing.

We mentioned our observations to the OT, and told her that we knew Molly wasn't afraid of a pool or of sitting down in a chair. This was out of the blue. It didn't make sense. The OT said it could be her increased awareness and frustration. Sara and I exchanged doubtful glances.

That night, back at the apartment with Mom, we compared notes about Molly over the past few days. Sara said, "We know what Molly's frustration is like, but this wasn't like what we'd gotten from her before."

The following morning, the rehab therapists told us they'd decided as a group to give Molly "win-win" exercises to reestablish her confidence to combat her growing anxiety.

I did my own mental checklist: She had aced getting dressed by herself, with only a little assistance. Now she was putting two socks on one foot and couldn't get her arms in her sleeves. Molly had known for weeks how to get to the hospital's elevators or to the bathroom. Now she became disoriented in the hallway and opened a closet looking for the toilet. She also couldn't remember what she was saying and she had trouble recalling what someone had just asked her.

Two weeks before, she'd mastered standing up and sitting down by herself, now she couldn't do it. Even when Sara and I lifted her by her elbows, her arms and legs wouldn't move into place and would seem to resist, as if her body was disconnecting. When I tried to help her take longer steps to walk to the chair in her room, she began making soft crying noises, whimpering, but no tears. Then her soft moaning became searing agitation. I recorded a piece of our conversation in the spiral notebook before she had dinner, the first time I was sure something was truly different:

"I hate peeing, I hate it. Why do I have to go pee?"

"Molly, you can do this. The bathroom is right here. I'll help you over to the toilet."

"I don't want to sit. I hate to sit and pee. I'm just not going to do it anymore."

Not only did she not want to practice the activities she had learned to do, she didn't want to do them at all for any reason. I thought, maybe she's just exhausted. For weeks, she's been conditioning and retraining her body and her brain every day, all day long, and it was a huge, demanding task. I was trying to be positive and hoped she was just having another bad day.

But she got worse. Even that night. Dramatic changes that couldn't be passed off anymore. She could not stand up, walk, or turn around. She hated brushing her teeth. She couldn't find the telephone on the nightstand.

"Where is it? Where the fuck is the phone?"

"Smith, it's right here. Right next to you. See? Who do you want to call?" I asked.

"You took it. You took everything! You are an evil, horrible person. I can't stand this! I can't do this."

I referenced the spiral notebook like a lifeline. No, I'm not crazy. She did read that chapter in the book 10 days ago and remembered what it said. She did go up and down the flight of stairs in the gym.

If a broken bone started to re-break or if a wound started to un-heal, the patient and her family would notice right away and react quickly to remedy the situation. Not so with brain injury—it is unlike any other injury. There is no scientifically proven treatment protocol, no tested guidelines about what healing should look like, no "what-to-expect" timetables.

I couldn't understand her regression. My mind wasn't accepting what was going on. I'm sure my optimism and hopefulness, as well as my piece of the collective family brain injury, got in the way. I also had no idea how potentially perilous her situation was.

Each attempt and new failure added another layer of confusion for Molly. Her brain didn't have the ability to understand why she used to run before, could walk all around Loma Linda last week and now, could not even shuffle herself across her room. We didn't know either.

Her short-term memory was iffy, but she had some recollection and she had muscle memory. She knew darn well she had walked six blocks to and from the post office the week before because she remembered how it felt and she wanted that feeling again.

I tried reminding her of the feeling of that achievement in an effort to encourage her to walk across the room with me to her wheelchair near the doorway. She looked at me with an athlete's determination. Then she looked straight ahead, then at her feet, then the door, her feet; they didn't move. She turned to me with an expression on her face like something she'd been holding in her hand had flown away, she was shocked and scared.

"This is horrible. It's so shitty, it's goddamn awful," she spat out.

"This *is* crazy," I agreed, lost for words. I braced Molly against the bed and I brought the wheelchair to her.

Molly hated having to use the wheelchair again after her victory of getting out of it before. Mary K. had reminded us just the night before how Molly had walked unassisted down the hallway five days earlier, while Mary K. pushed her empty wheelchair behind her. And now I was helping her to sit in it again.

"I despise that thing," Molly yelled at her wheelchair. "It's disgusting."

It didn't make sense to her. Or to me. Or to any of us. Healing, once it starts, is supposed to only go forward. I desperately wanted to believe this was temporary; a day or two and she'd be OK. It was so unexpected, so fast. I couldn't grasp the trouble right in front of me. Then I couldn't deny it. She was being sucked away, yanked in the wrong direction, pulled inside some dark vortex.

We family members told each other the odd things happening in our shifts with Molly. I was tentative for the first couple of days in these discussions, unwilling to let go of my mantra of positive thinking. But the similarities of our observances were terrifying.

One particularly unsettling condition common in brain injury had become much more frequent with Molly. That is perseveration: the uncontrollable repetition of a word or an action. The night before, Molly had begun rolling and unrolling her eight pairs of socks in the dresser drawer, over and over again, occasionally mumbling to herself. She would have stood in one place and done it for hours if I'd let her.

"Hey, Smith, your socks are perfect now, so you can stop."

"Nope. There's more, more, more, more..."

I wondered if it was comforting for her to stay in an automatic mode, in a good place of repeating a successful task. But she was stuck. When her dinner tray arrived I intercepted a pair of socks and put a spoon in her hand and led her away from the drawer.

I realized later that night when Molly fell asleep, that I had some perseveration, too. I was stuck in the idea that if I kept pressing forward and we kept doing what we'd been doing, Molly would get better again; new problem solved. After all, we'd already proven this worked with her once. Just repeat and repeat, to get the progress I wanted and was accustomed to from her. I wasn't thinking of anything else, even though this strategy was clearly not working now.

During the second week in March, whenever Molly attempted to walk, her steps were a tiny shuffle. Then all forward motion would stop. She'd gaze ahead, her sharp blue eyes blazing with intent to go, with one leg trembling and the other foot attempting to push forward but not even lifting off the floor. Molly's "walk" became almost pivoting in place, rotating around one shaky leg, her whole body quivering but unable to move forward.

She also lost her center and began to tilt, a little at first, and then almost constantly, whether she was standing or sitting. She wasn't aware of it and wasn't able to right herself if she was asked to try to sit up straight.

I arrived for my shift the afternoon of day 33 to find Sara in tears. "Something is desperately wrong. It's such a dramatic change," she said, trying to hold Molly's shoulders up from behind her wheelchair. "She's bent over and falling out of her chair. And they don't have any good reasons for this at all. I need them to do something! It's not just fear or frustration."

Sara was especially upset because she had a ticket to fly home that evening for nine days. It would be her first trip away from Loma Linda since we'd all raced to Molly's bedside almost five weeks before. Sara had told Walter, her boyfriend, that she didn't want to leave because she was so concerned about Molly. It felt like the wrong time to go home, she'd said.

She admitted to me that she was exhausted and had been excited about the opportunity to go home, be with Walter, and get her life back in order. "I'm going to the airport," Sara said, as she hugged me. "But I've gone from being elated to being devastated about Molly."

I realized later that night that Sara might have greater clarity about the severity of Molly's regression because she was leaving, which gave her urgency and insight. That morning, Mom had told me that she couldn't sleep because she was now extremely worried about Molly. She's a mother and has those instincts.

I propped Molly up that night so she could eat her dinner leaning on me and a stack of pillows, and she reverted to using the handle of a spoon to eat her meatloaf. That's when I first noticed that her hand had a Parkinsonian tremor; my mother had told me she'd seen it the day before. When I tried to help her use a fork and to steady her hand, she became weirdly angry, then laughed wildly, and made bizarre exaggerated faces—silly frowns and scary smiles. She seemed haunted. I wanted to hold her face in my hands and quiet the phantoms inside her.

She seemed so lost; like she didn't know who she was anymore. Worst of all was that Molly's "go-get-'em" spirit had flattened. At least her previous agitation and bitchiness were energetic and active. And I could excuse those difficult moods as her way of attacking and conquering the brain injury beast. Seeing her morose was defeating.

The next day I was searching my quote book for a new inspiration to hang on the apartment's refrigerator and I found this: "Depression is anger without enthusiasm." Maybe Molly felt deflated. It hurt to realize that even within the damaged cells of her brain, she knew she should be better, could do better, but couldn't figure out how to get better. She didn't know what was happening, why she was failing, or what to do about it. And I didn't either.

Molly's various therapists, who had worked with her for almost a month, almost every day, became as baffled by her regression as we were. They drew more up-arrows in her chart next to "impaired cognition," "muscle rigidity," "gait disturbance," and "frustration." They put down-arrows next to "compliance," "judgment," "focus and effort," and "ability to concentrate."

Even with all that, they were stuck, as we had been, in the belief that this was simply a new phase to contend with in the usual ways. One OT wrote in Molly's chart, "Molly's personality seems to have worsened over the past week. This may be due to an increased awareness of her deficits."

Trudy, however, was in agony over Molly; they had come so far together. As Molly's PT, she had been an integral part of teaching Molly to walk again, to balance, and to move up and down stairs. Now she was witnessing a horrifying breakdown and was distraught. Trudy told me that working with Molly the past couple of days was like grasping for a fish that kept slipping away and going deeper with each attempt to reach it. She told Mom that as Molly's confusion increased so did her frustration, which made her abilities decrease, which added more confusion. It would be a vicious cycle in anyone, but when intensified by a brain injury, it was a black hole.

Mom and I stared as Molly struggled to shuffle a few inches in the gym with Trudy.

"This whole thing is just terrible. My legs are so stupid. I'm an idiot!" Molly said, leaning into Trudy.

A look of distress came over Trudy's face; she was wordless. I leapt up and stood next to my sister. "No, Molly, you are not an idiot. This is just a really, really hard time."

"OK, we're going to get your legs going again, Molly." Trudy was back. "Lean this way onto me to straighten you up, and let's try again."

Molly stopped shaking and turned to face Trudy. "You must really hate my balance." Tears filled Molly's eyes. I sensed in that moment she was mostly upset because she wasn't delighting Trudy with any performance accomplishments that day.

Meanwhile, a look of fierce resolve replaced the tic on my Mom's face and her mother's instinct kicked it. "This isn't right," she said to me, as she stood up. "Something is really wrong with Molly and I'm going to get to the bottom of it."

In Molly's session that afternoon, Trudy thoroughly evaluated Molly in the same way she had established a baseline for her weeks before. She concluded that Molly's leaning, her bent rigid knee, and her stuck legs that prevented her from walking were not due to Molly's frustration level. Something else was going on.

I could no longer fool myself. Molly was failing. Declining. Extremely fast. Totally bizarre and scary. It was as if some stealthy, invisible invader was attacking, snipping away her hard-won abilities and maybe the very life she'd battled to repossess. Panic jolted me, that feeling of being on a cliff edge and unexpectedly teetering.

Mom transformed into a warrior. She gathered her troops and weapons. My sisters and I were now on full alarm. Our mission was clear: Molly could not fall away, not after all she'd been through, not after how far she'd come. We could not let go. We had to fight for a solution.

Mom, Mary K., and I were strategizing at the apartment, day 35. We got Sara on the telephone and she had talked to Walter about how shocked we were and that she had no idea why Molly had stopped improving and was actually going backwards.

Mom told Sara how Molly could no longer sit on the swing in the hospital gym, or move the big orange cone from one side of her body to the other. How she was struggling again to find simple words and couldn't make a connection between an object and its name. How she washed her left arm over and over again. How she got dizzy just standing up and couldn't keep her hand from quivering.

Suddenly Mom stood up. "Sara, I've got an idea. Do you think Walter could help us by doing some research in the medical library?"

"I don't see why not—if he can find the time," Sara said.

"If it's OK, I'll ask him," Mom said.

"Sure," and Sara handed the phone to Walter. He had special access at the libraries at Michigan State University as a staff PhD entomologist. Among other research, he was conducting his own study on medical conditions that might be improved by honeybee venom.

"Hi Walter. Thank you for taking such good care of Sara," Mom said, and paused. "If possible, Walter, could you please research articles about carbon monoxide poisoning and hyperbaric oxygen, and also mention sudden declines or reversals in cognitive and physical abilities, personality changes, trembling hands, maybe depression," asked Mom.

"I know about Molly's difficulties from Sara," he said. "I'll do my best."

"Thank you so much, Walter. Let me know what you find—soon. When you can."

The next day's notes in Molly's chart from the medical and therapy staff were distressing. *"Gait has become a shuffle, off kilter, leaning stooped posture. Ambulation required maxA (maximum assistance) to go 5 feet. Apraxia with cones, pegboard, stacking blocks. ADLs have relapsed. Patient has developed increased frustration and resistance."*

Molly also became incontinent, first at night, then also during the day. In addition to being demeaning for Molly, it also meant she could no longer have therapy in the pool. Her sense of defeat was palpable, at times silently, at times it shot out of her.

"I'm frozen here. I hate it! I just can't find my house anymore," Molly said, as I lifted her feet onto the wheelchair footrests.

"I know, Smith, it's a mess. It's terrible and I'm scared, too. But, we're going to work it out. We're going to help you."

"No! No, I don't want you, Smith. Why don't I just die? I *hate* this."

Overhearing this, an OT came and stood behind Molly, resting her hands on Molly's shoulders. "High frustration affects all other types of thinking," she said, looking at me. "It's not really a rejection."

"OK. Maybe," I said. "But it seems to me she has really good reasons to be angry."

Meanwhile, Dr. Strum described Molly as "resistant" and "irritable." The words felt like being stabbed.

Mom, Mary K., Amy, and I sat around the kitchen that night. We all needed to vent and brainstorm. Dad was with Molly on the dinner/evening shift.

"You know, most of the brain injuries in Loma Linda's rehab unit, and under Dr. Strum's charge, are older adults who've suffered strokes," Mom said. "It's clear to me that Dr. Strum and his staff are attempting to care for Molly with only their experience of geriatric patients."

"Yeah, except for a couple of people who were in car accidents and only have impact brain injuries, the rehab folks don't see people as young as Molly," Mary K. said.

"We also know they haven't worked with a patient with Molly's type of brain injury before—not with such a high level of carbon monoxide poisoning. They don't exist," I added.

"I hate to see Molly so down. It seems like her will is plummeting," Amy said.

"It's horrible," I said.

"OK, so let's decide right now that we'll do everything we can to boost her morale and protect her pride," Mom said, straightening her back. "It's important to her."

I knew we'd needed strong resolve not only to kickstart Molly's typical gung-ho spirit, but also so we could rally ourselves to fight the mysterious foe that was bringing her down.

Fortunately, Molly's support forces were widespread. Her friends, work colleagues, and neighbors, and well as FBI agents, Yale alumni, and Molly's buddies from the gym were all checking in and sharing news about her throughout their groups. Molly gained some other powerful advocates, too.

One morning, while Stephen was at the apartment with Abi, he answered the phone as we all did for our Molly information hotline. "Molly Weber Command Center."

"Well, hello. This is Louis Freeh, may I speak with Sally Shuler, please."

Stephen fell in line with his naval officer training and said, "I'm sorry, Director Freeh, Sally is at the hospital."

Stephen knew about Louis Freeh, the director of the FBI. Freeh said he was calling to find out about Molly. Stephen was impressed. He gave him the number in Molly's room.

Freeh was brief when he called, Mom said, but very personal and concerned, as if he were inquiring about one of his own family members.

Director Freeh called Dad and Martha's house, too. Martha said Freeh asked her to let him know if there was anything the FBI could do to help them, and he'd be sure to do it. Martha wished silently, but knew not even the FBI could heal Molly. But she was grateful for his call.

Meanwhile, the day after Director Freeh called, my mom wrote in the spiral notebook that she was sitting next to Molly on the edge of the bed, propping her up so she could eat lunch, when Janet Reno called.

"Hello, Sally. I'm Janet Reno. I'm the Attorney General, and Chief Executive in Charge of the FBI."

"I'm a big fan of yours, Ms. Reno. How are you?"

Reno said she'd been told great things about Walt from his supervisors and was deeply saddened at the loss of such a good agent and even more so, for such a good man.

Reno wanted to know about Molly and asked how she was and what we could expect so far in terms of recovery.

"Well, we're working on it, Ms. Reno. Two steps forward, one step back." Mom paused then got her bearings. "In fact, Ms. Reno, she's right here next to me, leaning on me. She's not doing as well as she had been. She's declined some, which has us very concerned."

"May I speak with her?"

"Yes, of course." Mom handed the receiver to Molly and she held it with one hand and leaned on her other arm.

Remarkably, Mom said that Molly seemed to know who Reno was and spoke sensibly to her. And Mom noticed that Molly listened really well, with more focus than she had demonstrated in days. She seemed to recognize that this person on the phone was significant.

Late that night, as I was helping Molly get into bed, she told me she'd spoken at lunchtime to "Walt's boss, Janet Reno."

"Really? OK. So, how'd that go, Smith?" I chuckled to myself and continued to adjust Molly's socks without even looking up.

"Janet Reno said Walt was great and I needed to work hard and get a lot better."

"That's good, Smith," I said, beginning to wonder. "Do you want a second pillow?"

After Molly fell asleep, I read what Mom had written about Reno's call in our spiral notebook. I was scared for Molly, but proud of her, too. Guilt was curdling inside me. I had to go home in a week and do a good paying job I'd scheduled, but I felt sick about leaving.

One tactic we decided to try was to bring Molly new, stimulating experiences. By now, after five weeks at Loma Linda, the warmth of spring was alighting like a sigh of relief. Hoping to air our spirits a bit, I arranged to take Molly on a walk one afternoon through a rose garden on the hospital grounds. I was already feeling buoyant—I'd received the day before a wonderful "missing you" greeting card from Brian with a really sweet note. It was exactly what I needed.

Lightly bumping over the brick pathway, I pushed Molly's wheelchair around the perimeter of the garden and she leaned over at each different color of rose bush to smell the blooms. "A little smell... No smell... Not much smell, but really pretty... Oh, big huge smell."

Our amble reminded me of some old family photos—Molly as a toddler pushing me, an infant, in a stroller. Mom said she sometimes pushed me right into the hedge, but ultimately, Molly practiced and her misaligned foot and faltering walk improved by pushing me around.

I got Molly out of the wheelchair and we sat on a little wrought iron bench amidst the blooms in the sun, holding hands, and watching house sparrows hop about. When the breeze would stir, we'd toss our heads back to embrace the freshness on our faces.

"I love it here, I really love it," Molly said. Then she gave me a serious look. "Smith, I'm getting worried about all my unemployed family members."

I laughed and patted her hand. "We're OK. I'm really happy to be here with you." I was surprised she seemed to know better than I did the strain I was under.

"Are you helping me?" Molly asked as the breeze jostled her bangs across her forehead.

"Yeah, I hope so. What do you think?"

"I wish I didn't have to be involved."

S e v e n

AT the family meeting with medical staff on the morning of day 37, Dr. Strum read from his notes, "The patient seems to be regressing."

Astonishingly, it was the first time Molly's decline was registered in her medical chart—not Molly being frustrated, irritable, or unhelpful—but an official medical regression.

Mom, Mary K., Dad, and I glanced around the table, not sure whether to cheer or cry. We'd been witnessing Molly's decline for what felt like months—it had actually been about seven or eight days. But now we were validated. We knew we were entering a new phase. We didn't know what it was or what was happening to Molly, but the affirmation fortified us to help her. It would not, however, be nearly enough.

Dr. Strum said they were going to stop asking the daily orientation and medical questions, because he felt her frustration could cause more behavioral problems. Didn't he just say "regression?" I thought to myself. On either side of me, I could feel Mom and Mary K. clench.

Then he added that the PT staff wanted to try some new strategies, too; some stretching to increase flexibility and some kneeling and crawling to improve strength and balance overall and stability in her hip flexors and trunk.

Mom jumped in. "Wait. If Molly is regressing, then what are we doing to find out why? We have to figure out what's happening. What's wrong with her?"

Dr. Strum admitted he didn't have any explanations yet, but he was concerned, and they would do all they could to shift her to forward progress again.

The ravaging problem was conceded, and it was obvious the medical staff was confused and shaken by Molly's predicament, too. Mom knew that the family would have to take the lead.

Meanwhile, without the convenience of the Internet (there was no Google in 1995), Walter used a medical database at the MSU library and worked his research magic.

Within a few days, Mom received a 3½-inch floppy disk that Walter had sent via Federal Express. It had several dozen article abstracts on it. Mom hunted through them on her computer at the apartment and selected 10 as the most relevant. During her shift that afternoon, Mom took Molly to the Loma Linda Medical University library and was able to locate six of the articles in the journals and publications there. Molly sat nearby in her wheelchair while Mom got dimes and nickels from the librarians and photocopied the articles.

We pored over them, discussing our observations of Molly, and by late afternoon, we were all convinced that the name of our enemy was a condition called "delayed neurological sequelae." Our diagnosis was terrifying, a dreadful ailment. But after a quiet time with Molly that night, I slept better on the apartment's pullout couch than I had in two weeks.

It was a strange comfort to read Molly's symptoms and bizarre reversal of skills perfectly described in several of the articles:

After recovery is demonstrated following initial CO poisoning incident, patients may present several days to several weeks later with delayed neurological sequelae (DNS), which causes deterioration and a relapse of cognitive abilities, personal and social behavior, and movement.

The exact mechanism that causes DNS is not known. It should be diagnosed by its symptoms, including a lopsided, short-stepped gait with loss of arm swing, akinesia ("freezing up," an inability to begin or maintain body motion), *apraxia* (loss of coordinated movement), *aphasia* (loss of power to use or comprehend words), *double incontinence, and sometimes a Parkinsonian tremor.*

Another of the articles listed other symptoms we'd seen: *increased rigidity in the body, stooped posture and imbalance, tilting, movement disorders, and a masked face.*

"Molly's face gets kind of weird sometimes," I said, showing Mom the list. "They call it 'masked.'" We were sitting around the table at the apartment, the articles scattered at hand.

"She looks drawn; she looks awful." Mom ticked off each symptom with a check mark. The tip of her pencil snapped, but she kept going with the stub. "Especially compared to how she was. She was showing all kinds of emotions before. Now I don't know where she is."

One article warned of *a mixture of emotional changes and instability, difficulty concentrating, confusion, disorientation, irritability, apathy, and depression.*

"Look, Mom. This says the DNS could cause depression," said Mary K.

"I know, I saw that, too," Mom said. "And Dr. Strum's been saying she's irritable and depressed, as if she would do that on purpose."

I sighed in relief when I read: *Also, peculiar behaviors, such as attempts to eat or bite non-food items like flowers or notebooks, also "drinking" solid food, muttering, disorganized dressing, inappropriate laughing or crying.* It all fit. It was both fascinating and horrifying.

The next morning, at Mom's request, her husband Harold was at Kinkos when their doors opened at 7:00 a.m. and made 20 copies of each of three articles that Mom thought were the most representative of what we saw happening with Molly.

Dr. Strum was away for the day and Murray Brandstater, the medical director of the rehab unit, was making the rounds that morning. Mom handed him the articles. "I think we know what's going on and why she's regressing. It's delayed neurological sequelae or D-N-S. Please, read these."

She circulated the other copies around the staff and left the articles for Dr. Strum in his office. Dr. Brandstater was the only one who ever responded. He walked in the next morning and faced Mom. "Sally, the articles—I think you're right."

He had a kind face with thoughtful creases and eyes that conveyed concern. His large glasses were often on top of a head fringed by a crop of white hair. His slight accent and soft voice made him seem meditative.

"We need to get her more hyperbaric oxygen," Mom said. "Right away. She needs more HBO."

"I'll consult with Dr. Lo about that and let you know." With a small, assuring smile, he fished his glasses out of his hair, put them on his nose and walked away, reading Molly's chart.

Later, at the apartment, Mom shared her victory. "I thought, holy mackerel, I'm teaching them something by just bringing them the right articles. And it just might save Molly! We've got to get her back in HBO with Dr. Lo."

It was great to have Mom in a more typical role. Gone were the facial tic and dull eyes; she was taking charge, commandeering Molly's care. Her eldest daughter was under attack and she was ready to do battle with DNS.

Mom eased my fears. I was bolstered by her confidence and surge of purpose. Her leadership was comforting.

Still, the stakes were extremely high. There was real urgency among us because Mom understood from what she'd read that Molly could die from DNS. I had a different interpretation of the article, but Mom had a specific memory of it.

"If a patient stops progressing and goes downhill over a couple weeks, like Molly has, then she'll probably survive," Mom told Sara, still at home in Michigan. "But if a sharp decline happens faster, more like a collapse, over two or three days, then the patient could die."

Mom rubbed her forehead as she spoke. "I thought Molly was alive and with us. She's already survived carbon monoxide poisoning and being in a coma for god's sake! I can't imagine losing her this way."

After she hung up with Sara, I took Mom's hands in mine and looked into her sharp blue eyes. "You're right, Mom. We've come so far, and we *absolutely* will not lose her now. None of us would let that happen."

I learned years later that, in fact, DNS doesn't usually lead to death. We had envisioned at the time that the dendrites in Molly's brain could collapse, shrivel up, and that would be that. It was not out of line for us to have this fear. Molly had fallen so far, so fast, with such a dramatic drop in her abilities, it seemed possible she could just fall off the edge.

But Molly's brain and heart were receiving oxygen and functioning; she had good vital signs. She'd had HBO soon after the CO poisoning and had come out of a coma. She was surrounded by medical personnel and in a hospital. Death from DNS was not likely. In fact, it simply isn't part of the syndrome. Never say never, one expert told me. It does happen; but death as a result of DNS is not usually a concern.

However, a huge range of neurological injury is, and rightly should have been a very legitimate concern. Current research indicates that our fears in this regard were extremely valid. The ongoing injury to the brain from DNS can range from a subtle personality change to complete debilitation to an immobile, uncommunicative, unresponsive state. We had passed that horrible phase almost six weeks earlier, and none of us wanted to go back.

To minimize injury, according to recent research on DNS, any decline in a patient's functioning must first be recognized.

Without our observations and Mom's dogged pursuit of an answer, this critical first step might not have been taken. The doctors and medical staff simply had not yet viewed Molly's regression as significant.

But we were stunned and baffled, wondering why Molly was going down the tube.

At that time, published reports about DNS occurring in CO-poisoned patients, like the ones Walter had found, were available—if the Loma Linda rehab staff had known enough to look for them. But they had an utter lack of experience dealing with CO poisoned, brain-injured patients like Molly. In a different place with different personnel, the thinking should have been that once Molly had survived CO poisoning and the initial brain injury— even if she'd already had HBO treatments—we should have been alerted that DNS was a possibility and been told about its symptoms. We should have known that she was still sitting on a gigantic time bomb of potential injury. But the Loma Linda staff couldn't teach us what they didn't know.

Even today, more than 15 years later, no one knows why DNS happens to some CO patients and not others, or how 50 to 75 percent of patients with DNS recover within one to two years, with only general rehab and supportive care.

The studies Mom dug up didn't cite a cure for DNS, but suggested that a variety of cognitive and physical therapies could be helpful in minimizing its impact. But Molly had been doing those kinds of therapies all day long for weeks and we had no evidence that any of it was working to stem her decline or help her recover. She was still spiraling away from us, losing more of her abilities, her rehabilitation disappearing. We were frightened she might become worse off than she was just after she came out of her coma. We had to do something more. Mom wanted new HBO treatments. It was the antidote we pinned our hopes on.

Since Molly's clash with it in 1995, more is known about DNS, but much remains mysterious. We do know that DNS is not uncommon. It occurs in up to half of the patients who have had CO poisoning, usually a few days to six weeks after exposure, and sometimes several months later. Risk factors for DNS are murky. However, older age at the time of CO poisoning (studies say age 36 to age 50 or older), loss of consciousness during the episode, and a long exposure to and intense level of poisoning may point to a greater chance of DNS.

Some scientists report there may be a significant correlation between cerebral white matter changes in a CO-poisoning patient's initial brain scans and the development of DNS. Others dispute this.

A higher measurement of carbon monoxide to hemoglobin, known as the COHb level, can be used to confirm CO exposure, but doesn't necessarily reflect the degree of cell damage. Even when CO poisoning is relatively mild, DNS can still occur. Therefore, COHb is not a valuable predictor of DNS, even in more severe cases of poisoning, like Molly's.

Molly wasn't very old, just 37; she was in a coma for almost two weeks; had a long exposure to CO (36 hours); and an extreme level of poisoning in her bloodstream (34-36 percent COHb). By comparison, a normal COHb level is 1-3 percent under typical environmental conditions, while smokers average 5-10 COHb. The higher the COHb level, the lower the amount of oxygen that can be delivered to the brain, heart, and other tissue.

In addition, Molly received her first HBO treatment within a few of hours of being found and also had 20 HBO treatments in 15 days during February before DNS seized her in early March.

Years later, Dr. Lo remarked to me, that in 1995 it was believed DNS might only occur as a result of not getting any HBO treatments and that it was very unlikely to happen with someone who had had HBO. So, in Molly's case, he said, even if the rehab staff had known about DNS, no one would have been watching for it, even if they should have.

Today, the debate continues about how to use HBO and its efficacy for acute CO poisoning, surrounded by conflicting clinical data and inconclusive evidence. Two points of agreement are: 1) a majority of physicians concurs that at least some HBO is critical to help a CO-poisoned patient and 2) nothing is known yet that can absolutely prohibit DNS or halt its assault.

Even without total proof or clear consensus, many scientists believe, through a number of studies that have been completed with CO-poisoned patients and lab rats, that HBO treatments significantly reduce the incidence of CO-related cognitive sequelae, be they delayed (DNS), persistent, or both. Nonetheless, for patients who received HBO the odds are still not zero. DNS can still develop, as it did with my older sister.

We were fortunate that Molly's DNS set in while she was still in a hospital, with medical care, HBO chambers, and advocates, like Dr. Lo and my mom on hand. In addition to the established symptoms of DNS, all of which Molly experienced, in rare cases patients could have seizures or slip into a coma, creating great potential for permanent damage.

With all this in mind, our fears of "losing" Molly once she began declining were not out of line. Even to lose what amount of "Molly" had emerged from her coma was a terrifying prospect.

Years later, I began to learn the science about what happened to my big sister. When CO enters the lungs, toxicity occurs because CO binds to hemoglobin 250 times more readily than oxygen does, and creates carboxyhemoglobin (or COHb), which thereby displaces oxygen in the blood stream. The result is cell hypoxia—oxygen starvation throughout the body, which is cumulative and particularly damaging to the heart and brain, and accounts for the symptoms and high mortality of CO-poisoned victims. Hypoxia alone, however, is not sufficient to explain DNS. Once the CO is flushed out and oxygen reunites with the body's hemoglobin, it seems healing should be straightforward. But it's not. Not for survivors like Molly. Experts' theories of how and why DNS occurs are multiple and varied.

One idea is that DNS may result from a recurrence of increased COHb levels due to a sort of "off-loading" of remaining and hidden CO that happens when the CO releases from myoglobin, a protein that stores and carries oxygen in muscle. This CO is the interloper lurking in the dark, hiding in the closet.

When breathed into the body, CO binds to: hemoglobin (reducing oxygen transportation), myoglobin (decreasing its oxygen storage capacity), and mitochondrial cytochrome oxidase (inhibiting cellular respiration). CO has a high affinity to bind with myoglobin, although not as much as it does with hemoglobin, but it has a slower release from myoglobin. Once it does release, generally later and, diabolically, as a patient is improving, then the CO is likely to bind, as it did initially, to hemoglobin and cause a "rebound" effect with a delayed return of symptoms.

CO, an especially perplexing and outlandish compound molecule, causes profound changes in MBP, or myelin basic protein, the protective sheath that surrounds nerve cells. Injury from a lack of oxygen caused by CO poisoning sets into motion an autoimmune response in which leukocytes, or white blood cells, the body's infection fighters, arrive, attach to the MBP cells, and activate. At first triggered to eliminate the altered myelin, the leukocytes continue to attack normal myelin, too.

The brain damage from CO is due in large part to this autoimmune reaction because the body simply doesn't know when to stop attacking what it views as a trespasser. The really bad news is the products that drive this initial injury continue to float around in the bloodstream.

The delayed, or DNS damage, arises from the overactivation of those gone-awry immune cells attacking MBP. The now-battered MBP is viewed by the body to be a foreign substance or an invader. Once the immune system is cranked up, the leukocytes again see normal MBP as abnormal intruders. As these immune cells lash out against the torn-up and the healthy MBP, further ravaging the nerve cells, permanent brain damage can result.

More recently, certain "pathophysiologic" mechanisms are thought by scientists to also have a major influence on DNS. These intricate processes involve biochemical changes and interactions between certain molecules in the brain's cells, inducing a cascade of immunological effects and, most critically, inflammation.

While on their rampage, the hyperactive leukocytes become little factories of dangerous oxygen free radicals, which prowl the bloodstream like gangs out to cause trouble. These roaming ruffians lead to leukocyte-mediated inflammation and brain lipid peroxidation—that is, the oxygen free radicals act like toxins by "stealing" electrons from the lipids, or fat compounds, in a brain cell, causing inflammation and destruction. This disrupts brain cell function and energy and causes a loss of proper immune reaction and grave tissue damage.

The end result of lipid peroxidation is that it causes delayed demyelinization, the pillaging and destruction of MBP, that all-important insulating myelin sheath surrounding each nerve cell. This injury precipitates neurologic dysfunction, including impaired cognition, movement, and sensation. Within the brain, it can lead to edema (excess fluid) and areas of necrosis, or cell death, in which cells swell up and break open. This can also harm other nearby cells and provoke inflammation.

Much of the latest research shows that HBO seems to mitigate this whole ordeal by inhibiting the leukocyte attachment, thus short-circuiting the autoimmune attack and minimizing inflammation and damage to MBP and other cells.

Still, the awareness of DNS in CO patients, much less the effectiveness of HBO to treat it, was very sketchy for many years.

A full 10 years before Molly's 1995 accident, some medical researchers knew DNS could occur in CO-poisoned victims, but wrote in a published paper that DNS was not recognized widely enough by the medical community to safeguard CO patients. This is what we believe happened to Molly at Loma Linda.

Also in 1985, a published study said that HBO could minimize and even eliminate "post CO exposure relapse," and detailed how a patient improved when HBO was used to treat DNS. Five years after that, a study group of CO-poisoned patients improved after receiving HBO for treatment of DNS.

However, research in 1994 showed that if patients with acute CO poisoning received HBO, most still developed DNS. One paper concluded: *"There seems to be no effective strategy to prevent and treat this tragic event."*

"Especially in early 1995, we didn't have answers or definitive studies to go on for what to do exactly," reflected Dr. Lo, in 2006. "With Molly, we had nothing to lose, so we stretched and did more HBO and got more benefits. Most doctors then were using only animal tests to find answers, but it isn't the same as having human tests. But we don't have two Mollys with exactly the same brain injury from CO poisoning to give one HBO to and not the other to find out who does better. It's logistically *and* ethically impossible."

By April 1995, a few months after Molly's accident, a study reported that HBO decreased the incidence of DNS after CO poisoning. At that time, it was known that the resulting brain damage from DNS usually occurred during a patient's rehab and that it might result in lasting cognitive defects and movement disorders.

One year after Molly's accident, new research stated that all victims of CO poisoning were at risk for DNS, that HBO reverses both the acute and the delayed effects of CO poisoning, and that additional HBO may produce greater improvement in brain function. By the late 1990s, scientists were piecing together the brain chemistry and physiology of how HBO for a CO patient was beneficial.

Nonetheless, the value of HBO for CO patients remains controversial, even as more research continues to show that HBO decreases the incidence of DNS. Many scientists today do believe that even if CO patients initially received HBO, they should be monitored for DNS, and if symptoms develop, they should receive additional HBO. Which was pretty much what Mom intuitively deduced in 1995, and insisted on getting for Molly.

When Dr. Strum entered Molly's room the next day, he wore a politician's smile. He was a younger doctor, maybe in his 30s, with wavy light brown hair, of medium build and height, and with a slight smugness, as if carrying a permanent secret. Mom called it his condescending air. He nodded at me perched on the windowsill and said hello to Mom who was standing at Molly's bedside. Molly was sitting in bed, propped up against the pillows.

Mom asked about the DNS articles she'd left for him and he said he hadn't had a chance to read them yet. She paused, and said, "I'd like a complete neurological workup for Molly, including an MRI to see how it compares to earlier scans and to find out what's going on in her brain now."

"I don't think that's necessary," Dr. Strum replied.

Just as Mom was about to flare up, Dr. Brandstater stepped into the room. "Hello, Sally. I should hear from Dr. Lo today about more HBO, and I'll work my channels and make sure Molly gets the head MRI done. We do want to rule out any complications," he said, looking to Dr. Strum.

Dr. Strum raised his eyebrows with a slight shrug and walked away.

Mom blinked slowly and then turned to Dr. Brandstater. "Why hadn't all of you considered that this might be delayed neurological sequelae with Molly?"

"The articles you found had probably been... excluded," he chose his words carefully. "Most of the research wasn't done by American doctors. Most were from other countries, developing countries, where they have more incidents of carbon monoxide poisoning each year, like China, Korea, and India."

"Well, it makes sense they're studying it then. Are you saying they aren't credible?"

"It's more complicated than that. Look Sally, I agree with your assessment from the articles. But we have not had anyone recover after being as seriously injured with carbon monoxide poisoning as Molly was. The vast majority who are that sick meant to do it and don't want to live. They're not fighting and they don't make it," Dr. Brandstater said. "Molly is different. She's a unique case."

"Let's see what the brain scan shows," Mom said. "And please let me know when you hear back from Dr. Lo about the HBO."

Just then Mary K. and Harold appeared at the door with Abi. Molly reached her arm toward Abi who skipped up to greet her aunt with a hug.

"Right now," continued Mom, "I've got to go to Disneyland. Lyrysa will be here today with Molly."

The trip had been planned a couple weeks before. Mary K., Mom, and Harold had promised to take Abi for her first time. So they were off to spend a day in the magical kingdom.

Molly quacked her best Donald Duck voice at Abi, making her giggle. "Bye-bye, Abi. Say hi to Mickey Mouse for Donald Duck and don't forget to write!" Molly clucked.

Hearing her Donald Duck imitation was like being 12 years old again. Astonishing.

I took in Molly's full range of DNS symptoms throughout the long day, day 39. She got tangled getting her legs into her pants, she used the wrong side of the hairbrush, she got vertigo moving in and out of her wheelchair. She stared at the elevator buttons but couldn't remember which floor the physical therapy room was on.

"Remember, Smith, you were in the PT room with George yesterday," I prompted.

Another patient in the elevator, a smiling man, also in a wheelchair, who had a wrapped stump for a left leg, piped up, "It's on 3. I'm like you, I was there yesterday, too."

"Third floor. Yeah, I know that," Molly snapped, punching the 3 button, and then leaned so far over during the short ride, she almost put her head on the man's shoulder.

She was good and grouchy during lunch, eating her salad with a spoon and dropping most of it in her lap. She peed before she told me she needed to go to the bathroom. I got her clothes changed and she took a nap before her afternoon therapies.

While she slept, I daydreamed, staring out the window at the snowcapped mountains in the distance. Molly's breathing provided a chant-like pulse. No distractions. A rare quiet time. I hungered for such moments, but didn't know it. There were just so many disruptions and so few opportunities. I was thinking of Brian's quick, joyful smile, his eager gratitude for my vegetarian cooking, his genuine desire for me. I thought of our house, our cats and the likelihood that all their toys were under the refrigerator because I wasn't there to fish them out with the flyswatter. I missed being needed and appreciated.

I thought about the documentary scripts that I wanted to be writing, the bosses I wanted to contact and reassure of my loyalty. I thought of the way Brian lifts me off my feet in a bear hug when he comes home from work, even if my hands are busy stirring a pot with a wooden spoon or filling cracks in a wall with a caulk gun. How he sets me down and looks into my eyes, grinning, and then kisses my cheeks, forehead, and neck—and I giggle and try to kiss him back without using my hands, which are full and held aloft. I thought about how I love the comfort and confidence his enthusiasm gives me. A place of not worrying. Assurance in abundance. No doubts at all.

The clouds had cleared, so Molly and I went outside with the PT to enjoy the warm afternoon. With assistance, Molly stepped over blocks laid out in a line on the hospital patio in an effort to get her to lengthen her steps. But she got peevish after she almost stumbled a few times and her gait got worse. The PT put an up-arrow in her chart next to "frustration," and a down-arrow next to "performance." She wrote, *Molly's apraxia has gotten worse over the past week, perhaps due to her increased awareness of her deficits.*

It was obvious that Molly was exasperated by her inability to do tasks she'd breezed through less than two weeks before, but I knew that wasn't the problem.

Before we went inside, I held Molly up, my arm wrapped around her waist. She stood and stared at the sidewalk that led away from the patio.

"That's the way to the post office, Smith," she said.

"Wow. Yeah, that's right, Smith," I said. "I know you walked there."

"Yep, that was me," Molly said. The PT put the wheelchair behind Molly, who plunked down into it.

That day she was trapped in a body wrangling DNS, but 11 days before, with only a little assistance, she'd walked to the post office. That ability, like many others, had evaporated like a light rain on a sunny sidewalk.

At dinner, Molly's hand rattled as she ate her peas. "Get away. I don't want your help!" she said, as she fetched the peas in her lap with a spoon. It took a while, but she found every one. She beamed like she'd climbed a mountain as she set her spoon down on the tray.

She was nice to the nurse who helped her roommate get a shower, and almost cheerful as we sat on her bed and reviewed some word puzzles and vocabulary from the speech therapist. I was eating a sandwich as we practiced and when I dropped part of it down my shirt, she laughed so hard, she cracked me up, too. It felt like we were in junior high again. I had always gotten a lot of teasing from my big sister.

After I helped her get the toothpaste on her toothbrush instead of squirting it into the sink, she seemed to relish the familiarity of getting under the covers and leaning back against the pillows.

"It's the frozenist time I've ever had, Smith," she said, as she took off her wristwatch and turned it top to bottom several times, held it to her ear, shook it, stared at it, and then put it on the bedside table. She pulled the blanket to her chin.

"It's the scariest, frozenist time. I have to get out of this... this freeze frame. I've got to get this freeze frame unstuck and get it moving."

I was dumbfounded. She'd called it "frozen" before. She had such poetic moments; and astounding insight. I could almost hear the good brain cells clinking together in her head.

Abi got out of bed when I arrived at the apartment that night to give me a *Lion King* "Hakuna Matata" T-shirt emblazoned with the animal cartoon figures. Abi had picked it out as a thank you gift for staying with Molly all day so they could go to Disneyland. Abi couldn't talk fast enough to share all she'd done and she couldn't believe all of her favorite characters were there, just walking up and hugging her. Mary K. said she and Harold took lots of photos and they'd get them developed soon so I could see Abi with Mickey Mouse.

Mary K. and I put Abi back to bed and Mom and I stayed up talking. She said she'd felt far away at Disneyland and was sad she couldn't interact with Abi as well as she should have. "But it wasn't what I felt like doing," she said, in a hushed voice. "It was OK, but with all the stuff with Molly on my mind—I just couldn't shed it for the day, even though I really tried to."

Abi and I both donned our *Lion King* shirts and walked to the hospital the next day. Abi was bursting to show Molly our shirts and she told Molly all about Disneyland and that Donald Duck was there. Molly asked Abi questions about Disneyland using her Donald Duck voice, making us all laugh. Then Abi sang songs from *The Lion King*, word for word. Molly joined in the "Hakuna matata, means no worries" chorus and sang "Circle of Life" with zeal.

Then Molly told Abi that she had been to Disneyland with Walt and Kristen, but it was before *The Lion King* movie. Molly said Kristen liked Tigger and the other Winnie the Pooh characters, and Walt had taken a million pictures. We all smiled, and I was grateful Molly had retained a good memory of a happy day from a few years before.

That afternoon, Molly got a brain MRI. According to Dr. Strum, the results didn't show any new bleeding or clots. It showed the same damaged areas and was essentially unchanged from the MRI she'd received just over a month before.

Even with today's better MRI technology, neurologists say that DNS is not revealed in a typical MRI image. DNS is not like a broken bone on an x-ray.

"Well, at least certain physical problems can be ruled out as causes for her decline with the MRI, right?" Mom said to Dr. Strum.

"For the most part," he said. He wrote a note in Molly's chart: *HBO ASAP with Dr. Lo*, and told Mom that Molly would get more HBO right away.

She looked at him and nodded deliberately, "Good."

That night the phone rang in Molly's room. "Maybe it's Brian," I said. Molly picked it up before the second ring.

Brian asked her questions about her day and she told him about getting an MRI. Then he got her laughing so much I had to shush her for fear of waking up the entire floor. Soon she said good night and handed the phone to me.

Brian always made Molly feel adored, and I told him how much I appreciated his attentiveness to her. He said, "I was telling her Irish jokes since I'm Irish, you know, and it's St. Patrick's Day."

"Geez, I totally forgot. St. Patrick's Day. It didn't occur to me all day," I said. "Wow, I just looked at my watch. It's after midnight there. I didn't realize how late it is either."

Brian admitted that he'd been out "celebrating the green." He was a bit tipsy and didn't tell me much about his evening, but he was funny and sort of sweetly sexy and lovable in his silliness. I wanted to talk to him about coming home in a few days, but it wasn't the right time. I was mostly glad he thought of us and took the time to call.

The next afternoon, I called Brian from the apartment, determined to have a connected conversation. I quickly updated him about Molly's decline, about our DNS discovery, and trying to get more HBO. "You would freak out if you saw her—you wouldn't believe how she's fallen apart," I said.

Brian was quiet. Then he said, "Really?... That's wild. Wow." He sounded distracted.

"I'm overwhelmed, Brian." Then I lost it. "It's so hard to be here with her and be away from you, and it's hard for you to understand what it's like here. And I'm afraid. This is a critical time for her." I gulped a breath. "I'm so screwed up. I wish I could see your face. I don't know how you're reacting to it all or how you're feeling about me," I sniffed back my tears.

"Try to believe me, Lyrysa. I know it's hard. I can hear it in your voice that it's scary. It'll be easier when you're home—just a couple of days now," Brian said.

"I hope so. I hope you can put up with me."

"I can't wait to see you," he said.

I didn't believe Brian could feel the enormity of my situation when he was in New York City working or in our messy, torn-up, half-renovated home—those were stressful situations, too. And I wasn't there to help him. But he couldn't possibly grasp the danger I was feeling. I was sure, too, that my piece of our collective family brain injury wasn't helping me communicate. Nothing was easy. I was displaced. Wherever I wasn't is where I wanted to be. I wanted to be with Brian and I wanted to be with Molly.

"I can't wait to be with you," I said, feeling drained. "I hope you can feel OK with the choices I'm making. Please be patient with me. For us."

"We'll be together very soon. It'll be great. I'll let you go now, OK? Love you, babe."

"Love you, too, Brian."

I wasn't sure he heard me. It felt like what was happening with Molly was happening to us—my sustaining, cheerful world with Brian was losing ground, slipping, collapsing.

When Amy and I arrived at the hospital the next afternoon, Mom said that the OT got Molly to wash her hair just fine that morning, but then Molly got "stuck" rubbing the soap on her washcloth and wringing it out without being able to stop. More perseveration. Molly did it a lot—in the shower, reading the same sentence over and over again, moving the ring on and off the cone in the gym even after she'd already completed the exercise.

Molly's afternoon sessions were tough, too. The PT had Amy stand across the room so Molly would look at her and keep her head up as she held onto railings on each side of the walkway. The PT and I crouched behind Molly, pushing her heels forward with our hands, trying to get her into a rhythm of initiating forward steps. On my hands and knees at Molly's feet, I felt shattered as I thought about how she'd wowed everyone, strolling around the gait clinic a few weeks earlier.

I stayed with Molly into the evening, and soon after she finished eating her turkey dinner with a spoon, Sara came to visit Molly. She had just returned from Michigan; I was due to fly home to New York in two days. We caught up about Walter, his sons, and her work for a few minutes, sitting at the end of Molly's bed.

"You know, you guys, I don't know if I'll ever get out of this weird world and back to reality," Molly said. "Do you hear me? You should goddamn listen!"

Sara and I froze and looked at our big sister. Angry outbursts and cussing from Molly were not uncommon, however, her recognition of her "weird world" was.

"Hey, we're here, Smith. And we *are* listening, I promise." I moved closer and rubbed her shoulder and tried to catch her eye, but she seemed lost inside somewhere.

"I've had a long day of traveling, Molly. But I'll see you tomorrow," Sara said, as she put on her jacket.

"See you later, Sara," I said, standing to hug her.

"See you later, Sara. I love you, too," Molly said sweetly, and nestled her head back on her pillow, smiling.

Finally on March 20, Dr. Lo welcomed Molly back to the HBO room with his exuberant smile. It had been one month since her last HBO treatment. He wrote a note in Molly's chart at 4:30 p.m.: *HBO x 10 tx (#21 today), due to regressions... Possibly residual delayed neurological sequelae from initial CO poisoning.*

It was the first time DNS had been mentioned in her chart, almost two weeks from the first signs of her collapse. Everyone in my family was relieved to have Dr. Lo back on Molly's case, DNS acknowledged, finally, and Molly scheduled for 10 days of HBO treatments.

But we remained urgent—Molly was still declining. HBO and persistent attention had saved her before; but she needed a champion. In this saga, Mom wore the white hat of a hero.

"I had called Molly's boss at Houghton Mifflin, Garret White, and told him about the DNS and how horrible it was," Mom explained. "I said we had to get more 'experimental' treatments and that we really need additional HBO approved by the insurance company."

These were the days when most corporations were self-insured through contracts with companies that managed health care insurance for the business's employees.

Mr. White reflected on his conversation with Mom and said it was clear to him Mom was intent on helping Molly beat this thing. "I wasn't terribly surprised," he said, "knowing what a strong, tough person Molly was to see that in her Mom, too. Molly's no shrinking violet, she was smart and impressive. Whatever she took on, it was bang-bang-bang—done."

But the real reason subsequent rounds of HBO were approved, Mr. White said, was because of Nader Darehshori, the CEO of Houghton Mifflin. He knew Molly and what had happened and insisted on frequent reports about her.

"I spoke directly to him," Mr. White recalled, "and he said, 'If it's what she needs, we'll take care of it. We're not going to let anything get in the way.'" Mr. White said, "Nader was very prominent in the whole situation. He got it done."

By the time Dr. Lo had Molly on the HBO schedule again and Loma Linda contacted the health insurance company, everything was approved, Mom said.

"We still don't have all the answers, and certainly at that time we did not," Dr. Lo said, many years later. "So I utilized my gut feelings, along with my medical knowledge and clinical experience. I have my patient's best interest at heart. If HBO won't cause harm, and if there's even a tiny possibility it might help, then I must try.

"But really, it was quite novel back then to give a patient HBO for DNS," Dr. Lo said. "More kudos to your mother for twisting arms to get them to approve it. She's extraordinary."

For the record, physicians today state there is no sure-fire solution or proven treatment for DNS and no "official" data with humans that prove HBO helps, even though many of these experts strongly believe that it does. Research continues and hopes are that one day some anti-inflammatory medications may be effective against DNS, and that neuropsychiatric testing may be fine-tuned enough to ascertain the risk of DNS in a patient.

In 1995, I had no idea how long healing Molly's brain from DNS would take, I only believed HBO would help. I didn't know if her brain would go back to progressing like it was before DNS set in. That's the expectation with a broken bone; after treatment, it should function the way it did before. But it's not the same with a broken brain.

I asked Dr. Lo about it when I came to get Molly after a treatment. He explained it this way: You may learn to walk as a child, with your brain neurons connecting A to C to E, but learning to walk again as a 37-year-old woman with a brain injury, and then again after DNS—we hope for *any* pattern of rewiring, whatever works. It might be G to Q to M to E to Y. With HBO and therapies, we try to get neurons to fire again; if they fire, they might rewire.

Hearing all this, I thought I should feel utterly daunted. But instead, I felt OK. Optimistic, even. I nodded my head and smiled. "Cool. Thanks, Dr. Lo," I said, and gave him a high-five.

"Yeah, you're cool, Dr. Lo," Molly said, as I wheeled her out the door.

By 2005, some scientists using mice showed that HBO may help prevent DNS because it partially prevents biochemical alterations in MBP— that is, it keeps the autoimmune "attack of the leukocytes" from beating up on the normal myelin sheath that's just doing its job protecting nerve cells.

While new HBO research is promising, the critical first step remains the same: to be knowledgeable about the possibility of DNS after a period of recovery from CO poisoning. Today's prudent advice from experts is that DNS must be anticipated and that medical staff, especially in emergency departments, intensive care, and rehab units should be familiar with DNS symptoms and monitor for its development consistently for every CO patient. There are no handy guidelines as to how long the watch should go on. The symptoms of DNS simply need to be widely known, and observation for them encouraged.

We never received such guidance. In early 1995, the medical community was less aware of DNS, and the Loma Linda staff seemed unaware of it at all. They didn't know enough to look for symptoms, or to direct us to look for symptoms.

It was also tricky because Molly had made such stunning progress. No one was thinking something could go wrong. She was sailing along.

But her family noticed her sudden regressions; small at first, then quickly profound. In this case, the advantage we had was vastly more important than any official medical knowledge. We knew the patient. We had close, detailed knowledge of her. We'd been watching her intently every day for weeks and sharing our observations. Nothing, not tests or MRIs, nothing was more valuable. What really mattered was seeing what Molly was doing.

We'll never know what would have happened if we had not complained about why Molly was falling apart before our eyes. If we had not stomped our feet and protested that Molly declining was not typical. Or without Mom's fervent mission to figure out what was wrong with her. I only know we knew what mattered.

After midnight, I boarded my cross-country, redeye flight. It wasn't easy. I didn't want to leave at such a critical time for our sister. Sara had said the same thing 10 days earlier when she flew home. I harbored some hope that Molly was on a better path now. An article I'd just read in a science magazine at the hospital gave me confidence about her ability to bounce back.

It described a study with one group of mice in a cage with toys, pieces of carpet and ropes, and a running wheel, and another group of mice in a bare cage. After a week of the same feeding routine, all the mice were then given the same brain injury. Only the mice that had the stimulating environment of texture, play things, and exercise equipment recovered.

We all believed Molly's earlier progress had been boosted by her healthy body and because she'd always kept her mental jukebox jumping. Before the accident, Molly was not only managing a group of sales people and traveling around to college campuses across the U.S. for her full-time job, she was taking notes for her first book, contemplating becoming a lawyer, running, cycling, kickboxing, learning to fly fish and water ski from Walt, and studying to discover the best ways to help Kristen, her stepdaughter, become a better reader. Every summer and Christmas holiday, in fact, Molly became a full-time stepmom, too.

Now even the simplest things were out of reach—getting dressed, sitting upright, holding a pencil steady, walking 50 feet. Maybe those busy-brain, busy-body mice recovered, but I wondered if DNS had ruined recovery for Molly—or if "recovery" was even an appropriate wish. I felt harsh for thinking this, but I didn't like "recovered" as a measurement anymore; it felt unrealistic and judgmental.

Perhaps we couldn't rescue Molly as we knew her. Perhaps we should strive to preserve as much as we could.

It eased my guilt somewhat, knowing that Molly was in good hands with Mom and Sara and Dad. Mary K. and Abi were home with Stephen in Colorado and Amy and her fiancé, Steve, were together in northern California. And I needed to do my job in New York City. I wanted to hang on to the nice client and the good-paying gig I'd had for a few years of writing an educational TV show.

As I watched a lovey-dovey couple on the plane, I was warmed by the butterflies I had about being with Brian again. I was excited and nervous. I wasn't sure what kind of reaction I was going to get from him, but my jitters were pleasant.

I settled back, took a few deep breaths, and tried to relax in my middle seat. I actually welcomed the time to think surrounded by sleeping passengers. In addition to tantalizing notions about what it would feel like to sleep with Brian, I thought about what to say to friends. They'd ask, "How is your sister?" How should I respond?

"Oh, she's getting better everyday. Thanks for asking," I could say.

Or, "I barely understand how she is and it changes constantly. I don't always recognize this Molly or how I feel about her."

Or, how about an upfront approach? "She was getting better, and now she's not so good at all. She's lost a lot of her mental and physical abilities again. She's aware of some of her deficits, and she's confused and really pissed off. Sometimes she realizes Walt is never coming back, sometimes she doesn't. She's sad and frustrated, and she's often a real drag to be around. But, she's alive. And now I hope she's getting better again."

Brian met me at the gate around 7 a.m. as I stepped off the plane. He swooped me up into his arms and swung me around. It was so delightful and spontaneous; we must have looked like a scene from a TV movie. We kissed deeply and his body pressed against mine felt solid and sure. We went home and ate breakfast, chatting and catching up. Then we spent the day hanging sheetrock on the bedroom ceiling with the radio turned up, singing the songs, grabbing a few sexy touches, and laughing together. It was productive and joyful. We made dinner together about 10 p.m. and even slept in a little the next morning on our futon on the dining room floor. We didn't make love, but it was cuddly and cozy to be home with him.

But by the second mug of coffee that morning, I was jolted back to reality. It was as if the kitchen floor had cracked and shifted overnight. We sat at the counter and had a bumpy discussion about our mortgage, IRAs, and overall finances—even our commitment to each other. For the three years we'd lived together, we'd kept separate bank accounts but shared all of our expenses. Sometimes I'd earn more money and pay for more "extras," sometimes he did.

"I think we have to minimize our spending, outside of the real essentials," I said. "Like, we should hold off buying any new tools and we really can't afford the new camera and enlarger you want. Can you get by with what you have for now?"

"I need the medium format for the photography work I want. I don't think I'll get the jobs unless I have it," he said.

"It's just that until Molly is more stable, I can't predict how much I'll be able to work or how much time I'll need to spend out there with her."

"I guess I can borrow some stuff for awhile and just make do," he said. "What about skipping a few monthly payments into our IRA?"

"That's our future together, babe. It's our only retirement fund right now. I don't want to stop saving for our old age together." I smiled, trying to tease him. He didn't smile back. "Look, I'm committed to us—long term," I said. "I'm committed to supporting your photography career and helping you buy what you need. I just need you to be patient until I know more about what's happening with Molly, OK? We probably have another year of renovation on the house, too."

"At least. That's why I want to keep trying to do both carpentry and photography work."

"I'm sorry, but I think cutting back is the right thing for now. I'm hoping she'll be a lot better soon."

"Yeah," he said, "me too."

With a sigh, Brian gave me a tight smile and squeezed my hand as he stood up and got ready for work. It sure wasn't much to lean on; I felt frayed by our conversation and at fault. After a moment sitting alone, I decided I had to swallow it and just be OK with that tiny bit of assurance he offered me. I went to New York City the next day and plowed full-steam ahead into my writing job. I called Molly late after work. Sara was in her room and had been reading to her.

"It was Walt's birthday yesterday, you know, Smith," Molly said.

"Oh, that's right, Molly. I wish he was with you to celebrate," I said, carefully.

"Yeah, that's what Mom said, too. I felt like—oh good, what am I supposed to do? Have a party at the hospital? I've been left behind."

I winced. Then she told me about a dog that had come to the rehab art room to "play with her and the other sick people." I could tell she was getting sleepy as her words began to drift.

"He's just there, he's connected and he won't go, he just stays there," Molly said.

"Who, Smith? Are you thinking about the dog or about Walt?"

"I like the skiing part the best," she said.

"Why do you like the skiing part best?"

"Skiing with Walt. That was great."

"You were very good together," I said. "He taught everyone in the family how to ski. Well, except for me; but he tried!"

Molly chuckled. "Yeah, you're terrible, Smith."

"What made him such a good teacher do you think, Molly?"

"Purpose. He had purpose."

Sara took the phone and said Molly had closed her eyes. I told her what we had been talking about and Sara said that Molly seemed to have floated back in time and place; she had no doubt that Molly was with Walt as she drifted off.

Sara spoke quietly and said it had not been a very good day. Although we felt glad to have a name for Molly's decline, Sara thought the therapy team was really alarmed by the idea of DNS, and the problems were continuing. She read me her notes from the family and medical staff meeting that morning.

"They said Molly had 'regressed in the areas of transfers and self-ambulation.' You know, like moving in and out of bed or her wheelchair, or even just walking," Sara said. "Also, in dressing herself, hygiene and grooming, shower skills, and she's still incontinent. They also noted motor and verbal perseveration."

Listening to Sara, I suddenly realized how we used these odd terms like pros now; they'd become part of our everyday vocabulary.

"Well, she's only just gone back to HBO. What else are they doing?" I asked.

"They're working on improving her walk, as always, but she's still shuffling in place, sometimes on her toes, and she's still tilting to the right, too. And they *still* say her increased frustration is what decreases her abilities overall. It's crazy," Sara said. "On top of all that, Dr. Strum thinks she's depressed, so he started her on Ritalin today."

"What?" I blurted.

"I know!" Sara sounded exasperated. "He said it would help her cognitive and mobility skills. But I don't like it, and Mom *really* doesn't like it."

The next day when I called after work, Mom told me that Dr. Strum said Molly was being "uncooperative." "I couldn't believe it. I told him, 'You don't know my daughter. She's never had an uncooperative day in her life!' He was arrogant and acting like a know-it-all, and I had to tell him he was wrong."

Mom felt that some doctors were looking for other medical reasons for Molly's regression, but her lab tests were unchanged. "And I'm telling them that for Molly, even now, this isn't normal. I know my daughter. This isn't typical. It's not her usual spirit. This is DNS."

When I called the following night, Sara said that Molly threw her shoe across the room while the OT was with her. "She expressed herself pretty darn well, though," Sara said. "She said, 'I'm confused, perplexed! And I'm frustrated and embarrassed. I can't get my body or my brain to do what I want them to!'"

The OT picked up the shoe and helped Molly put it back on, saying, "You're right, Molly. It is perplexing, and I get frustrated, too. Now, let's get to work."

"Molly liked that idea," Sara told me. "And I did, too. And she'd shown great self-awareness! After that, she let me help her get her arms through her sweatshirt sleeves."

Mom and Sara believed the therapists couldn't bear to not have Molly improving, yet they seemed mystified about how to help her improve again. She was their rising star, their big success story, and they felt their efforts were at stake, professionally and personally. Worse still, they didn't seem to know what to think about DNS.

I wanted to feel positive and be proud of my big sister again. Her initial quick progress after coming out of a coma, after surviving the CO poisoning, was standard for Molly in my mind. Of course she'd pull off these amazing feats. Molly was a competitor. When Molly started swimming at age 12, she was coming from the back of the pack, with more obstacles to overcome and less time. She pushed harder and that motivation gave her grit. She became a late-blooming champion swimmer at Yale, clambered her way up the ranks to a big-deal job, found an amazing guy in a cowboy bar to marry, and pedaled a150-mile race to Baja, Mexico on her mountain bike—on a dare.

This falling down and not getting up wasn't like Molly. I wanted my idol back. I needed Molly to get better again.

There was one upbeat note. Sara told me that Molly was really trying to impress George, her current favorite PT. She'd always seemed sweet on him and it didn't surprise us, but not because he was her only male PT. George looked like Walt. Deep brown eyes, a receding hairline, and a moustache. A lean and muscular build. He also had a similar quiet but powerful disposition, and a warm, handsome face that could melt your heart.

"Molly said to him—I think only half-joking, 'I'm dead, I'm dying. I feel like I'm dying,'" Sara said. "She was out of breath and looked into his eyes, pleadingly. They'd just walked down a flight of stairs together and he had his arm around her waist. And George said, 'What are you talking about Molly? Life and death?' And Molly said, 'Oh, that's a mean topic; very, very mean.'" Sara paused. "Then Molly just laughed and laughed, leaning in on George—so, we all laughed. It was wild."

The days went by. I called my family and wanted to hear their stories whenever I could catch someone. But I was on overload. My life sensors were blaring "Tilt." I was living in a split world. I couldn't be fully in one place or the other. I was busy and happy to be back home, but I hated not being in California to witness Molly's results from HBO and to help out. I felt invigorated being with Brian and doing my writing, even though I was constantly distracted and had a terrible time getting much done. Then I'd have work in New York City for a few days, and Brian would be home. We'd overlap at the house for a day or two and then we'd switch places.

One rainy night, I was alone at home sitting on a cardboard box in what would one day be our living room. I was folded over with my elbows on my knees, staring out the large picture window with only a candle for company. I felt so overwhelmed I thought I would collapse. I had an urge to throw something through the glass. I wanted to run in an all-out sprint. But I couldn't move.

I imagined it was a glimpse of being Molly—wanting to burst out, but being stuck; alternating being present and not present at all.

Dr. Strum increased Molly's dose of Ritalin over the next few days and she continued to get daily HBO treatments. Amy was back for a few days and, among other things, helped Molly get on and off a stationary bike at physical therapy. Although Molly seemed familiar enough with the bike, Amy had to remind her to keep pedaling during the 12-minute session or she'd go into a fog and seem to forget what she was supposed to be doing. On the bright side, Amy told me that Molly also walked several long steps—not shuffling—with only a little assistance.

Sara went to an occupational therapy session at which Molly was supposed to tear up lettuce to make a salad. Molly would "fade away," staring at nothing and drop whole pieces of romaine into the bowl without noticing. Sara told me the entire scene made her feel anxious. Then she joked that Molly would have probably been happier to make pizza.

At the end of the week I received an angry letter from my dad's wife, Martha. The misunderstanding between us that had started weeks ago when I was in Loma Linda was raging on. Dad and I had been writing letters to each other. I was trying to untangle the mess. I was shell-shocked by Martha's letter and utterly exhausted by the whole ordeal. Their sharp words penetrated my head like a toothache. I'd made a colossal mistake. I'd apologized for it. Now I wanted to throw the whole fiasco out and start over.

When I look back on her letter now, and all of our correspondence from that time, our inability to communicate effectively, much less to understand each other, is hugely evident. The words on the page are sucked dry and fall flat. Like trying to retell a terrifying nightmare the next morning, words don't convey the disturbing impact. But the emotions remain. At the time, my disputes with Dad and Martha felt so crooked and deeply set, I didn't know if we could ever smooth them out.

I believe we were riddled with our pieces of the family's collective brain injury. I wasn't aware, nor were my family members, of how this was affecting our reactions and judgments. Like Molly, we only knew the frustration of things going unexpectedly awry. Brain injury threw us off balance. This was a whole new way for our family to try to function. We weren't thinking about being extra cautious in our discussions and decisions, trying to move delicately, stepping gently, counterbalancing our weak spots and compensating elsewhere, as a person with a broken leg would; asking for help when moving along a bumpy road.

None of this was visible to us, as most injuries would be, but it affected everything we did or said. And by its very nature, people with a brain injury are the least able to understand its impact. Like someone who might watch us stroll by on the street, we, too, constantly underestimated the impact of the injury to our world and relationships.

On Sunday evening, after a weekend together of working on our house, Brian wrapped himself around me as we stretched out on our futon. He barely said a word, but listened attentively as I tried to unravel the argument with Dad and Martha and find the magic words to finally solve it.

"Maybe you should just let it go for a while; don't write back right now," he said, after I'd spewed all my thoughts into the dark room.

"But I feel like I need to respond and counter the mistakes. Their assumptions are unfair. I just want to end it."

"Well, at least sleep on it for another night... or a few more nights," he said, and slipped into his dreams.

The next morning he went back to New York City. I felt empty the minute he was gone.

My interactions with Molly, Brian, Dad and Martha, my work—mirrored how I felt. Happy, then lost. Discouraged, then hopeful. Frustrated and scared, then trying to be positive. Energized, then beaten down. And it just kept coming. I felt uneven and uneasy, like I was staggering back and forth across a trampoline. I wanted to leap gracefully. I wanted a solid landing and to feel joy again.

Meanwhile, Mom had decided Molly needed a better hospital. She felt Loma Linda's rehab wasn't good enough. They weren't asking enough questions, or the right ones. Dr. Strum seemed to have a disturbing lack of interest in Molly and, as we now knew, neither he nor the rehab staff had been aware of the potential for DNS to occur in a patient like Molly.

Even if the Loma Linda medical staff had been fully knowledgeable about DNS and the risk of it for Molly, it will forever remain a mystery how anything might have been different. Some experts believe it would not have mattered. An earlier diagnosis may not have stopped DNS from occurring in any other way than how it did. But recognizing the symptoms sooner might have helped Molly get additional HBO more quickly, which some scientists today believe may have spared her brain tissues some inflammation and damage. It certainly would have saved us all from some confusion and angst.

Nonetheless, I had qualms about moving Molly away from Loma Linda. It was what we knew. Molly was comfortable there, with Dr. Lo and HBO, her favorite nurses and therapists. Moving felt risky. However, I was too far away to be useful, and I trusted Mom's judgment. She had solved the mystery of DNS, with Walter's help, and she was in charge. I tried to let go and focus on Brian and my writing. But distraction clung to me like a bad cold.

Mom contacted the caseworker from Molly's health insurance company and said she needed a different brain injury rehab hospital with access to HBO, and soon. She explained about Molly's DNS and that our research had uncovered the problem and the articles pinpointing the symptoms. The caseworker asked Mom to send her the most relevant articles and asked where the next hospital should be or if there were any geographic limitations.

"It doesn't matter at all; they just need to really understand severe brain injury from carbon monoxide poisoning. It's about competency," Mom said.

At the hospital, Sara showed Dr. Strum the way Molly was still leaning as she sat in her wheelchair. He admitted it might be due to the Ritalin and ordered a reduction in the drug over the next few days. He thought she would straighten up as it wore off. Mom had told him she didn't like Molly taking Ritalin. She believed it was wrong to focus on depression and wrong to mess with the chemistry in her brain, especially with the DNS ongoing. Now Mom felt validated, and we were all relieved.

At a meeting with my family in late March, one week after Molly started receiving HBO again, her therapists spoke about her improvement for the first time in three weeks. She was still incontinent, but she got dressed with "minimal assistance." Her heel-to-toe motion at the gait clinic was better, even though she only walked a few steps. She even went up and down four stairs with assistance from George. It wasn't much to go on but it felt huge to me in New York.

Mom told me that Molly was still tilting, but her therapists said she was "cooperating and seemed more relaxed," and had less frustration overall. She was even humming and singing songs. These smallest notions of progress, and a few notes of typical-Molly happiness, made me want to dance across the rooftops.

I called the next day and Mom answered the phone. She was ticked off.

"Strum wrote in her chart—here, I wrote it down, that her 'functional decline remains unaccounted for despite physical and neurological workups' and that he'll 'request a neurology consult to help clarify this issue.' Can you believe it?" said Mom. "He's out of it. He's not paying attention. He's pretending the DNS doesn't exist! He's never said a word to me about the articles I gave him weeks ago. I doubt he even read them."

Over the next couple of days, Molly was leaning less and taking even longer steps. Mom read to me a neurologist's note in the chart: "Major concern is 'post-hypoxic delayed leukoencephalopathy,' (a more detailed name for DNS, I learned later) ...Maybe fluctuation in baseline brain scan, but obtain new MRI for white matter changes... No benefit from HBO."

Mom scoffed and said, "Ha! We'll see about that."

Molly received the last of 10 scheduled HBO treatments and was also completely off Ritalin by the end of March. She was continent day and night, and although she required some assistance getting dressed, she initiated the tasks and only needed help finishing them.

Sara told me that Molly sat up straight in her wheelchair and was more confident with her walker, too. She still wasn't really walking, but she was stepping forward more consistently without shuffling. And, at last, Sara said, she seemed more cheerful and calm. After doing some sit-ups and walking 150 feet twice with Sara's assistance, Molly seemed surprised by herself and said, "That was good!"

"And you knew she meant it," Sara said. "It *was* good; she was right."

"Maybe she's happier because she's getting back some of her abilities and feeling more in control, too," I said.

"Maybe," said Sara. "I hope so." Then I got off the phone so Sara could call Walter.

It was so heartening to get good news from Sara and Mom. I needed it; my world in New York was splintered. Brian was in New York City so I was working on our house by myself and also trying to write. I found plastering walls much easier and more quickly gratifying than sitting at my computer and writing, so I wasn't moving my work projects ahead much.

I also had a confounding and disappointing phone conversation with my dad about the letter from Martha. This beaten-down misunderstanding was so messy and clogged; nothing new was coming out of it. No insights. No solutions. I felt like I was thrashing around, drowning in it. My only journal note that day: *Sad, sad, sad.*

At the end of the week, I picked Brian up at the train station and did my best to be really present with him now that we were both home. I needed his comfort and solace. I wanted to celebrate being together. I made nachos and we sat on stools, eating from one plate, and drinking champagne from coffee mugs amidst the renovation of our kitchen-to-be. He listened patiently as I tried to catch him up on everything, but I think I smothered him. He looked into the bottom of his mug and then ran his hand over his face and through his long black hair. He finally stood up and began clearing the table.

"Well, I'm glad Molly's doing better, and your mom will find a really good place for her to go next—you know she will," Brian said, taking my empty mug and smiling warmly. "And I know you well enough; you're a problem solver. You'll work it out with your dad and Martha."

I recognized his words as an effective way for him to pat me on the back without wading in too deep. I suspect he didn't know what to say to help me. He left to work in the city again two days later. I didn't miss him as much as I had the week before. I was pulling my tough-chick independence on like an overcoat. Alone, not lonely.

I caught Sara on the phone that night. Molly had walked that day, holding on with just one hand for support, and took pretty smooth steps. She'd followed instructions and was more aware and tuned in. She even sat up straight all on her own. Sara sounded tired, but pleased. The heavy burden of stress on her and my Mom seemed to have lifted slightly, but Sara was nervous.

"I'm not happy about leaving Loma Linda," she said. "I get Mom's point about it, but we'll go someplace where the people don't know Molly or have appreciation for how far she's come. At least here they know us, we're comfortable and together like a family."

"It *is* a big change," I said, "and we don't know where we'll end up."

"We also don't know if we'll find something better at another hospital," said Sara.

Soon it was obvious, though, that hope was in the air. Molly picked up her heel when she stepped forward and didn't drag her right foot as much. She was managing two-step commands with little trouble. She still had a tremor in her hand sometimes, especially when she was eating. But she was using a fork when she was supposed to, and just seemed more chipper.

Molly was also delighted to receive a letter from Attorney General Janet Reno. She wanted to read it to me one night when I called.

"'Dear Mrs. Weber,' that's me, Smith—oh, you know that," said Molly, rustling the paper. "'I was so glad I had a chance to speak with you and tell you how much I admire you for the strength and courage you have shown in the face of tragedy.'"

Molly paused, and sniffled. "'We are pulling for you and I want you to know my thoughts and prayers are with you. I hope I will get a chance to meet you in the not too distant future. Sincerely, Janet Reno.'"

"Wow, Molly. That is *so* nice. What a wonderful note. She's really great, isn't she?"

"She's really good. Her prayers are with me," Molly said.

"I hope you do get to meet her one day, Smith. She'd be even more impressed with you."

"I just hope I don't stop walking forever or fall on my face or something."

"Well, I know you'd be fine with Janet Reno. You're getting better every day, now."

"You're so overtly... so overly not ever negative," Molly said.

"Why, thank you,... I think," I said.

Molly laughed, and I joined her.

The neurologists ordered another MRI and told Mom not much had changed, but added that Molly's decline had likely been due to "traumatic delayed leukoencephalopathy." They seemed to be dancing around the DNS label, which made me suspicious.

Then, a note from Dr. Brandstater in Molly's chart also seemed strange: *Over the last one or two days, patient has shown steady improvement in functional levels, which seems to make diagnosis of late leukodystrophy unlikely.*

"But it's after weeks of decline. What are they doing? Backing off?" I asked Sara.

"Mom and I think there's some pretty serious denial around here about DNS," Sara said.

Now that DNS was loosening its grip on Molly, they were behaving as if nothing unusual had been going on at all. It was weird and maddening. Just because she was getting better again didn't mean DNS didn't happen. I felt *glad* to know what had caused Molly to fail so rapidly and even better to feel like more HBO was helping her get better again, but it seemed like others were seeking ways to avoid the DNS diagnosis and the benefits of HBO entirely.

What I believe, as does my family, is that HBO helped Molly survive CO poisoning and helped her get through DNS, possibly even reversing the destructive cellular activity and limiting the damage. At the time, we thought we were saving Molly's life. What we were actually doing was making the rest of her life as good as it could be by trying to protect the progress she'd made and working hard not to let her slide any farther away. I know our interventions, especially my mother's, were critical to preserving much of Molly's functional abilities.

I also believe Molly's core essence, her tenacious willpower and sturdy determination to overcome limitations and obstacles, as she did to survive CO poisoning, and had done throughout her life, played a huge role in seeing her through the DNS battle, even if she was unaware she was fighting it.

E i g h t

AT the end of March, the caseworker from Molly's health insurance company called Mom back with a suggestion for a brain rehabilitation facility.

"I'd already put Molly's life and mine in her hands, so I said, 'Just tell me where it is,'" said Mom, her voice sounding tired over the phone. "When she said, 'Craig Hospital in Denver,' I just about fell over. I would have gone anywhere, but this was amazing."

Craig Hospital is a few miles from where Mom lives. She knew they specialized in rehabbing back injuries. Willie Shoemaker, the famous racehorse jockey, had been treated there; so had George Wallace, the former governor of Alabama, after he was shot. She didn't know Craig's other specialty was brain injury rehabilitation, or that Craig had HBO treatments available for patients through nearby Porter Hospital.

Mom called a physician friend in Denver and asked his opinion. He told her Craig was a wonderful hospital and if he had known we'd decided to leave Loma Linda, he would have recommended it sooner.

Mom flew to Denver the next day with Molly's medical reports in hand and met Mark Cilo, a neurologist who helped to develop the original traumatic brain injury team at Craig. Dr. Cilo showed Mom around. She was impressed with the bright, modern facility and the energetic staff. Dr. Cilo said he could take Molly the second week in April, and not to expect a day less than six months of rehab, given the severity of her injuries. Mom was thrilled.

Mom visited one other brain rehab facility she'd been told about. "It looked like a bad hotel that had been left out in the rain," she said. "Dreary and depressing. Too many people sitting around, vegged out in the dark, watching TV." Mom had been through enough in the past two months that she also wanted a full-fledged medical facility. My gut told me she was right.

Mom returned to Loma Linda and told the medical staff that Molly would leave and go to Craig. Mom told me that they didn't want to lose her, and several of the therapists said as much. Molly had declined under their watch, but she was progressing again and they didn't want to let her go until she had regained her previous level of accomplishment. That was a high point, however, that she would not reach again at Loma Linda.

Molly was taking small steps on her own now. At the gait clinic that week, she walked about 100 feet, twice, with four rest breaks. She advanced one foot past the other to about a half-length stride, but there was still toe drag with one foot and quivering in her legs. Her walking still needed a lot of improvement, but the shuffling motion had decreased.

Sara told me that Molly sounded more like herself, too, even in frustration. She described how Trudy, the PT, was in front of Molly instructing her to stand on one leg in a balance exercise. Sara was at Molly's side, encouraging her through several "almost" attempts.

Finally, Molly leaned fully on Sara's shoulder with both arms, and said, breathlessly, "Look, Sara, I want to do this and I've got the balls, I just don't have the backbone."

Sara said they couldn't help it—they all cracked up, including Molly, who laughed the longest once she realized she'd said something so funny.

The next afternoon, I raced up the basement stairs and grabbed the ringing phone. "Hey, Smith," I heard Molly say. "Dad is here in my room, but I wanted to call you all by myself."

"Wow! Fantastic! Thank you," I said, "It's so great to hear from you."

Molly reminded me it was Paw-Paw's birthday. (My father's father was born April 1st and had died several years before.) "No fooling, April Fools! I mean no April Fools, it really *is* Paw-Paw's birthday," she laughed, and I could hear Dad chuckling in the background.

Then she surprised me with a laundry list of questions about my life; she asked about Brian, my work, and the house. When I explained that I was catching up with some bills by working a lot, she got worried about finances.

"There can't possibly be enough to cover all this. There isn't enough money," she said.

"Now, Molly, you've got to focus on getting better and don't worry about that stuff. You've got good health insurance and Mom is keeping track of it all." I wanted to shift to something more positive.

"Well, with the money, you know…it probably would have been better to just get it re-upholstered," Molly said, matter-of-factly. "There can't be enough money, there just can't be."

"Hey, I'm saving my money to come see you again, Smith. And this will all work out, OK? Don't worry. We'll take care of you and we'll find a way to afford it."

When I told Mom later what Molly had said, she thought Molly might have been thinking of the new couch she and Walt had bought several months before the accident. Molly had told Mom then, that it had been a stretch for them to buy it. Mom wondered if maybe they'd discussed fixing up their old couch instead of buying a new one. It made me smile to think of how Molly had connected financial concerns in her mind, and, best of all, that she'd made the connections at all.

Over the next few days, Molly began taking slightly longer steps. When family and PTs complimented her improvements, Molly insisted, "Oh, I can do better, even better, much better than this!" Sara happily relayed this to me and it was a relief to hear it, like a cool breeze on my forehead. Molly's competitive nature kicking in; she knew it and she wanted it.

At a final meeting with family, Amy, and the medical staff in early April, Trudy read from her chart notes: *Molly's shuffling and getting "stuck" has decreased. She's on an upswing and improving in most of her therapies.*

Other therapists added that Molly was progressing nicely with ADLs and expression of emotions. They said she was also initiating more and had a longer attention span—at least 20 minutes with agility tasks and exercise equipment in the gym.

It was also discussed that after leaving Loma Linda, Molly would go with the family to her home in Saugus for a couple of days and also visit Walt's grave so that she might better understand his death. Tony Benjamin said he didn't believe Molly would process this very quickly, but visiting these specific places was a good place to start.

The final write-up from Dr. Strum said that Molly *"would be transferred to Craig at the week's end to be close to home for extended therapies."* This was not accurate. Molly had never lived in Denver; she lived north of Los Angeles in Saugus. The fact of the matter was that Mom meant it when she'd said she would go wherever necessary for Molly to get the best care.

Amy gave me this update when I called to thank her for being at Loma Linda and for all she'd done for Molly and for us. She was heading home to northern California to stay; to be with her fiancé, and return to her work and her life. Even so, she offered to continue as liaison with Molly's publishing colleagues. She admitted feeling anxious about Molly leaving Loma Linda, too—all the adjustments to a new place, she said. Plus, Molly would now be farther away than a day's drive down the coast. I could tell, even over the phone, that Amy was misty-eyed.

She said that after the meeting she was pushing Molly's wheelchair back to her room and was quietly preparing in her mind how to say good-bye for a little while to her best friend.

"So, Amy," Molly piped up, "when is this vacation—that doesn't feel much like a vacation at all—ever going to end? It just seems like forever!" Amy smiled and then answered that one day soon they'd take a *real* vacation somewhere really nice.

The two close friends wore their hair long and then would get shorter cuts at the same time. They had similar wardrobes, favoring jeans and T-shirts whenever possible, but had comparable taste in business clothes, too. They found the same things funny and had similar laughs. In photographs, they looked alike. They had often organized their travel for work to coincide so they'd both be in Boston or Seattle at the same time and could have dinner. With Walt and Steve, the two couples had spent many vacations and long weekends together over the years, sometimes simply visiting each other's homes.

Just before Molly and Walt's accident, Amy and Steve had scheduled their upcoming wedding for the day after the date in July that Molly and Walt had been married 10 years earlier. That way, Amy and Molly figured, the foursome could celebrate anniversaries together—fishing and skiing on Walt's boat or hiking and camping in the mountains.

At home in New York, despite good news in daily phone calls, my stress was unabated. I had cold sores on my lips that looked like bad movie make-up. My writing, the house, the problems with Dad and Martha, catching up, staying afloat, were all like whining noises in my head. I was facing deadlines for a documentary I'd produced, scripts for the educational TV show, freelance articles—everything was due, and I was still terribly distracted. Working on renovation projects around the house, like painting or even cleaning up, was rewarding. It didn't require the mental game of pushing back "Molly stuff" so I could be focused, creative, and able to write. But I needed to write. Even as I'd catch up and send my work in, I knew it wasn't up to my usual efforts. That bothered me, too. I got little sleep.

Brian was working in New York City and I missed his adoring touch and the way he provided ballast in my life. I tried to quell my anxiety with phone calls to Mom and Sara that made me feel connected to them and to Molly. Brian would call in the evenings and we'd have sweet, small conversations, and that felt good. When he'd come home for a few days, it would be warm and wonderful and then get bumpy just before he'd leave again. I think we were both exhausted. A lot of work, a lot on our minds. I was moody. He was distant.

"I can't believe it's already Sunday afternoon and you have to go back to the city in the morning. I miss you already," I said, as I put away leftovers from our brunch.

"Don't sweat it. I'll be home again in a few days that will go just as fast," Brian said. "Besides, you're busy, too. You won't even notice I'm gone."

"Ha! Fat chance. But maybe you'll notice you miss me, too?"

"Yes, of course," he said, without looking up.

On the last Friday at Loma Linda, Mom received a case review and a discharge summary from Dr. Strum. They didn't sit well with her at all and left her "frankly mystified," she said.

The review from neurology stated, *the patient showed little improvement in the first five weeks* ("We would have said going from a coma to walking and talking was more than 'little,'" said Mom). *Then the patient suffered a rapid decline, physically becoming rigid in the trunk with small shuffling steps* ("And we would have included her dramatic cognitive decline as well," added Mom). *New medical factors were ruled out, and it is likely that this was a "delayed relapse," though it occurred somewhat later and without diminished cognition as reports and articles suggest is more common.*

This made Mom so angry. She had supplied the articles about DNS to the medical staff. The articles and our observations most definitely had Molly in the time range for DNS symptoms, and they most certainly included cognitive decline.

Mom continued reading the discharge summary. *After two weeks, the patient began to spontaneously improve.* Mom didn't hide her outrage. "Can you believe that? Spontaneous!" she said. *Patient was walking better, becoming continent, and verbal expression improved in accuracy of vocabulary and complexity of thought.*

At least Dr. Strum's discharge summary also included that HBO was reinstated and even said that Molly's decline could be explained by *delayed neurologic sequelae*. But he still said Molly was *limited in progress by her frustration level*. It all made Mom spitting mad, but she didn't dwell on it. An exit plan was in place.

I wondered aloud to Mom if perhaps these doctors were purposefully not completely honest to protect Loma Linda or themselves somehow. That to reduce Molly's initial progress could make her decline seem less severe and her slow improvement afterwards better. We agreed that we would never know. Mom would take Molly away in a couple of days and we'd move on.

"My greatest misgiving is that, as far as I can tell, those in Loma Linda's rehab have not accepted responsibility for missing the DNS or for not knowing about DNS as a possibility," Mom said. "I felt like I was teaching them something they had no awareness of."

"But I think we know now that that's true. They didn't know," I said.

"Well, that's why I wanted a better hospital, with a different kind of depth and experience with carbon monoxide brain injury," Mom said. "Maybe if they had tapered off HBO more gradually for Molly, maybe the DNS would not have been as deep or damaging."

I realized Mom was grasping for answers, and I understood why. Was it a coincidence that Molly's decline happened about two weeks after HBO had stopped? Or that her improvement from DNS began just days after she started back on HBO? In fact, the DNS was horrifying, HBO was started again, and she got better.

We'll never know another scenario. We do not have two Mollys, as Dr. Lo had pointed out. And no two brains or brain injury situations are similar enough to even speculate.

Mom came to believe that immediately following the DNS episode, Molly's brain was worse than it had ever been, and that she had to recover again from that point; a more difficult place than even her initial CO injury and coma.

Years later, Mom told me she had thought about suing Loma Linda, but didn't because Dr. Lo had saved Molly's life, after all; and he had advocated successfully for more HBO for her, and he didn't have to. "I'll always be very grateful for his efforts," she said

Molly and George, the PT, worked all week on Molly's "traveling" skills. She practiced getting in and out of her wheelchair, standing and turning around in place, getting into a car—and hardest of all—climbing up and down stairs.

Meanwhile, Mom and Sara arranged for Molly's Siamese cats, Sugar and Pepper, to come for a visit with Molly in an enclosed room at the hospital. "They've done so much to brighten our world here at the apartment," Mom told me. "We're hoping maybe they'll do the same for Molly and help connect her to her life."

In the photos I saw later, the cats are scattered, exploring the small office at the hospital and Molly is strapped in her wheelchair, looking off into space. In her lap is a life-sized, toy Siamese cat she'd named, "Sugar-Pep"—a gift from one of Molly's neighbors. But she barely noticed her real cats that day, Sara said. It was the first time she'd been with them since the afternoon she'd left for a ski weekend eight weeks earlier.

The enormity of what had occurred seemed bottomless; how could it be just two months? Hit with a tidal wave of shock and trauma, we'd still packed so much in. Grief and glory, hope, failure, and progress each day, moment to moment. Our world was rearranged in a deluge, but it often felt like simply treading water, in place, just treading. Time passed and it didn't.

Brian and I had some quiet time face-to-face, sitting on the floor, our legs wrapped around each other, our arms stretched out as our hands rested on each other's shoulders. Looking into each other's eyes gave me such relief.

"So, I think we can push through this messy time and find our usual ease and joy and grooviness of being together," I said, with a teasing smile. "How about you?"

"Most definitely," Brian said. "Definitely. We'll settle in. Soon."

"We can be together, like this, and separate..."

"...and still together," he finished. He rolled us onto the floor, our arms and legs intertwined. I kissed his neck, his ear, and his mouth before he could speak.

Brian spent the next week in New York City working a carpentry job. We connected every night by telephone. I was productive—getting my scripts written and stories done. Over the weekend, he came home and we did yard work together, took a drive to explore back roads, and, with me acting as his assistant, worked in his "kitchen darkroom" until 2 a.m. We played fun music on his boom box. He asked my opinion a few times on cropping his photos. And we kissed in the unnatural glow of the red darkroom light. Once his photos were on the line to dry, we collapsed onto our futon and made love by candlelight.

On Sunday he returned to New York City and I worked late writing. I found I could focus and find words again. Just like Molly was, too, I thought to myself.

On April 9, 1995, nine weeks since the day she'd arrived, Molly left Loma Linda—with George, the PT pushing her wheelchair, Dad and Sara carrying her things, and Mom taking photos. Sara described an exchange between George and Molly as they went down the hallway:

"So Molly, are you happy?" George asked, leaning around from behind the wheelchair.

"Yes," she said, smiling up at him.

"What's making you happy?" said George.

"Happy—because all the parts of my life are working out," Molly said, looking straight ahead.

I hoped that Molly's response might have put Sara's mind at ease a bit. She hated leaving Loma Linda. "It was such a big change," Sara recalled. "I'm sure I was trying to make the best of it, but I found leaving extremely painful."

Mom had packed up Molly's room that morning. She'd pulled down all the photos and greeting cards and mementoes of Molly's life that we had taped to the walls, and put them into a small suitcase with sweatshirts and socks. It was quiet that Sunday at the hospital, Mom said, and she had time to think. She'd arranged everything; a couple of nights in Saugus at Molly and Walt's house, a visit to Walt's gravesite, and then a flight to Denver.

Dad brought Mom's SUV to the hospital's front door. Molly practiced her travel moves one more time in the hallway with George and Sara. Then as the group was assembling outside, Molly paused amidst the bustle and looked up from her wheelchair at Sara—tall and slim, with long blonde curly hair, wearing a denim jacket and jeans, carrying a bag of Molly's clothes.

"You're so perfect, Sara. Look at you," Molly said, "you're perfect." Sara halted, standing right next to Molly, and watched her face. Silence. Then they both laughed and, once again, everyone joined in.

Finally, Sara caught her breath. "I'm not perfect at all, Molly. I can't even imagine it."

When Sara told me about the comment, we thought it might be a moment when Molly was aware of her place in the wheelchair and being "on display" with her entourage as she was moving out of Loma Linda. Maybe a sense of herself being unwieldy in public, instead of the agile, graceful person she once was. Perhaps simple recognition of her differentness. Early on, Sara, Mary K., and I were "little sister" reminders of her dependency and deficits and we became the focus of her intense resentment. Now, at least, her comment to Sara was not hostile. It was, I believe, a true compliment.

Molly had completed her HBO sessions a few days before and said good-bye and thank you to Dr. Lo with a big hug. Now she was moving out into the world, climbing into a car to go away from the confines and comforts of Loma Linda for the first time since her new life had begun.

Molly, Mom, Sara, and Dad, and Sugar and Pepper moved into Molly and Walt's house for a few days. Word spread fast, and the neighbors stopped by to welcome their neighbor home with hugs and a few tears. They said how much they missed her, how great she looked, and how glad they were to see her. Molly greeted everyone with big smiles and her eyes welled when they expressed condolences about Walt and gave her their good wishes.

Photos Mom took at the house show Molly sprawled on her bed cuddling with her cats, everyone sitting around the dining room table, and Dad and Molly outside in the small backyard looking out over the valley. Molly's roses were in bloom along the fence and her signature plastic pink flamingos were in place, just in front of the pink flowers.

Molly had given Dad a variety of pink flamingoes through the years— little wooden statues and on greeting cards and coffee mugs. "It was a theme for us, and I pointed out them out in her yard, but it didn't hold any significance for her," said Dad. "Or maybe it held a lot of significance and she shut it down.

"She didn't seem connected to her house at all, and that surprised me," Dad said. "When I'd been there before with Walt and Molly, it was a different place. This time we were just passing through and she seemed to know it."

Sara says she's pretty much blocked out the whole time. "I can't even imagine being there, even though I know I was. But Walt wasn't there," said Sara. "I was resistant about going to Molly's house with Molly and the cats and hanging out without Walt. I just can't remember it. It was too sad."

Sara held in her mind the images of Molly, full of beauty and vitality, and Walt, strong and kind. Years before, during a particularly rough time in Sara's first marriage, Walt had reached out and become a true big brother by creating some security for her when she needed it most. Sara never forgot how he saved her.

Between snapping photos, Mom was busy digging through file drawers in the office and boxes in the garage, trying to pull up the important paperwork she thought she might need sooner than later. The logistical details of Molly's move to Colorado were overwhelming, she said. In truth, it was just the beginning of an ongoing massive paperwork mountain that Mom would scale many times.

When I spoke to Mom after they'd returned from an early dinner, she admitted it was a confusing and disconcerting time for everyone. The first night Molly had wet her bed, which she was sharing with Mom, and was very embarrassed. It hadn't been a problem for a couple of weeks. Mom did her best to comfort Molly and quietly changed the bedding.

They'd been to Walt's gravesite, and though it was hard, Mom thought Molly had done really well during their time there.

Dad pushed Molly up the hill and placed her wheelchair close to Walt's gravesite. In one of the photos Mom took, Sara is standing next to Molly with her hand on Molly's shoulder as they look down at Walt's marker.

"The grass had grown in pretty well since the funeral," Sara explained. "It was windy up there, no trees, just a long open hillside. I wished there were more trees."

The graveyard has only flat gravestones, so it appears as rolling grassy hills with an expansive view. In the distance is a busy highway and mountains with mature evergreens. Just up the hillside from Walt's grave an American flag snapped in the wind from atop a tall pole.

"We had talked to her about going there and I had the feeling that she understood," Dad said. "She was very sad. She didn't expect to see Walt. She seemed aware he was gone.

"We all let her just be alone there for a little while," Dad continued. "I walked around the hillside and was keeping an eye on her. Your mom and Sara were sitting on the grass nearby. I sensed she was communicating with Walt in some way. I know it was hard for her, but she seemed lucid. She knew what was going on and why she was there."

When Dad came back to join her, she looked around and said, "What a pretty place; it's a nice hill." Dad felt it was her transition from being alone with Walt to being with them again.

Sara thought Molly was at times not putting it together; then there were moments when she cried. "She was understanding it, and then in another moment, not understanding again," said Sara. "We had brought flowers and we laid them near Walt's marker. We stayed a long time; it was quiet. Then it was time to go."

I heard protectiveness in Mom's voice. "Your dad was talking to Molly about Walt and remembering him and the funeral," Mom told me. "I thought Molly understood already and has enough sadness in her life; she doesn't need it to be emphasized."

Anyway, they were all leaving the next day, Mom said, and she was hoping it would be a better one.

It hadn't been a good day for me, either. I'd woken up that morning, without my alarm clock, in an agitated state. Instead of sleeping, I'd been thinking about my family going to Walt's grave later that day. I imagined Molly being there, trying to make sense of it all. The last she knew of Walt was that they'd crawled into bed together, kissed good night, and thought they'd spend the next two days skiing. I felt crappy that I didn't know if or when I would ever go to my brother-in-law's grave, especially without any family in California anymore. It was a missing piece for me. I felt horrible that Molly and I had Walt's grave to visit in the first place. The whole situation didn't have to be, and yet, it was reality.

The rest of my day did not improve. The newsletter I'd submitted to one of my clients was riddled with errors, theirs and mine, and I ended up working very late to fix the problems. Sara called around 11 p.m. and said they were set to leave early the next day to go to the airport. Sara sounded out of sorts, quiet and sad. We spoke briefly about my misunderstanding with Dad and Martha—I said it felt unending. But I was crushed with work so we kept the call short and I tried to put my problems aside. It was clear, though, that neither Sara nor I was coping very well with our stress.

Even though I was cranky, Brian was sweet and supportive all day. When he got home from work, he heated leftovers for dinner, sat with me at my desk while we ate, and chatted about his carpentry job at a neighbor's place. Later he brought me a big mug of tea before he went to bed. He massaged my shoulders, kissed my forehead, and said good night.

I faxed and mailed the repaired newsletter to my client and left for New York City before dawn the next morning for several days of work on the educational TV program. I'd had practically no sleep and tried to nap on the train, but my heart was elsewhere. With Brian asleep in our bed. With my family as they were leaving California.

Later that day, my family put suitcases in the car and wheeled Molly out through the garage door. Mom told me they'd arranged for the Hott's teenage daughter to take care of Sugar and Pepper again for a week or so, until Mom and I would return to pack up Molly's house.

Craig Hospital had made the arrangements for the private plane and the nurse who traveled on the flight. When they arrived in Denver, the nurse would accompany my family and Molly to the hospital.

My family was met at the regional airport near Los Angeles by Nancy, Walt's colleague, and our FBI "goddess," as we'd come to call her. She'd done so much over the past couple of months to help Molly and all of us. She'd come to bid farewell and assure Mom that she and the FBI were standing by ready to lend a hand.

When the nurse met Molly at the bottom of the flight of stairs that led up to the small plane, she was elated about the good shape Molly was in. The description on paper of the severity of Molly's brain injury and her use of a wheelchair often belied how Molly appeared in person—smiling, athletic, and determined.

"Molly couldn't do the stairs very well, and we'd practiced and practiced," Mom told me later. "Finally, with Dad and the nurse, one on each side, Molly climbed up. Of course, we found out later it was easier to go up than to go down."

The nurse, Dad, Mom, Sara, and Molly arrived in Denver at a small county airport where they were met on the tarmac by Harold and Mary K., Stephen, and Abi. The whole family entourage arrived at Craig Hospital around 4 o'clock in the afternoon. While Mom handled the paperwork, Molly was shown to her room and she stretched out on her bed. Abi kept everyone entertained with her chatter and singing.

Once the Humbers left to go home, dropping Dad off at his hotel along the way, Molly wanted to move in. "She was unpacking, packing, unpacking—perseverating," Sara told me. "She knew she wanted to put things away, but she couldn't make the full connection. She'd put things in the drawers but couldn't leave them there, so she'd put them back in the bag."

Mom and Dr. Cilo came in. He introduced himself to Molly, who didn't look up. He watched her as she unpacked and packed again. He stopped her by touching her arm and leading her away from the dresser as he calmly explained to her what was happening. This is perseveration, it's repeating an action, and it's hard for you to control because you're probably pretty tired after a busy day. "Molly really liked that," Sara said. "She'd only just met him, but I think she felt understood."

Dr. Cilo told Molly he'd see her later. Sara then helped Molly put her clothes in the dresser without a hitch. After a light supper, Molly was ready to sleep and Mom and Sara left for the night.

However, when I spoke with Sara later on, she was not so settled. The transition she'd been so helpful with was wrenching for her. "Leaving California, leaving Walt, leaving Molly's home, and her friends, leaving all of her life behind—it's this big confirmation of Molly not returning," Sara said, her voice cracking. "She's making her life elsewhere now. I hadn't gone through the mental process of Molly *leaving*, taking her away from all that she had before."

"I think I left that Molly behind in California already," I said quietly.

After we hung up, I stared at the frenetic flowered wallpaper in my tiny room in the women's hotel on the upper east side of Manhattan. I was staying there while I worked because it was inexpensive and had a phone in the room. Never again would I stay in a cheap hotel room without a phone as I had for that one night—the one night my family was trying to reach me in New York City when Molly and Walt had been found.

I thought about what Sara had said. I, too, had thought that some semblance of the former Molly would return. Get the physical body back and the brain and personality would follow. So far, it wasn't working out like that. Maybe it still would.

Pangs of anxiety shot through me as the four walls and their pointy flowers moved closer. I was worried, too, about Molly moving to the Colorado rehab program. But I was distanced from it, embroiled in my life in New York, unlike Sara and Mom who were hands-on, face-to-face, day after day. New fears encroached.

Could DNS come back? It might sneak up and hijack Molly, again, sending her—and us, her supposedly stable family members—into a nosedive again. What could we do? We might be even less able to rescue her and keep her from crashing this time. We were worn down from our battles; I know I was weary. I turned out the light to stop the florid walls from crushing me.

While I worked hectic, long days the rest of that week in New York City, Sara and Mom got accustomed to Molly's new schedule chockfull of rehab therapies and evaluations. Happily, the risks and persistence began to pay off right away.

When Molly arrived at Craig that Tuesday, day 61, the many deficits from her CO poisoning and episode with DNS were very evident. She needed her wheelchair. She had little short-term memory. She displayed an array of cognitive problems.

But Sara said Molly hit the ground running at Craig, "as if she was training for the Olympics." Her attitude and determination came on strong. She worked through a variety of therapies all day and met with neuropsychologist James Schraa daily. The therapists and Dr. Schraa reported dramatic improvement in Molly each day to Dr. Cilo. By the end of the week, which happened to be Good Friday, Dr. Cilo reduced his proposed time for Molly to be at Craig from "not a day less than six months," to three months.

Without a moment's worry about the two-hour time difference between Denver and New York City, I stayed up late Friday night talking with Mom and Sara even though I had to be at work before sunrise. They were energized and joyful and I drank it up like my morning coffee.

I called Brian at home at lunchtime the next day with the good news and to thank him for a greeting card he sent to me at the TV studio in New York City. "That was a wonderful surprise, getting a love note from you here," I said. "That was really sweet. Thank you."

"I'm glad you liked it," Brian said. "And that's fantastic news about Molly."

"Yes, it is such a relief."

"And it should help you, help *us*, feel better about focusing on our projects together since she's really getting better," he said.

"I agree. It does feel like a brighter, easier place for us, too." I wished I could see his face, but I imagined him smiling warmly.

"Yeah, absolutely, babe," he said.

Mom arranged for Molly to get day passes to leave the rehab center and spend the Easter weekend with family. Martha had arrived in Denver, and she and Dad were to pick Molly up on their way from their hotel and bring her to Mom's house. Then Sara, Dad, and Martha would take Molly to Red Rocks. This beautiful park, just west of Denver, is famous for its huge, red sandstone boulders that shoot up at remarkable angles, and its renowned open-air amphitheater. In addition to being spectacular, the park was also a good choice for an outing because it has many smooth paths accessible for wheelchair-users.

When Dad and Martha arrived at Craig, however, they couldn't find Molly. She wasn't in her room or around the central desk on her floor. Finally, one of the nurses realized she had left her in the bathroom. When the nurse opened the door, Molly was there, dressed for her day, with her hands tied to her wheelchair. She had wet her pants. Apparently, Craig was lightly staffed for the holiday weekend and a nurse who had meant to help Molly use the toilet was called away, got busy, probably thought she would get back to Molly in time, but forgot her behind the closed door. It had been protocol in the four days Molly had been at Craig to use restraints when she was in the wheelchair to keep her safely in place.

Dad had called Mom when they couldn't find Molly to make sure he hadn't misunderstood the plans. When he called back and told her what had happened, Mom was furious at the staff at Craig. But she put her anger aside and spoke with Molly to reassure her.

"Molly was terribly upset and so frustrated. It broke my heart for her, especially after such a good week of improvements," Mom told me. "She didn't want to go back to Craig that night—or ever—because she knew what they had done to her and she was afraid the nurses would mistreat her again."

After talking with Molly, Mom called Dr. Schraa and told him what had happened and how upset she was and that Molly was beside herself. "He was wonderful about it," Mom said. "He gathered the nursing staff together that morning after Molly had left with your dad and lectured them about how smart this patient is, and that even though she has a brain injury, they shouldn't treat her as stupid."

Mom said his "lecture" made a difference and that Molly was given more attention and respect after that.

Despite the rough start, that day ended up being a nice one. Photos I saw later show Sara pushing Molly in her wheelchair near the Red Rocks stage where performers were preparing for an Easter service the next day. Three crosses hung above the stage surrounded by the canyon of vibrant red rocks and a deep blue sky. Later that afternoon, Molly took a nap in the upstairs bedroom at Mom's house, while Abi colored Easter eggs at the kitchen table with the whole family watching and helping.

Easter was a sunny, beautiful day, and Molly was all smiles after a good night's sleep when Dad and Martha picked her up at Craig without a hitch. The Humbers went to church, then everyone gathered in Mom's backyard, including Molly in her wheelchair, to watch Abi, in a flowered dress and matching Easter hat, hunt for Easter eggs.

Everyone squeezed in around the dining room table, with Molly at the head, for an Easter supper provided by Mom's favorite Chinese restaurant. Everyone loved it and it was much easier than cooking up a big ham dinner, Mom said, with a laugh.

I'd returned home to Copake from my work in New York City on Saturday night. Brian picked me up at the train station and that night I helped him in his kitchen darkroom until about 1:00 a.m., and then I fell into bed.

After some clumsy lovemaking after he came to bed, Brian and I got some much needed cuddling together after the sun came up the next morning. Sometimes finding our place to connect intimately took a little time to rediscover, especially with so much going on in our heads and beyond our four walls.

I put a small "nest" of chocolate eggs next to his morning coffee as an Easter surprise. And even though it was cold and grey, we worked happily, side by side, in our yard putting up a fence, planting a birch tree, and hanging a new bird feeder. A hot shower together was luxurious.

Mom and Sara and I coordinated our upcoming travel plans on the phone that night, and after they told me about their Easter weekend with Molly, I felt a little left out. Mostly, though, I felt uplifted to be home with Brian, delighted to hear a chorus of spring peepers, and revived with optimism—even though I knew I'd be leaving in a couple of days.

Brian and I caught up over a late dinner. We were giggling and still chatting when we crawled into bed. The bedside candle's light made being naked romantic and sexy.

Monday was a whirlwind. I only had one more day at home to be with Brian, catch up with business calls and assignments, do laundry, send invoices, and pay bills. Early Tuesday morning, I would fly to California and be gone three weeks. Mom and I would meet in Loma Linda and move out of the apartment there, then go to Molly and Walt's house and pack everything but the large furniture. Brian would fly out a week later and he and I would drive two cars and a U-Haul trailer filled with Molly's belongings to Denver and Mom would fly home.

I did not get to bed at all Monday night and, after a delay in Albany, almost missed my connecting plane in Chicago. I hadn't been in California for almost four weeks and it was odd to be back. No visits to the hospital. No clusters of family around. No Molly.

Mom almost missed her plane, too. Molly had called her that morning from Craig hospital because she'd remembered being stuck in the bathroom and was afraid to be there. Mom told Harold as he put her suitcase in the car, "Molly needs me. I have to help her. If I miss my flight, I miss my flight." They drove to Craig and Mom assured and soothed Molly; then Harold hightailed it to the airport.

Mom and I spent the afternoon packing out of the Loma Linda apartment. It was a relief to lock the door, turn the key in at the apartment office, and close that chapter.

We loaded Mom's car that the FBI had left for us at the apartment and decided to go to a little Italian café near the hospital for dinner. After we ordered, we sipped our glasses of wine, and chatted about going to Molly's house in Saugus that night and how to accomplish the packing there. We were pretty quiet, really tired, but as we sank into our booth, we began to overhear a conversation at a nearby table. Certain words pierced our space, impossible to ignore.

"...Emergency ...potential donor ...young ...age 37 ...she was really fit. Perfect health. Skiing... ...carbon monoxide ...clinically dead. Husband dead... ...She got hyperbaric oxygen... we assessed her organs... contacted... hospital... ...recipients. Dr. Lo said wait. He thought... ...some reason... ...pull through. She walked out of here. Like a miracle."

After straining to listen and giving each other looks of "Did you hear that?" and "Can it be?" Mom and I couldn't sit still a moment longer. The two women were discussing organ donations. They were talking about Molly.

We got up and introduced ourselves and explained we were Molly Weber's mom and sister. The women looked stunned. They told us they were shocked that Molly had recovered and truly elated she'd left the hospital in such good shape. One woman said she worked for the local organ procurement organization and the other said she had just started with the group. They said they had been notified about Molly, a strong potential donor, arriving at Loma Linda that night in early February. They had heard that Molly had very present, very attentive family members. They wanted to know how Molly was. Mom gave them an update. They said they were amazed by Molly's story. They said they were really happy she was getting back to normal.

As we ate our dinners, we shook our heads at the incredible coincidence of this exchange. "Can you believe it?" said Mom. "What are the odds?"

"It's really crazy," I said. "Sometimes, in this whole odyssey, it seems there's this powerful pull of fate or destiny directing us all."

We drove to Walt and Molly's house, went right to sleep, got up early, and started sorting through the artifacts of Walt and Molly's lives and packing the pieces and evidence. I had Walt's boom box tuned to NPR and the Morning Edition program was interrupted with the news of the bombing of the Oklahoma City federal office building. We stopped packing for a few minutes to listen, stunned. Then we quietly went back to work. As the FBI took over the investigation, and the hours and horror wore on, we thought about Walt and agreed he would have wanted to be there to help.

Mom and I worked 16-hour days, quitting just in time to run down to the local restaurant for a quick bite before they closed. We'd take short showers, fall into bed, and start all over the next day. We wore the same clothes, had instant coffee and fresh fruit for breakfast, and peanut butter sandwiches for lunch.

The cats, Sugar and Pepper, were glad for our company, but they sensed their world was shifting around them. They were unusually skittish, and after a little cat chow in morning would spend the day in the master bedroom, trying to ignore our packing commotion. I'd rub their chins and pet them, but they seemed happiest curled up together on the bed near Molly's pillow. Mom enjoyed their presence at night. It reminded her of being home with her Siamese cats, Mama and Lil' Darlin', the mother and sister of Sugar and Pepper. Years before, when Molly had offered Mom two of the family of four she'd adopted, Mom chose Mama and Lil' Darlin' because she knew the scrawny, runt sister would need a mother's special care.

The packing was an awesome, monstrous job. Digging through the drawers and closets, deciding what to save, who to give things to, what to donate. Sorting. Organizing. Making piles. Wanting to be quick, efficient, and smart. Really trying to understand and appreciate the bits and pieces and substance of Walt and Molly's lives. Emptying their house to be sold.

In our packing flurry, Mom and I were careful to set aside some special items. Family photos for Walt's mother and daughter. Walt's wristwatch and several of his flannel shirts for Molly. Even today, she wears them in the colder months. "They are so very Walt," Mom said.

I have Walt's Navy field jacket; an olive drab coat with a "WEBER" name patch over the right breast pocket and an illustration of a "Sea Bee" on the left. When I wear it, which I do frequently, it always feels like a warm hug from my first brother-in-law. Walt was not a huggy kind of guy, at least not to me. But I always valued the hugs I'd receive when I arrived for a visit and when I departed. Walt wasn't distant, but he was reserved. I'd tried to be closer to him, but as I packed his things I thought I should have tried harder. In reality, though, it didn't seem like an effort he would have welcomed. We were close enough, especially in humor and teasing and when we were doing an activity together as a group, and that seemed to be enough.

Meanwhile in Denver, Craig hospital had arranged for Molly to begin a series of 10 HBO treatments at nearby Porter Hospital. Sara took on the task of getting Molly there each day. One morning, after the third HBO visit, Sara got Molly back to Craig and went up to her floor.

"Dr. Cilo was there at the central desk, and Molly said, 'Hello Dr. Cilo, how are you?' I was stunned!" I could feel Sara's excitement over the phone. "She was happy, in a good mood, and right then she started to get out of her wheelchair because she wanted to get up and walk. It was automatic, she just stood up! But I was still shocked, trying to digest the fact that she'd remembered Dr. Cilo's name. I was trying to get everyone's attention. I wanted to jump up and down and yell, 'Hey, you guys, this is astounding! She just said Dr. Cilo's name!' And Molly stood there grinning."

In contrast to her foggy memories of leaving California, Sara remembers a lot about Craig. "Molly got well there, very quickly. She was talking, remembering stuff, wanting to walk. Her fast improvement made it much, much easier for me to be OK in this new place."

But Molly's progress also put her in jeopardy. She was ready to get up and go. She was well aware that her rehab time had been cut in half already and she liked that "award." And with her typical zeal, she was determined to get up and walk anytime, even though she wasn't stable enough to go very far. So, the staff at Craig still had to use the restraints on the wheelchair to keep Molly safe. Sara said they explained it to her, and they treated her with respect and never left her alone again as they had before, but it frustrated Molly. She was like a 16-year old with a brand new driver's license who thinks she's ready to drive fast in heavy traffic in a Porsche.

By the weekend, Mom and I were using the two-car garage as a staging area for our packing. We raised the door during the day as we worked and neighbors stopped by to say hello. We appreciated the pitchers of ice tea and kind words they offered. They helped keep us steady.

Mom would also talk to Harold, Sara, and Mary K. almost every night. They'd tell us about Molly's progress and I could see that Mom functioned better in the day and slept peacefully at night after their enthusiastic reports. I was emotionally drained; adrenaline kept my energy high. But knowing my family members were part of this team effort helped me focus and keep my head on straight.

Early Monday morning, after six days of packing, I washed my hair, put on a clean T-shirt, and picked up Brian at the airport. He looked so good to me; his bear hug and kisses were sweet succor. We went to U-Haul and hitched up the trailer to Walt's SUV. Even after his redeye flight, Brian was in great spirits and gave Mom and me a fresh boost.

Over the next two days, Mom and I wrapped up the packing and Brian filled the two SUVs and U-Haul trailer with boxes and small furniture. On Wednesday morning, I put Sugar and Pepper in their carriers and nestled them between bags of linens on the backseat of Mom's SUV. We locked the windows and doors of Molly and Walt's house, and pulled away.

Brian drove Walt's SUV with the trailer and waited at a rest area on the highway as I drove Mom to the airport. Her SUV was packed so tightly, cats and all, Mom had to hold her suitcase on her lap and fold herself around boxes at her feet in the passenger seat.

"It will make your airplane seat seem so spacious," I joked, as she crawled out of the car. "We'll see you in a few days at your house, Mom."

"Be safe. Drive carefully," said Mom. "And thank you. I love you."

"I love you, too, Mom."

I joined Brian at the rest stop and we began our road trip to Denver. It was long straight days and roads, dusty desert, diner food, and small motels. We spent the first night in Barstow, California. Mom was back home safely and amazed by Molly. "She's excelling, Lyrysa," said Mom, when I called her from a pay phone in a diner. "You won't believe it, she's really doing great." I could hear Mom's joy and relief.

At the little Mom-and-Pop motel, I put my battery-operated CO detector on the nightstand. Brian had installed CO detectors on each floor of our house in New York immediately after Molly and Walt's accident, and all of us now traveled with portable CO detectors. The window that faced the gravel parking lot was open, letting a warm breeze in through the screen.

About 3:00 a.m., the CO alarm blared, jolting Brian and me out of bed and the cats under the bed in a flash of fur. I grabbed the alarm and we scurried out of the room in our bare feet. We discovered that a truck driver had left his rig running in the corner of the parking lot. The truck's exhaust was putting CO into our small room with every puff of wind. I couldn't believe it.

We woke up the motel manager and he got the trucker to turn off his truck's engine. The manager gave us a fan for our room and the CO detector remained quiet. Brian fell asleep again right away, but I lay in bed petting the cats for a while. Luckily, they were fine and their purring was soothing. I fell asleep staring at the smoke detector on the ceiling.

Just because I could, and we were there anyway, I called Sara the next night and sang, "Well, I am standing on a corner in Winslow, Arizona..." Sara and I rang out a few more lines of the famous song as I stood at the pay phone.

"Are you really in Winslow, Arizona?" Sara asked.

Yes, on a dusty corner. Just like you can imagine it," I said. "Pretty cool, right?"

"Very cool," Sara said. "And you're in for a treat when you get here, too. Mom is totally thrilled with Molly's progress. She can't believe it. Molly's come a long way in 10 days."

Sara also said that her Walter was driving into Denver that night. They were going to take a weeklong vacation in southern New Mexico. We made a plan and two days later the four of us met for breakfast at a truck stop in Raton, New Mexico. After lots of coffee and laughing, we snapped a few photos of our rendezvous and they drove south and we drove north. We got to Mom's house in time to unpack the U-Haul trailer into Mom's garage and return it.

Since it was Saturday, Molly was spending the day at Mom's house. When we got back, Molly heard us in the kitchen and walked downstairs to greet us. She held the handrail and took one step at a time. She'd been taking a nap, but she was alert. I was astonished to see her move so well.

"Smiiiiith!" Molly yelled. "Smith, I can't believe you're finally here." She gave me a big hug. "What took you so long? Did you use a wheelchair, slow-poke! You are so slow, Lyrysa! Hooray, you made it."

"I missed you, too, Smith. And look at you. You are doing really great!"

"Yes, of course. I'm stupendous, naturally."

I hugged her again and she tousled my hair. "Brian!" she squealed, reaching out to him. He lifted her off her feet in a gigantic hug. "Whooopeee!" she yelled.

We all went to Mom's favorite natural foods restaurant for dinner. It was the first time since her brain injury that I had been in public with Molly except in a hospital. Mom and Harold had had only a couple of experiences so far. I learned a lot at that meal.

Molly has extraordinary hearing. She could hear conversations in the kitchen beyond a swinging door 20 feet away and a baby whimpering across the room around a corner. I was unaware of these sounds. It was like she was wearing some super-charged hearing aid that picked up every sound far and wide. In a way, she was, sort of.

I learned years later that we "hear" with our minds. For some people with brain injuries, it's like they're being barraged with sound. Molly could not tune in or tune out; she heard everything equally. She could not select a particular voice she wanted to hear from the array of surrounding sounds. She could not filter out other diners' conversations, laughing, or the clattering of their dishes.

At the restaurant, Molly quickly became overwhelmed with the all the noise assaulting her. She became irritable with the waitress, she cursed about the crying child and mimicked its whining, she became indignant with the kitchen staff, who didn't even know she was there.

"It's soooo noisy. Noisy! It's bombarding me," yelled Molly. "I do not want to be bombarded. Stop smashing pots and pans."

I know she felt attacked, but I felt embarrassed. People shot glances at our table. Even after Mom gently tried to settle her down, Molly continued imitating the voices she heard and banging her fork against her plate. The restaurant got quiet and Mom suggested we have our dinners wrapped to go.

"Hey, Smith," I said, "Have you had enough to eat for now? Let's get away from this noise and walk outside. I'd really like that."

"Yeah, I'm ready. Let's get out of here," Molly said. "I like this restaurant but it's too vociferous. It's uproarious. Like voices exploding."

Brian, Molly, and I walked outside while inside Mom and Harold gave the waitress a short explanation and a big tip. She handed Mom a bag of leftover dinners to go. As soon as we were in the car, Molly was calmer, and by the time we got to her room at Craig, she was sleepy and very sweet. My heart was restless until I gave Molly a hug and kissed her good night. I needed her peacefulness to assuage my guilt about feeling so unnerved earlier.

On the drive home, Mom said, with her typical quick-study confidence, that Molly gets exhausted easily, and when she does, she gets cranky. "Then it's hard to placate her," Mom said. "I was worried we might have gone out a bit too late. It's better for her if we eat dinner earlier."

"That's wild about her hearing," I said. "I couldn't hear what she was hearing."

"Your brain automatically filters out what's not important," explained Mom. "She can't be selective yet in that way, so a noisy place can be way too much for her. I didn't think it'd be so busy there; it's not usually."

"Well, she's still light-years better than when I saw her last," I said. "Five weeks ago, she couldn't walk into a restaurant and sit down at a table. It's amazing how much she's improved."

"Yes, that's true," Mom said, pausing. "I've decided that the first miracle is that Molly lived. The second miracle was that Craig Hospital is in Denver. And here I was thinking I would sell our house and move wherever it was necessary to go."

"I'm glad that didn't have to happen, Mom. And I'm glad they have HBO here, too, and that they use it with brain-injured patients," I added. "It's the right place for a lot of reasons."

Then Mom announced that Dr. Cilo had told her, a couple days before we arrived, that Molly was ready to become a day patient at the end of the first week of May.

"Wow! That's great, Mom. And I'll still be here," I said, enthusiastically, patting Brian's knee and exchanging smiles.

"That's pretty incredible—and fast," added Brian.

"Yes, it is. Now I just have to figure out how to get ready," said Mom. "And what to do when she comes home." Harold glanced over to Mom and she returned his gentle look. He drove on quietly with one hand on Mom's.

I understood then that this notion of Molly leaving Craig was not an altogether carefree prospect. It wasn't just that Mom had only a short timeframe to reorganize her house, her life and Harold's—her world—to accommodate Molly. Also just beginning to set in was what it would mean to have her eldest daughter, now 37 years old and severely brain injured, living with her for the first time in more than 15 years.

Back at Mom's house, we finally sat down to eat. Mom told us she had a friend in Boulder who worked with people with traumatic brain injuries. She'd called her friend when Molly first went to Craig Hospital and reached out again when she learned that Molly would be checking out of Craig earlier than anyone could have imagined. The friend knew enough about the challenges ahead to give Mom honest advice.

"Do not take an emancipated child back into your home," she told Mom. "Just don't do it, Sally. I know what I'm talking about. You won't have a life of your own. There will be nothing left of you."

Mom said her friend's words ran through her like ice water. So, she shared her concerns with Dr. Schraa, who suggested a facility where Molly could live.

"It was very expensive, though," Mom said, as we sipped our tea. "It's in Bakersfield, California. Really out of range, financially and geographically. So I told Dr. Schraa that I was thinking I'd bring Molly to my own home.

"I told him that Molly had made it clear that she wants to come to my house when she leaves Craig," Mom said. "She's been here every weekend. It's comfortable and familiar for her. She really enjoys the cats, the big windows, and she takes naps in the upstairs bedroom."

Dr. Schraa asked Mom directly: "Is this your decision? That you will bring her home to your house?"

Mom said she believed she understood the cautions coming from her friend and Dr. Schraa. But she also knew it wasn't the last decision she'd make. It might not last forever. And if it was a disaster, then she could make another choice. I loved hearing this from Mom. She had always taught us the same thing: Make the best decision you can and then make a new one if and when you need to.

"At that moment," Mom told us, "I thought to myself, 'I gotta do this.' Yes. I'll make it work. She's my daughter. I'll find a way."

◀ Molly, age 2, and me.

▼ Dad and Molly, around age 4, loved to play together.

▲ Sara, 1, me, 3, and Molly, 5.

◀ Family
portrait for
the directory
at the church
in Phoenix
where Dad was
the minister.
Mary K.,
newborn,
Sara, 4,
me, 6, and
Molly, 8.

▼ Molly and me,
around age 19
and 17, goofing
around in our
noncompetitive
swimsuits.

▲ Molly, about 15, with our
dogs, which she took through
obedience training and also
taught them to do tricks.

◀ Molly at Yale, 1975-1979,
on the cheerleading
squad (left) with her
friend, Suzie; on the
swim team (middle row,
third from left) (below);
and a national champion
swimmer (below left).
Photos courtesy of Yale
University Library,
Manuscripts and
Archives, and Yale
Banner Publications.

▲ Molly at Stanford earning her master's degree during my senior year there.

▼ Molly visits me in New York City, about 1982.

▲ Molly, 25, and Mary K., 17, were the two coaches for a local swim team, summer 1983.

◄ Molly and Walt's
wedding day,
July 13, 1985.

► Molly, Walt, and
Kristen, age 9, on
a ski vacation in
Colorado, 1990.

▲ Molly and Walt, January 1995, one month
before the carbon monoxide accident.

▼ Molly, declared clinically
dead from carbon monoxide
poisoning, in a coma and in a
hyperbaric oxygen chamber at
Loma Linda University Medical
Center, February 1995.

Sketches by Harold Shuler.

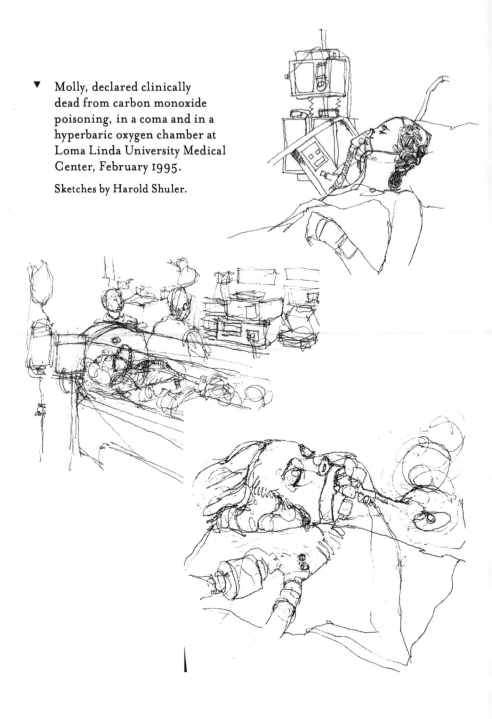

◀ Mom and Mary K. with Molly at Loma Linda soon after her coma ended, February 1995. Molly has a feeding tube in her nose and is using a wheelchair because she had not yet re-learned how to swallow or walk.

▶ Abi, age 3, and me with Molly at Loma Linda, March 1995. Molly is feeding herself and walking again.

◀ Sara and Molly at Walt's gravesite the day before Molly moved from California to Colorado, April 1995. Molly's ability to walk had disappeared due to her episode with delayed neurological sequelae.

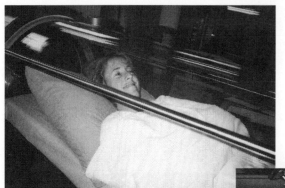

◄ Molly in the hyperbaric
oxygen chamber as part of
her continuing rehab at Craig
Hospital in Denver, April 1995.

► Molly and me at Craig Hospital
in Denver, April 1995.

◄ Molly and Mom at the annual
FBI ceremony honoring fallen
agents in Los Angeles in May
1995, four months after the carbon
monoxide accident that killed
Walt and injured Molly. Molly is
holding Walt's FBI credentials.

◀ Mom and her daughters
celebrating her 70th
birthday in 2004, in
Crested Butte, Colorado.

▼ Molly and me in Salt Lake
City, for her hyperbaric
oxygen clinical trial in 2007.

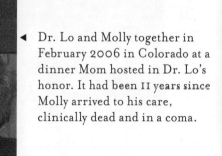

◀ Dr. Lo and Molly together in
February 2006 in Colorado at a
dinner Mom hosted in Dr. Lo's
honor. It had been 11 years since
Molly arrived to his care,
clinically dead and in a coma.

◀ Molly and Mom traveled to
▼ Hawai'i in 2012, their dream
trip. They visited several of
Walt's relatives, learned to make
leis, and enjoyed the warmth
and magic of the islands.

◀ Molly and me during
a family gathering at
Christmas 2011.

▲ Mom and Molly sat for a portrait together,
▼ and Molly posed with her cats, 2013.
Photos courtesy of Sandy Puc Photography.

N i n e

THE next morning, Brian and I arrived early at Craig to pick up Molly, who had finished breakfast and was ready to go. Back at Mom's house, the three of us took a long walk on the bike path. It was Sunday, so the path was busy with runners, cyclists, and people strolling with their dogs. Molly didn't walk quickly, but she did walk well for about an hour, including up and down a steep hill, and she enjoyed seeing the activity. It was hard to believe that she had left Loma Linda in a wheelchair just three weeks earlier. Brian took several photos of us in the sunshine wearing our sunglasses. We pretended to be movie-star glamorous and Molly delighted in Brian's attention.

Afterward, we were drinking tall glasses of water sitting with Mom in her living room—a sunlit, quiet room with high ceilings and several of Harold's large landscape paintings that reached far up the walls. Molly looked at a wedding portrait of her and Walt that hung near Mom's piano. Harold had painted it a decade before.

"Mom," said Molly, "Where's Walt?"

We froze. It had been more than 10 weeks since Molly had come out of her coma. She had been at Walt's grave 20 days before. Brian's eyes locked on mine. Mom rose from her chair and sat down on the couch beside Molly.

"Molly," Mom almost wailed, "Walt is dead."

Molly's mouth dropped open. I found my breath, moved closer, and put my arm around Molly's shoulder. "Remember, Molly, Walt died from carbon monoxide poisoning in the hotel room that you were in," Mom said, gently.

"Mom—I had no idea," said Molly. Bewilderment settled on her face like a shadow.

"We've told you many times, Molly, you just haven't remembered."

So Mom painted the picture again, stroke by stroke, of what we believe happened. Molly looked at the floor, at the backyard through the sliding glass door, back to the floor, up to the painting of her and Walt in their wedding clothes, Walt's arms wrapped around Molly.

Mom reminded Molly that after she left Loma Linda hospital, they had all visited Walt's grave. Molly listened quietly and then squinted.

"But why didn't Walt call 911? He knows he should call 911. He taught Kristen to always call 911." Her eyes welled up. "I don't get why he didn't do that."

"Molly, he couldn't," I said. "He was very, very sick in the hotel room, like you were. And he probably did try to call 911 to get help, but he just… couldn't."

I fell silent. Molly stared at the floor. She didn't blink.

"We all miss Walt so much, Molly," Mom said, softly. "And we will always love him."

Mom and I were now weeping, our arms around Molly. Then Molly cried, too.

A few minutes passed. Mom brushed Molly's cheeks with her hands and suggested a short nap, and they went upstairs. Mom said she fell asleep almost instantly.

We had an early dinner and Brian and I drove Molly back to Craig. After her nap she'd bounced back; pleasant during dinner, laughing with Harold, and yawning in the backseat as she teased Brian about his driving.

I slept fitfully that night. Molly had not grasped Walt's death, or if she had, it slipped her mind. My head churned, imagining her confusion. She must have all kinds of questions banging around in her brain that we didn't have nice, pat answers for.

Maybe Walt is going to come see me next weekend? Didn't Dr. Lo fix him, too? Doesn't Walt need HBO? Why am I alive and he isn't? Where is he?

I realized that Molly, with a severe brain injury, was trying to understand why the most precious person in her life wasn't there to protect her, laugh with her, and love her, the way he was in the wedding portrait hanging on the wall.

It was the last time Molly wondered aloud where Walt was. "I think her hippocampus, that part of her brain, was healing," Mom said. "I never had to tell her again that Walt was dead."

Monday morning I let Brian sleep in and I went to spend the day with Molly. In her morning physical therapy sessions she used exercise machines and stretched with the PT, and in the afternoon a different PT tested her range of motion and balance. I was astounded to see how much she'd improved since I'd seen her go through similar routines at Loma Linda.

She also worked with an OT doing kitchen and cleaning skills, and a speech therapist on reading and comprehension. I was even more amazed. A strawberry-banana smoothie in the blender, all the dishes washed and put away, and about 10 paragraphs read and retained.

I worried that my following Molly around all day was adding pressure on her to "perform" for her little sister, but she seemed at ease and remained positive. Molly introduced me to Dr. Schraa at his office before she had her daily one-hour appointment. She was comfortable with him; in fact, she liked him well enough to tease him.

"Smith, did you know that Dr. Schraa did not own a CO detector until he met me?"

"Really?" I said, smiling at Dr. Schraa. "Thank goodness you came along to educate him about how important they are."

"Poor Dr. Schraa," Molly said. "He needed me to educate him and I'm a half-brain. Are you less than a half-brain Dr. Schraa?"

"Sometimes, Molly, I think I am," said Dr. Schraa, playing along. "It's a good thing we work together. We can add up to one brain."

"I don't know, Dr. Schraa. I don't think we add up to a full brain, yet." Molly laughed.

I called Brian from a pay phone in the hallway while I had a few minutes on my own. He was relaxing with Mom and Harold after helping with a few house repairs. We had planned to drive to Castle Rock to have dinner with Mary K. and Stephen. I told Brian I'd pick him up so we could leave when the rush hour traffic had died down.

After seeing Dr. Schraa, Molly had one more session with a speech therapist who tested her reading skills, memory, and reaction speed. A few times, Molly was surprised when she wasn't correct. She immediately told the therapist she wanted to do it again and get it right, "like a normal person." But once her frustration was up, her cognitive skills went down. The therapist intervened and gently guided Molly to solve the problem.

Molly worked hard all day. She had high expectations for herself and treated the back-to-back therapies like workouts. She was challenged, but dedicated. And despite some missteps, she pulled through and found a reason to laugh, usually at me. Teasing was still a Molly trademark.

By the time I left, Molly had had her supper and was tired. The therapies and all-day concentration had taxed her. I was worn out, too, and told her so as I gave her a kiss. She stretched out on her bed and said, "See you tomorrow, Smith, if you're not too pooped out."

During the 35-minute drive to the Humbers, I thanked Brian for helping out at Harold and Mom's and told him about Molly's day and her progress. Mary K. had prepared vegetable shish kabobs and while she put Abi to bed, Stephen, Brian, and I huddled under the eave of their house in a steady rain to grill the kabobs on their patio barbecue. It was fun, and no one ever complains about rain around Denver. It was a wonderful evening and relaxing, just what I needed.

On the drive back to Mom's, we talked about our time ahead. Brian was flying home the next morning. I would fly home a week later. I remember feeling calm and content.

"Molly's improvement makes me confident that I can turn more of my attention back to me and you—us together," I said, raising his hand in mine. "Our world, our way."

"That's awesome, babe. I love that," he said, smiling.

The next morning, I went directly to the hospital after dropping Brian off at the Denver airport. Molly seemed to appreciate my being with her again and even "showed me off" by introducing me to several nurses and other patients she'd come to know, even if she couldn't remember names. Each day at Craig brought Molly some frustration and some discoveries.

One day after Molly had an EEG and a check-up with Dr. Cilo, he proclaimed, with a twinkle of pride in his eye and a hand on Molly's shoulder, that everything was looking good for her to move home at the end of the week.

"You know, I've never felt that Dr. Cilo is an especially warm person, at least not to me," Mom said, when I shared his comment, "but I believe he really cares about Molly and wants her to succeed."

Mom spent the week organizing and preparing the house and herself and Harold. Molly would be a lot to take on and she knew it. Harold had been supportive of Mom and steadfast helping with Molly. Now he was spending a lot of time at his art studio and Mom admitted they weren't connecting very well. She wanted to feel closer to Harold again, and thought if she could just get Molly settled, she'd have time to bond more with Harold and focus on their relationship.

I tried to call Brian every day and also pushed myself to make at least one call a day to line up freelance jobs back in New York. I needed the work desperately, but it was a bit crazy thinking how I could get back to juggling my work, Brian, our renovation, my family. I fought against the feeling that I was cheating everyone—stealing time and attention from here and there so I could manage it all. During my early morning runs, I'd coach myself: "OK, just adjust to feeling overwhelmed. You're not out of control. Be positive."

At night I would sit with Molly as she had dinner in her room and stay with her until she was ready to sleep. It was so much easier now to say good night and leave. She was stronger and more complete. Less scary. More Molly.

On that Thursday night, May 4th, just 12 weeks since the accident, Mary K. and Abi came to Mom's house for pizza and salad, and we created a huge paper banner to welcome Molly home the next night. Mary K., Abi, and I stretched a long piece of butcher roll paper on the floor and decorated it with colorful hearts, stars, flowers, and animals while Harold and Mom watched from the kitchen table and took photos of our "mural" in progress.

After the sign was finished and Mary K. and Abi left, I stayed up late making Molly's favorite foods to serve at her "Welcome Home" celebration dinner party. It was a smorgasbord—guacamole, vegetarian chili, pesto pasta, tabouli. Brian called and I chopped parsley while he chatted about his work and things happening in our village. He felt close. I was relieved to hear him happy and involved in our community. I told him how much I missed him and wished he could share the homecoming festivities with us. He said he really appreciated what I was doing for Molly. I felt loved.

The next day, Mom had a meeting with a good friend who was also her attorney and was working on the lawsuit filed on Molly's behalf. Mom said she would go to Craig and bring Molly home after she finished her therapy sessions. I spent the day making phone calls to New York. Luckily, the job front was looking more promising.

Mary K. and Abi came in the afternoon and we pinned up the banner we'd made across the kitchen wall. Abi said, smartly, that it would be the first thing Tia Molly would see when she came in the door. (Mary K. had taught Abi to use the Spanish word for aunt, "tia" for her three sisters, and to use "aunt" for Stephen's sisters.)

When Mom and Molly arrived, Harold, Mary K., Abi, and I yelled "Welcome Home!" Molly beamed and held her hand held delicately over her heart as we applauded. Then she read the banner aloud, "Welcome Home, Tia Molly."

Mary K. and Abi clapped and cheered. Harold took photos. Molly was radiant. Mom dabbed at tears.

I took in the scene from the kitchen with a wooden spoon covered in pesto in hand. It was difficult to reconcile the image of Molly standing there in Mom's house. It had been exactly three months to the day that she had arrived "clinically dead" at Loma Linda. February 5th to May 5th. A lifetime. A new life. An ongoing odyssey.

"Thanks so much, you guys," Molly said as she tickled Abi and tousled her hair. She kissed Mary K. and Harold and gave Mom a kiss and a long hug. "Thank you, Mom, for bringing me home."

"You're so welcome, honey," said Mom.

"We're glad you're here!" Harold said. "We're really glad you could make it!" And we all laughed at the ironic truth of his comment.

"Hey, it's Cinco de Mayo," Molly said. "Mexico's Independence Day and mine, too! Whooo-hooooo!" Molly raised her fists high over her head.

Mary K. and I exchanged looks of surprise, and I shook my head in wonder. No one had mentioned the date or the holiday.

"You're incredible, Smith, the way you always remember dates," I said.

"Of course, I'm fabuloso, perfecto, muy bien!" she said, high-fiving my free hand.

No one enjoyed the eclectic feast more than Molly. "Oh, Smith, this is all so good. I want to keep eating, but I'm stuffed."

"Don't worry, Smith," I said. "We'll be eating leftovers for days."

Mary K. and Abi headed home and I put away food while Harold filled the dishwasher. Mom and Molly went upstairs to get Molly situated. She cooed, petted, and spoke sweetly to Sugar and Pepper, but Mom said Molly really just wanted to go to sleep. She chose the twin bed closest to the bathroom and the window and crawled in.

When I tiptoed in later, Molly was sound asleep, with her cats on top of the comforter. As I lay in bed listening to her soft breathing, I realized that, with the twin beds and two Siamese cats, it was like when we were kids and shared a room for more than 15 years. Only the black light and the Beatles, Jimi Hendrix, and Linda Rondstadt posters were missing.

The weekend was quiet. Molly slept in. We ate leftovers and went for walks around the neighborhood. Mom had moved her home office downstairs to a corner in hers and Harold's bedroom. We unpacked a few boxes from the house in California and added a boom box, some music tapes, and a few framed photos to Molly's room. We even set up her computer on the desk near the bay window. Mom and I shrugged and said, "Who knows?" and "Why not?"

Mom had done so much to prepare for the move, but I could tell it was both a relief and a little unsettling. Mom's eyes looked tired. It was a huge change for her and for Harold, too. He'd been so helpful and Mom let him know how much she appreciated his cooperation. Still, I knew it couldn't be easy on the two of them and that adjustments in their lives would keep coming. But no one was letting on. We were all happy to have Molly doing so well. It kept spirits high.

Molly had gone from "not a day less than six months" that she was to be at Craig, to three months, to a total of five weeks. I hoped that once she got into a routine as a day patient at Craig, Mom would feel more at ease.

My last night in Denver, I slipped into bed after Molly had been asleep for more than an hour.

"Smith?" Molly whispered into the darkness.

"Yes?" I said softly.

"I thought that was you. Just checking. I wanted to be sure."

"Sorry. I didn't mean to wake you up. Do you need anything?"

"Nooooo." She paused. "Maybe a new brain. I'm a widow, you know. Maybe I need a new husband."

"You had a great, a really great husband, Molly. We all miss Walt a lot."

"I know. I wanted to talk to him."

"Well, you should Molly. You can think of him and—just close your eyes and talk to him, if you want. What would you say?"

It was quiet for several moments. "You're my best friend. I love you. Don't leave me."

Her words floated in the darkness. I pushed my head back on my pillow and pressed my lips together. I didn't want Molly to hear me crying.

Finally, I whispered. "He loved you very much, Smith." She was silent. "I love you, too."

Soft rhythmic breathing came from the other twin bed. Molly was sound asleep.

I flew home on Sunday. On Monday Molly became an outpatient at Craig's rehab unit. Everyone settled into the new routine that first week, Mom said. She or Harold would take Molly to Craig in the morning to spend all day in therapies and to meet with Dr. Schraa. She also saw Dr. Cilo regularly. Molly would be at home in the evenings and on weekends.

On my flight home to New York, I wondered again what words to use when people asked, "How's Molly?" I needed the review, to straighten out my head.

"Molly is healthy and strong, and back on track," I'd say. "She's different. This version of Molly, this rendition, is sort of unfamiliar. It's not like she's a stranger; she pretty much looks the same. She looks great, in fact. But she is new to me, with unpredictable reactions and sometimes startling behavior. And that can be unsettling and a little weird."

I could add: "She holds her face in a distinct way, a little cockeyed and uncertain; not the forthright, secure woman I've known. She's in between, with reminders of who she was, and the new person forming. Sometimes she just seems a lot like the old Molly, especially when she's laughing. Other times she's raw, unpolished, the intractable new Molly."

Trying to wrangle my shifting impressions of my older sister into something coherent was tricky. I could not have fathomed how tempestuous Molly would become. But at the time, she was a willing outpatient at rehab, and she was often compliant and sweet.

I had been away from home for three weeks and now it was springtime. I felt optimistic as our tulips began nudging up through the cold mud. I loved springtime in upstate New York, when nature gives her best color, energy, and hope. It's a short season; gone before you can appreciate it all you want—or all it deserves.

After dealing with the initial rush of bills, paperwork, cleaning, and phone calls, I happily moved back into my life. It felt good. I did some writing work and managed to secure a few new assignments. Most of all, it was great to be with Brian. We worked on the house and in the yard. We visited friends and walked to the post office holding hands. We talked and laughed late into the night. We were in synch. I felt our world was charmed.

Sara and Walter returned to Denver from their getaway to New Mexico soon after I'd left. She called me from Mom's house and said she and Walter had decided to split up. I was blown away. The next day she called again and said they were back together and trying to work it out. She said their conflict was about place and flexibility. Walter was entrenched in Michigan. Didn't like to travel, would never move. So different than Sara.

"Life will change. And I realized Walter won't," said Sara. "But he's agreed to at least think about compromise, so we'll see."

I was struck by how unstable and scary it all seemed. She and Walter had chucked it. Now they were trying again. But what was the damage done?

Here we were, all of us, attempting to settle into our lives. Maybe "danger" warning signs were staring me down in my relationship and I wasn't seeing them. Like Sara, my focus had been elsewhere. But now, I was trying to connect with Brian and re-enter my world fully. I was determined to be attentive to him and to stay positive.

Sara hung out with Molly in Denver for a couple of days. When she and Walter left for Michigan, they had Molly's cats in tow. Mom explained that she, Sara, and Molly had decided that Sara should take Sugar and Pepper to live with her, at least temporarily. One problem was that Denver has a city ordinance that allows no more than three animals in a residence. Mom already had her two cats, Mama and Lil' Darlin'. Sara loves cats and adored Sugar and Pepper. Molly was glad that Sara could take care of them.

"Molly just wasn't enthusiastic about caring for them," Mom said. "She wasn't possessive about leaving her house, and she's not possessive about the cats either," Mom said. "She just lets it all go."

I thought afterward that perhaps Molly's home in Saugus and Sugar and Pepper reminded her of "family life" with Walt.

The week after I came home, I sold a brand new video camera to the owners of our favorite camera store while Brian was in New York City. Mom had given me the camera five months before when most of the family, including Walt, Molly, and Kristen, were all together for the holidays in Winter Park, Colorado. It was an extravagant Christmas with especially luxurious gifts from Mom. Even at the time, it felt "over the top" for me and I doubted I would use it.

I spent the money from the sale of the video camera towards the new equipment Brian had been wanting for his work as a photographer. It paid for nearly all of it. I was happy to have the money go to something meaningful.

A week later, Mom sent me snapshots of their Mother's Day, a celebration for her and Mary K. The photos showed everyone in the backyard enjoying the sunny day. The Humbers, all dressed up, had come over after church. Abi was so cute in a sailor dress and hat. Mary K. (always the most photogenic sister) was glowing; her pregnancy a little more than half way along. Molly also looked beautiful. She was sitting with Abi on a lounge chair. She had on a little lipgloss and mascara, her haircut was short and chic, and even from the photos, she seemed bright and calm. I was relieved to see such cheerful pictures.

In her note, Mom said that Molly was going up and down the stairs with ease. She'd been worried that the stairs might be a troublesome obstacle. I called Mary K. to hear how she was doing and ask how she thought Mom and Molly were getting along.

"You know, I think they're doing pretty good," Mary K. said. "I'm only there once or twice a week; I take Molly to HBO and then stop in to visit. And Abi always likes to take a ride over to Oma's."

"Yeah, I bet Oma is pretty good about spoiling her grandchild," I laughed. "Soon she'll have two to dote over."

"My baby's getting big." I imagined Mary K. looking down and patting her belly.

"I saw the photos from Mother's Day, and you look radiant, Mary K., totally gorgeous."

"Thanks, Lyrysa. I feel good. We took more photos when Mom and Harold and Molly came over for dinner here last Sunday. We ate on the patio, had corn-on-the-cob and ice cream bars—it was a nice time. And Molly wasn't grouchy at all."

"That's good. Maybe those mean-Molly episodes are behind us."

"She even did her Donald Duck voice for Abi and Abi *loved* that. We all cracked up."

I called Sara next. She said that things with Walter were good and that the cats seemed happy in their new home. Walter and Sara were now living together in his house, and Sara said she was feeling comfortable with that, too.

"It's weird. I'm finally home with Walter and working again on my dissertation and teaching classes, but I'm still anxious about Molly. Like I'm stuck. Being away from her is hard. I can't believe it. I guess I'm just used to seeing her every day."

"And helping her get better every day. Sara, you did so much for Molly for a long time."

"Well, she's doing well at Craig. I know it's a good place and they're doing a lot of HBO, which is great. I just hope she keeps improving so she can be more like herself."

I understood that Sara hoped a complete Molly, or at least more of old Molly, would break through. "She *is* a lot better than she was," I said, "even from a few weeks ago."

"I just don't want to give up."

"We're not giving up, Sara. We're just trying to get used to the new routine and this new... this current version of Molly."

Sara was quiet for a moment. "I miss her. The old Molly."

"Yeah, me too," I said.

When I was with Molly at Craig, I realized that what was going on was rehabilitation, not recovery, at least not yet. The distinction meant a lot. It protected me from looking for someone who might not show up.

But over the past three months, Sara was with Molly more than the rest of us sisters. She took only one short break away from Loma Linda. Mary K. was around a lot, but she had Abi, Stephen, and her pregnancy to take care of. I went back and forth to New York a couple of times. I had occasional distance from Molly, which had its pitfalls for sure; I was torn a lot. But I adjusted to the new Molly each time I was with her, seeing her with fresh eyes, perhaps faster, and more easily. Sara had been face-to-face with her oldest sister almost every day for weeks, searching for the Molly she knew to return.

Not only did I have more distance, I also had finality. While Mom and I were packing up Molly and Walt's house in California, I never saw Molly, but Sara was at Craig with her that whole time with a clear vision in her mind of who Molly once was. I had spent all those days digging through Molly's previous life. Smelling her sweaters. Sorting her jewelry. Packing up the novel on her nightstand with a bookmark half way through and the drawer filled with special, undecipherable mementos. Chatting with her sad-eyed neighbors who saw us stacking boxes in the garage. Reading her lists of things to do stuck to the refrigerator. Finding the partly written greeting card to me. She probably thought she'd mail it the day after their skiing weekend.

It was eerie and I toiled there in bottomless sadness. But the pressure to quickly finish the job helped me slog through. And being in their house, among their possessions, in their community, was decisive. It redefined my understanding of the situation. I felt the permanence. It felt final. It was the mindset I needed. I concentrated on all the evidence of Molly's former life, and I knew deep down she wasn't returning to that world. No more than Walt was.

Now, my sisters and I were going forward with our lives; we had time with Molly and time away, we had our own environments. It was the sister advantage. But Mom didn't get away, ever. She had no distance. She couldn't. She wouldn't. Not as the mother. She said she felt ultimate responsibility for her first child. Every day is Mother's Day.

Molly received an invitation from Nancy, our wonderful FBI liaison, to attend a ceremony a few days before Memorial Day for fallen FBI agents. Walt and other agents who had died in the past year would be honored. Mom decided she and Molly could make the trip to Los Angeles. "This time, we're going to fly United," Mom told me, laughing.

Amy came down from northern California and met them at the airport. Molly was elated to see Amy, which delighted Mom. Nancy said she and all of Walt's colleagues were so happy that Molly would be at the ceremony. They'd been afraid she wouldn't be able to make the trip.

The ceremony, attended by FBI agents and agents' families and friends, was typically for agents killed in action. But even though Walt was not on duty when he'd died, the FBI and his fellow agents wanted to honor him.

Walt and his partner, Don, had been working on a major case, a kidnapping, and the agent in charge said one of them had to work the weekend. Don had plans and Walt did, too—to go skiing with Molly and a group of friends at Mammoth. Walt suggested they toss a coin and Walt lost. He worked that weekend and the group of friends went skiing without him and Molly. The case was successfully solved and Walt arranged to go skiing with Molly the following weekend instead.

Agents didn't work that many weekends. It was just a coin toss, Don said, that had turned into a terrible, unfortunate chain of events.

At the ceremony, Don escorted Mom and Molly to the front and stood with them and the other family members of fallen agents. When the time came, Molly, on her own, walked up several stairs to the stage to accept Walt's credentials, beautifully framed, and a plaque from Charlie Parsons, the FBI official who gave the eulogy at Walt's funeral. As she stood in front of the crowd, Mr. Parsons said that Molly had come the farthest to be there that day.

Mom and Don stood nearby and walked with Molly after she left the stage to return to their seats. Molly was quiet, very gracious to everyone, and walked beautifully, even on the stairs. Molly told Mom and Amy at dinner that she was just praying the whole time that she wouldn't do a "face-plant."

"She said didn't want to embarrass Walt by falling," Mom told me. "It was very important to her that she did well to honor Walt."

Mom, Molly, and Amy also went to the house in Saugus. While Mom made arrangements for the furniture to be shipped to Denver and for the house to be sold, Molly and Amy sat at the dining room table, drank iced tea, and talked and laughed, just like old times.

When they were ready to go, Molly walked out the front door, leaving her and Walt's home for the last time.

Finally, they stopped by Loma Linda hospital to visit Dr. Lo and the nurses and therapists in the ICU and rehab.

"Molly had to introduce herself to everyone because they barely recognized her," Mom said. "They needed help to understand that this was really Molly."

They had dinner that evening with Dr. Lo, who just shook his head at Molly in wonder, and said, "She is very impressive; truly amazing."

On their last day together, Amy took a photo of Mom and Molly, and Molly playfully put two fingers up, like rabbit ears, behind Mom's head. Mom's photo of Molly and Amy shows them with their arms wrapped around each other, their heads together, with huge smiles.

The week after Mom and Molly returned from Los Angeles, another note from Janet Reno arrived:

> *Dear Molly,*
> *I was so happy to get your note and to learn from your mother how well you are doing. I was also in California last week and got a great report from [an agent] on your progress.*
> *Your strength, and courage and perseverance motivate us all to our very best.*
> *Sincerely,*
> *Janet Reno*
> *U.S. Attorney General*

Molly was very pleased with the letter and asked if she could hang it on the wall in her room. Mom suggested they frame it with the first note Reno had sent and Molly liked that idea.

I'd call Mom a few times a week, and when I could talk to Molly, she'd be cheerful but would hand the phone back quickly to Mom. Mom said Molly didn't like to talk on the phone too much but was very pleasant around the house most of the time. She was working hard with her therapists at Craig every day, and getting some HBO treatments. "She still has a tendency to get cantankerous when she's tired at the end of the day," Mom said. "That's when I try to get her to go to bed as soon as I can."

My month of June had some dark patches. A friend's fiancé committed suicide, and she and her family were devastated. Another close friend was going through a horrible divorce. My workload quickly became overwhelming. And the continuing discord with Dad and Martha was like a thorn in my foot. One Wednesday I wrote in my calendar: *Stressful day. Work demands bad. Call with Dad for 2 hours. So hard.*

I thought I was gathering enough insight to recognize the impact of the "family brain injury" on me, and on Dad and Martha, and the harm it had done. We still weren't expressing ourselves in speech or in writing effectively, or listening well. Plus, we had the ironic, almost impossible task of comprehending our problem of family brain injury while in the midst of it. It is an impediment unlike any other. We were impaired and unaware of it; attempting to function normally, but unable to understand why we couldn't. Like trying to stay on the road when driving drunk and without knowing you've been drinking.

I tried to tell Dad and Martha about this predicament; I'm not sure they understood me. I so wanted to be back in their good graces, to be at ease and happy again. I kept pushing for that. But I couldn't understand why they persisted in assuming the worst of me when I'd been the daughter who for years had done the most to be close to them. I'd really hurt them and felt terrible about it, but where was their acknowledgment of my apology or faith in my history with them? It was weeks before I could get any clarity on the whole murky mess.

I was aware, too, that these stressful situations, highlighting my piece of the family brain injury, didn't make it any easier for Brian to deal with me. I did my best to shield him from my emotional tangles and quite consciously presented my best positive disposition to him as much as I could. I still got knotted up, but he understood without me having to say much. He rolled along steadily and gave me affectionate support; the spontaneous bear hugs, the shoulder massages, and the way he'd sit across from me as we'd hold each other's forearms. He'd deliberately hold my eyes with his gaze for a long time. It often felt better than breathing.

Meanwhile, I was trying to find new ways of interacting with Molly. She didn't like phone conversations and wasn't writing letters. It was frustrating; as if we were speaking two different languages. She didn't seem concerned, but I was desperate to reach her.

I ached for my big sister, as I'd known her. I wanted to pick up the phone and gab with her for an hour while I chopped vegetables for dinner. To know my thoughts before I could speak them. To tease me, ask my advice, challenge me. But reconnecting for Molly was readjusting for me. I knew I needed to be patient. So, I'd handwrite a note and fax it to her. Mom and I both had fax machines in our home offices. It wasn't as good as a phone call, but I hoped this one-sided communication was temporary. I needed some way to "sister-yak" with Molly.

"I saw you sent Molly another fax today," said Mom. "She absolutely loves those, Lyrysa. It seems to be her favorite way to communicate."

"Well, she doesn't fax me back," I said. "But I'm glad she likes mine to her. Since she doesn't like the phone, I had to find a way to reach her."

"She especially likes your drawings at the end—the little smiley face with curly hair."

"Yep, that's me," I said. "And that's a picture I can't send over the phone."

I resolved to approach Molly as I would any new relationship. Start with small steps. Use what you have. I didn't choose my family members, but I had nurtured our friendships. I'd especially tried to cultivate closeness with my sisters; I could use my life-long sister connection with Molly to build anew.

I decided to talk to her like I used to, even if it was one-sided or on a faxed page. Every now and then she'd answer the phone when I'd call and talk to me for a minute or two. I did my best to always be up and encouraging—whether by phone or fax. And Mom told me that she looked for faxes several times a day, like letters in a mailbox. I sent greeting cards, too, hoping she would reinstate her good habit of sending cards.

I wanted to be grateful for whatever I had with Molly. I worked to keep perspective. But the simultaneous loss and celebration of Molly, happening back and forth, was like a drawer opening and closing, opening and closing. I had no assurance how long each stage would last. I could not be certain of the contents. I just didn't want it to slam shut for good.

As I looked over my diary, all the usual stuff was there—appointments, work hours, thoughts about Brian, plans, lists of things to do, check marks, and circles. But my largest, brightest handwriting was always reserved for Molly—stars, hearts, exclamation points, underlining, notes about every fax and phone call leapt off the page. Molly was my focus.

She was doing great at Craig. Mom sent a few photos of her swimming in the rehab pool with perfect freestyle form and riding a horse at a nearby farm. The PT had arranged the riding because it helps many brain rehab patients improve their balance and regain a natural rhythm to their gait. In the photos, Molly looks at ease both in the saddle and stroking the horse's head as it nuzzles her neck.

In a list of goals Molly had written several years before her injury, I was surprised to read that she envisioned owning horses at a home she and Walt would build in Jackson, Wyoming on a mountain with a view of the Grand Tetons. She wrote they'd ride daily, year round. Molly has always loved all animals, but I'd never known her to enjoy riding. It was a dream for her future and now it was helping her to walk better.

Mom also included a few photos of George, the PT from Loma Linda, who'd come to Denver for a weekend visit. He stayed in Mom's guest room and hung out with Molly. In one photo, he's jogging alongside her as she rides a bike. He'd managed to get her riding her bike in just over an hour, despite her fear of falling over. They also did some sightseeing walks in town.

I asked Mom if she thought he had a more involved interest in Molly than we'd realized. Mom said she wasn't sure, but there was fondness there and maybe he'd flirted with her a bit. At Loma Linda when Molly was in the worst of her DNS, Mom recalled that George was gentle and persistent when the other therapists were stunned and discouraged by her setbacks.

"George was relatively new on the scene then and he hung in there and pushed ahead, bringing the other therapists along with him," Mom said. "Here, George has been really kind to Molly and enthusiastic about her progress." And even though his Denver visit went well, Mom believed it satisfied his urge to see Molly continuing to improve, as well as his curiosity about her beyond that of a patient and friend.

By late June, the strife between me and Dad and Martha was finally dissipating, like a dense fog lifting. The discussion had warped far beyond the original mistake I'd made and the resulting mistakes we'd all made. It reminded me of one of the worst fights I ever saw my parents have, when one of them burned the toast one morning. They yelled at each other in the kitchen; I don't remember their words. I couldn't look at them. I stared at the still-smoking blackened squares in the toaster. Their argument, that day and ultimately, was about everything but breakfast, but on that day, burned toast ignited the battle.

Each time in the recent months when I thought I'd done all the explaining I was capable of to Dad and Martha, and that maybe it was enough, they would raise another point I'd have to address. It was like an inescapable maze. Tons of effort, no path out. Finally, it may have been more exhaustion than time that cleared the air.

Dad and Martha even came to visit us at our messy house for two days at the end of June. They slept on a futon mattress on the floor and helped us install a joist, choose paint colors, and frame a new window. We took a hike and made good meals together. It was a sincere and warm time together, and confirmed a way forward. It was a wonderful gift to me.

Over the next months, not being with Molly but in my home, I further realized the impact of brain injury on my life. No matter how much I accepted my situation, it felt as if my wings had been clipped and I would never fly unhampered again. Every thought process was different: how to spend my time, which job to pursue, what to buy, how to organize my finances, whether I could take a vacation or not. My choices were, as far as I could see, unavoidably couched in the bigger picture of being there for Molly and ready to help my Mom whenever I might be needed.

Luckily, Brian and I were busy—jobs, renovating, and still making some time for fun and togetherness. However, while I set about consciously trying to simplify my world and limit my undertakings, Brian embraced a new assortment of activities. In addition to his carpentry jobs, he was excited to have his new photo equipment. He spent days shooting and many evenings in the kitchen darkroom. He pulled his beloved 442 Oldsmobile muscle car out of storage and began rehabbing it in our driveway, with the hope of drag racing. He joined a spelunking group, which held monthly meetings and organized weekend trips through wild caves in upstate New York.

I was trying to avoid being overwhelmed, but I wondered if Brian was trying to distract himself. I reminded myself that I had always admired his "Renaissance man" qualities. So, I made an effort to be supportive. I learned a bit about an 8-cylinder engine, dual exhaust, and went with Brian to the nearby drag strip once. I even crawled in a couple of caves. None of it was for me. I told Brian so, and said I was glad for him to do what he loved.

I recalled during this time another thing Tony Benjamin had told us at Loma Linda: With brain injury, there's an intensifying of pre-injury traits. Characteristic qualities are magnified, he said, because the restraints on behavior are impaired by the injury. Personalities are exaggerated. He meant this phenomenon would exist for Molly, and perhaps for her family members as well. I saw this in Molly, sometimes in Mom, and now in Brian and in me.

Molly's sharp edges were exposed more easily and more often. Her harsh anger would unnerve me. Mom's determination to be in control and manage all situations was at times unbending. Brian seemed to thrive with near chaos surrounding him. It was how he'd grown up as a child in a big, raucous family always teetering on the edge of breakdown. Now, in our house and in our lives, it was as if he'd loosely arranged stacks of blocks at elbow height—each ready to tumble and crash with a sideways move. He'd stabilize for a moment, then he'd be off.

I'm a problem solver and an optimist. I like order and practicality. I pay the bills and balance the checkbook, each time to the penny. Reorganizing the kitchen pantry and tidying my desk help me function better. I believe I can figure out just about any problem with a go-get-'em, positive attitude and a creative solution. This had long been my way. I didn't usually stop to consider whether I was being realistic, annoying, or constructive. I craved a clear path. I wanted to focus on my work, my family, and on Brian.

But some of my struggles surprised me. For several days, I suddenly found myself so sad about losing Walt, I couldn't get any writing done. I couldn't focus. It was the 4th of July weekend, Independence Day—red, white, and blue. Friends visited. Flags waved. I tried to work. Backyard cookouts scented the air, fireworks splashed in the sky. I couldn't eat, I couldn't play. Five months since the accident, and I was grey in grieving.

By the end of that week, I discovered comfort in studying photos I had of Walt, which usually included Molly or Kristen. Brian also printed some black and white photos he had of Walt. I saw Walt's hands, his eyes, and his face. I saw him so happy with his wife and daughter. I saw how they looked at him. I discovered I missed him most of all for Molly's sake.

And there was my reality, distorted. Molly still looks a lot like Molly in the photos with Walt, but in significant ways, ways that really mattered, she was not that Molly at all. Yes, she is still slim and attractive with pretty hair and blue eyes and a brilliant smile. But now her face often seems numb, her eyes blank, her confidence quivering. From deep inside, her appearance was altered. Not so much what I see, but what I feel from her.

I was lost in this weird, convoluted scene. How do I let go and mourn the loss of Molly while she's still around, and, at the same time, actively celebrate the Molly that's here? There were no neat boundaries or consoling ceremonies. No right words to say or traditions to hold on to. No closure. I couldn't simply look at photos and trick myself into believing that Molly had died and a similar person replaced her. It wasn't like that at all.

I swatted away negative thoughts of Molly not coming back 100 percent, fully recovered. After all, she was getting better all the time.

I clashed with my own guilt. After Walt and Molly's accident, there was horror, then a celebration of life, and now I had to admit I wasn't always so thrilled about the existence of this Molly-with-brain-injury. It was messing up my life—I shuddered with shame.

I missed Molly, but I wasn't confronting her loss because she was still here. It was maddening. I couldn't express my sticky turmoil clearly, even to Brian. I fought the gloom that was pulling me down.

I wanted to feel cheerful about Molly, to regain my comfort zone. To do otherwise felt like defeat, especially after we all had given so much and tried so hard to help Molly be Molly again. To do otherwise, I thought was a huge, disrupting failure.

I began to see it for the first time; the stretching, staggering, ripple effect of Walt and Molly's accident. I began to understand that none of our lives would ever be the same.

And precisely because Molly was still here, I wasn't sure how to go on—I sure as hell didn't want to lose her. Could I mourn and disengage with the old Molly while in the presence of the still-living Molly? Could I forget while being reminded constantly? It wasn't a matter of packing up Molly's things and putting them in Mom's basement. This was a different kind of loss. No five stages would cover it. I needed a new way of coping.

Because everything had changed. Walt had died. And Molly had died. And lived.

T e n

MOLLY went for various therapies at Craig five days a week, worked hard all day, and went home to Mom's in the late afternoon, just a like a job. She worked on stretching, balance, and strength, reading skills and retention. She used computer programs that tested her attention and tweaked her visual and mental acuities. She was given brain puzzles and games to play on her home computer.

She continued to impress Dr. Cilo and he told Mom that he wanted her to have another round of HBO, which would bring her total number of treatments to 80. So far, each round of HBO had seemed to bring improvement. However, Dr. Cilo doubted that Molly's insurance would pay. Mom was ready for this.

"Just call them, Dr. Cilo, you'll see," Mom told him.

He came back 15 minutes later and said, "Well, Sally, you know something I don't know. They said yes, immediately, they will pay." I imagined Mom's satisfied smile.

Mom admitted to me that she would have mortgaged her house or whatever it took to get the HBO treatments paid for, but it was a huge relief to have them approved.

"So Molly started more HBO the next day. That was almost a week ago," Mom said. "And I give Harold a lot of credit. He takes Molly to Craig and gets her to HBO. He's done so much of the transportation all along, which is a big help to me. He's been really great about it."

Meanwhile, Mom put the brick, early-1900s townhouse she owned in downtown Denver up for sale. She'd bought it a few years earlier to be Harold's art studio. Brian and I spent several months working for Mom renovating the building. But now she needed the money to pay off the debt she'd incurred while we were all in Loma Linda for almost three months.

"I wasn't surprised or even unhappy about that debt. It was spent for all the right reasons," Mom said. "But I wasn't willing to just sit on it, either."

Mom had to make a number of life-changing decisions. When we were living in Loma Linda, she utilized the Family and Medical Leave Act to hold her position as vice president of strategic accounts for a big computer company. She told them she didn't know when she'd be back. Occasionally, her secretary would call to keep her abreast of what was going on in the Denver office, which Mom was in charge of, and Mom tried to read the memos and newsletters the office sent her.

"But I couldn't get my brain around it at all. I didn't care," Mom said. "All of that just faded away, it was so yesteryear to me. Next to what we were living every day at Loma Linda, all the company news, corporate business, and office politics were inconsequential."

In June, her boss at the company's California headquarters called Mom at home in Denver and said they needed her and she could have her job back. Mom told him she needed to think about it.

"Molly was sitting at the kitchen table and I told her that my boss just offered me a job," Mom recalled. "Molly said, 'Tell him you have a job.' I thought, 'She's right. I do.'"

Mom called her boss back and told him that Molly said she already has a job. "He never argued. He was really good about it. He understood."

Mom says now that if Molly had needed to live in an institutional home, she probably would have gone back to work. She'd enjoyed her job. "It wasn't a good or bad thing, it just wasn't right for me at that time."

A few years earlier, Mom had won a settlement from a previous employer in an age and sex discrimination lawsuit, which paid a monthly stipend and covered her health insurance for the rest of her life. It also gave Mom some preparation for the lengthy and difficult experience of Molly's legal case.

"After I turned down going back to my job, I thought, 'Thank you former company and bosses for being such jerks,'" Mom laughed. "I had the settlement money. I knew I didn't have to work and that was the greatest help I had. Molly was what mattered to me. Otherwise, I would have been distraught, like all of you were then."

Mom was keenly aware of the struggles we three younger daughters were going through to get reintegrated into our lives. She understood that we were stretched between Molly, family, trying to make a living, our careers, homes, relationships. She may have understood more about my life than I did.

Now that I was keeping up by telephone, with no plans to travel to Denver, I thought I'd have a clear head. My friends and coworkers, and maybe even Brian—hell, maybe even me—expected everything to be A-OK. Ta da.

But it wasn't. I was supposed to settle in, go on, and re-inhabit my life. I tried. I jumped back into my writing work and scheduled jobs in New York City. I made plans to hang out with friends, did stuff in the community, planted a garden, and established a game plan with Brian for our house renovation. Above all, I created time to be with him.

We didn't do anything out of the ordinary, but we had time together we hadn't enjoyed in months. Day after day, night after night was our rhythm again, and I wanted to be in tune with him. I made a point to be helpful and caring to him. It felt great to listen face-to-face and respond right away. I was adventurous and enthusiastic for him. We laughed and we loved. The simple stuff; the essentials.

I did the things I wanted to do to be home, to be me, to be with Brian. But I remained unsettled. Even at a distance, away from Molly and her daily care, I was struggling to get used to my altered world. I thought the changes were in my background, that they would stay under my newly calm veneer, but they rose to the surface like bubbles. Molly with a severe brain injury, lucky to be alive, living at Mom's house, and not really the sister I'd known my whole life. These realities were muddling distractions. I hoped I'd adjust.

Mom, meanwhile, embraced Molly and her new life. In mid-July, one day after what would have been Molly and Walt's 10th wedding anniversary, they attended Amy and Steve's wedding in San Francisco. Molly was happy to see her best friend, Mom told me, and really seemed to enjoy the wedding festivities. During the toasts at the dinner, Amy announced to the gathered family and friends, that the person who had truly come the farthest to celebrate their marriage was Molly.

That month, Molly's therapy at Craig was reduced to about three hours per day, usually speech therapy and meetings with her neuropsychologist, Dr. Schraa. She was also exercising a couple of hours a day, and had a more intense regime than anything Craig hospital had ever envisioned for her. Dr. Cilo said that the four months she'd been treated at Craig were like two years for most people. They attributed her progress in part to HBO, but mostly to her competitive, determined spirit. Each time they'd ask her to climb another flight of stairs, read a little more, total a longer column of numbers, she'd say, "Of course!" or "That's easy, piece of cake," or "I absolutely can, no problemo."

Before the accident, Molly would have said that swimming was what instilled her competitive nature. There's no doubt that swimming did positive things for all of us, including discipline and focus. Molly received Yale's highest team award, Most Outstanding Swimmer, not because of records set, but in recognition of her dedication and determination. She was as proud of that honor as any award, she'd said, because she realized that with passion, she could do anything. I'd add that the bigger the challenge, the more indomitable she became.

So now she was walking well, even running a little, and riding her mountain bike for short distances. She was enjoying reading, which Mom encouraged by giving her the novels she'd just read. And Mom, Harold, and Molly went to a movie or play almost every week.

She still didn't like to carry on a conversation over the telephone, or send faxes or letters, but she liked to receive calls, faxes, and mail from me, Mom said, so I kept it up.

In late July, the medical team at Craig said it would be a good time for Molly to take a break. Mom decided that an end-of-summer vacation would be a stimulating adventure, so Harold, Mom, and Molly hit the road.

"I thought, 'What to do?' and it seemed easier to take a car trip than to fly," Mom recalled. "We had folks to visit and lots to see."

In mid-August they drove north to Sheridan, Wyoming, where I was born when Molly was a toddler. It was where she had first run away from home, on her red tricycle, only to be found hours later in the cowboy bar downtown on Main Street. Her trike was parked out front, and Molly was entertaining the afternoon crowd, dancing on the tables in return for Coca-Colas. It was an innocent time, a friendly bar, a safe town; no harm done. Dad thanked the bar patrons, collected Molly and her tricycle, and went home. Molly used to chuckle about how she got a spanking and was "grounded" to our yard and not one foot beyond.

From Wyoming, they drove farther north to Glacier National Park, which they had all wanted to see. Then east through Canada to Michigan to visit Sara and Walter in East Lansing. Driving farther east, they visited Niagara Falls, another first, and then came to stay with me and Brian in Copake.

After a couple of days, they headed up the coast to Bar Harbor, Maine, then south to visit Molly's colleagues at Houghton Mifflin in Boston. When Mom called Molly's boss to say they wanted to stop in and say hello, Mr. White put them up at the nearby Ritz Carlton and met them for dinner that night. Mom said Mr. White and several of Molly's coworkers joined them for a lovely meal, and that everyone was very kind and complimentary.

Their last planned visit was to Maryland, just outside Washington, D.C., to see Molly's mother-in-law, Ah Mee Weber. Although they'd kept in touch over the past six months through letters and phone calls, the last time Ah Mee had seen Molly, she was in a coma.

Mom said Ah Mee and Molly hugged for a long time. "Ah Mee was always very sweet to Molly, and they were very loving to each other that day," said Mom. "They shed some tears remembering Walt, but most of their conversation was warm and easy and filled with smiles."

Over the following years, whenever any trip took Mom and Molly to the East coast to visit Dad in Virginia or me in New York, or to Mom's family reunion in North Carolina, Mom made a point to fly in and out of Washington, D.C. so they could visit Ah Mee.

Throughout that first extended vacation, Mom recalled moments of celebration, but there were also waves of grieving. On their last night at our house, we were all sitting around the table, having just finished a feast of grilled vegetables from my garden, and tabouli, which Molly had helped me to make, tearing the parsley into tiny pieces with great concentration. In the flicker of the candles on the table, we noticed Molly had begun to weep. I was surprised because we had all just been laughing over something funny Harold and Brian were talking about.

"Hey, Smith, what's wrong? Why are you crying," I said reaching across the table to her.

"This song, this Bruce Cockburn song."

The radio was playing softly in the background. I knew there was music but I had not been listening.

> *... Nobody's here beside me*
> *I can talk about it to*
> *All the ways I want you.*

"It reminds me of Walt," she said, rocking forward and back with her hands clenched together in a fist. She sang the words softly, staring into space and weeping. "I just miss him so much. I think he should be here. He should be here with me." Molly broke into sobs.

I had not seen her cry so hard in many years, maybe not since her rape, or after her cat, Grey, had to be put down a week before Molly and Walt were married.

"We wish Walt was here, too, Molly," I said.

"We all miss him very much," Mom added, touching Molly's shoulder.

Molly stopped crying, wiped her eyes with her hands, and looked at us, pleadingly. "But how do you choose a motel... or a restaurant? How do you choose a motel?"

I guessed she was trying to piece together the puzzle of Walt's choice of the hotel they'd stayed in that weekend and why he wasn't with her. But the warped picture in her brain jarred me. It was like being hit in the face with a brick. I was sore with grief for days after.

This event seemed to precipitate some bumpy talks with Brian over the next few weeks. I don't remember what they were about, but I noted in my calendar that they kept me awake at night. I also wrote, *Is he fearful? It's awkward love, cozy love, distant love.*

I called Sara to debrief with her about Molly's visit. Like me, she was thrilled with Molly's continuing improvement and crushed by her stunning gaps.

"I want her to make a full recovery, she's come so far; but I don't know if she really can," said Sara.

"You know, I hate to say it, Sara, but I don't think she'll ever be like she was." I stopped. Sara was quiet. "I'm learning that she's not, and may never be, the same person I knew and loved before the accident." Sara was still quiet. "I mean, I yearn for that sister; I want her back, too. But I also realize more and more that that person may be gone."

"It is like she's a different person with a familiar face," Sara said.

"Yes, that's what I mean. She's at once intimate and a stranger. She's not really the sister we grew up with. She's the same and she's not. She sounds the same when she laughs, but she laughs at weird stuff; it's just odd."

"I just want her to keep getting better, and end up being Molly again."

"Me too," I said. I wanted to tell Sara to get over that, to accept the loss and find ways to embrace a different Molly. But I needed to convince myself first.

I knew Sara and I were both missing parts of the old Molly that had changed or disappeared. But I was trying to shift away from looking for that person, while Sara seemed to be clinging to the hope that more of the "big sister" Molly might return—the close confidante we could talk to about anything, the wise advisor, the charming and thoughtful one.

And the bad stuff from Molly was more glaring than the many good things she was doing. She was still fiery, stubborn, and full of teasing, but it manifested in hard new ways—she'd be snippy, childish, and mean. She was still as moody as she always had been, but now she could switch in a moment from cheerful to cursing and slamming things around. We'd been told this was a part of brain injury.

I knew I wanted to be close to Molly again, but I didn't know how to deal with this version of her yet; how to interact with her and love her like my older sister. I had figured out that acceptance was difficult but vital. I'd also learned from Mom's example that acceptance was possible and unconditional love was the one essential.

A few days after they returned home to Denver, I received a thank you note from Molly. It was the first card, the first written anything from her since her brain injury. I stared at the shaky but familiar handwriting as if it were a favorite old photograph I'd not seen in a long time.

The next day Molly called me. Another surprise. I thanked her for calling and for sending the card, and I told her again and again how glad I was to hear from her, how happy I was she'd come to visit, how much she meant to me. We were on the phone for maybe 15 minutes. I felt like someone had finally opened the drapes on a sunny day.

Once Molly was living at Mom's, the one person she would regularly speak with on the telephone was her step-daughter. Kristen would call every week or so and talk like there was no tomorrow—to Molly and to Mom. They agreed that Kristen sounded lonely and needy, so they did their best to be there for her and talk with her about school or family. Molly enjoyed it.

Then the calls stopped coming. "We tried to call her for weeks, but it was hard to get through," Mom said. "Mostly the phone would just ring, no answering machine. We might have gotten through once or twice, but Kristen barely said two words."

Mom and Molly's theory was that Kristen's mom wouldn't let her call anymore. Calls from Hawaii would have been expensive, and no one had Internet or email at home yet. They figured out that most of the calls they'd had from Kristen before were probably made when she got home from school, when her mother may have been at work or out.

One time, before I'd learned what was happening, I asked Molly what she'd heard from Kristen lately and how she was. Molly got defensive. "She doesn't call anymore. Not anymore. She's acting like a brat. Her mother hates me and hates Walt and won't let Kristen call me. I don't care. She doesn't like me anyway."

"Maybe Kristen's mom doesn't like you, Smith, but I'm sure Kristen still likes you."

"Well, whatever," Molly said, glumly.

Mom and Molly continued to send Christmas gifts and birthday cards to Kristen for several years, but there was never a word in return. Ah Mee told Mom that when she spoke with Kristen she'd encourage her to communicate with Molly. But even with her grandmother's wishes, Kristen did not respond.

Fortunately, other connections to Walt came along that were joyful. Jacob Walter Humber was born on October 5, 1995.

Mary K. and Stephen had known that a boy was on the way after an ultrasound tech had let it slip, and said they knew they wanted to name him Jacob.

"We also knew immediately that we wanted Walter to be his middle name, to honor Walt's memory," Stephen said. "It was perfectly clear to us, it was what we both wanted."

A few weeks before the baby's birth, they decided to ask Molly about naming their baby after Walt. "Molly said, very sweetly, 'That would be nice, really nice.'" Mary K. said. "It didn't seem that big to her, it was bigger for us, it was our opportunity."

"Mary K. asked me if Molly and I would like to be present for the birth," Mom recalled, "and we told her, 'Yes!' Then, a few days later, she called in the wee hours of the morning and said they were on the way to the hospital. So I woke Molly up and we left right away."

"I just remember being in the delivery room with Mary K. and the doctors and nurses, and Molly and Sally were suddenly there," said Stephen. "They reacted to every little thing, very quietly, identifying with Mary K. on every contraction and every breath."

"We were calm, but very interested," said Mom. "Stephen was comforting Mary K., and we were sort of behind the doctors. It was the first time either of us had witnessed a birth—well, at least someone *else* giving birth. Molly was happy and quiet. We were observers."

"When Jacob was finally born," Stephen said, "I saw Molly and Sally across the room, holding each other and crying—laughter mixed with sadness, but in near silence. The medical staff was busy, but it was still so quiet in the room. And Molly and Sally were there, brimming over, tears streaming down their faces but trying to contain themselves."

Stephen said it was "life moment" for him and he was so glad for them to be there. "It was exactly right. It felt very appropriate."

The day Jacob was born, I was home working. Mom called that night and gave me the good news. A few days later, I spoke with Mary K. at home. Her voice was smooth and lilting and I could hear Jacob Walter cooing in her arms.

"And here's something really neat and affirming," said Mary K. "Jacob was born on 10/05/95 at 2:05 a.m. Walt died on 2/05/95."

"Oh, wow. That *is* neat," I said.

"It's really great," Mary K. said. "And we feel the linking of those numbers as part of the commemoration of Walt."

"It's wonderful, Mary K. You've made all the right choices."

A few days later, I finally got Molly on the phone. I was keen for her to tell me about Jacob's birth, but she was blasé about it and quickly handed the phone to Mom. Mom explained out of earshot, that one obstacle for Molly is when something is particularly emotional—happy or sad, or in this case, both. "She sort of shuts down," Mom explained.

"I understand," I said. "I've noticed that deep stuff is hard for her to cope with."

"I took some photos at the hospital," Mom said. "We dressed in a hurry to get there, but you'll see in the photos, Molly is wearing one of Walt's flannel shirts. When she held little Jacob Walter in her arms, I cried all over again looking at them, both snuggled in Walt's cozy shirt."

That same night, I had a good, but difficult talk with Brian. I don't remember why, but we had some tension about my going to New York City the next day for a week to work with the TV production I'd been with the day Brian got the call about Molly and Walt. Later, I had a bad dream and woke up panting. In the morning, I had car trouble on the way to the train station, missed my train, caught the next one, and was late for my job. I couldn't call the crew until I arrived at Grand Central Station and got to a pay phone. I missed Brian terribly the whole time. Hard times were harder without him.

"Hey, it's great you're back. How's Molly doing? Is she fully recovered? Is she back to normal?"

It felt as if my chest would cave in every time business acquaintances or friends in the city would ask. It wasn't easy to explain and mostly, I didn't. I'd simplify and say, "No, she's not recovered, but she's alive and she's improving."

To myself I'd say: "She's not her former self; not a stranger, but not always familiar, either. And there won't be any back to normal, for Molly or me, for a long time.

In mid-October, more than eight months since the accident, Mom and Molly made a trip to visit Dr. Lo in California. Mom had commissioned Harold to do a painting of him as a gift.

"Our trip was only for a couple of days, but Harold didn't want to go, which I thought was strange. I'd really wanted him to come with us. His painting was excellent," said Mom.

Dr. Lo is in the center of the canvas, facing the viewer and smiling confidently. He's just outside an open doorway, holding a folder with the name "Weber" on it. Inside the room, a technician looks at a patient inside an HBO chamber. Through the room's large window, sunlight pours in and the view is downtown Loma Linda and the snow-covered mountains beyond.

A photo of Molly and Mom presenting the painting to Dr. Lo and an article about him and his remarkable HBO patient ran as a feature in the Loma Linda University Medical Center's bi-annual magazine. The article is titled, "Molly's journey back to life." Never once does it use the word, "normal."

Those weeks of summer and autumn of 1995 were Molly's honeymoon period. None of us knew that. Our adjustments were already difficult—and complicated by the fact we didn't know what might be next for her. Fortunately, before the accident, our family was very tight-knit. Even through problems over the years, our bonds remained strong. Then, to help Molly, we came together like never before and our usual closeness was enhanced. But the dynamics of our relationships were strained, too. Just as the neurologists had said about brain injury—the good stuff was great, and the bad stuff was terrible.

But I was clinging to my optimism and anticipated continued progress for Molly. I wasn't yet generating the deeper connection with her that I wanted, despite all my faxes and phone calls. At least, she took some initiative with an occasional card or conversation. But I really wasn't thinking about what a long-term picture of life with Molly and her brain injury would be like.

In early November, Mom sold the brownstone building that had been Harold's studio. It was a relief for Mom. She could pay off her bills. She said Harold understood but wasn't too happy about it, or with her, either. Mom thought maybe Harold felt she was giving more attention to Molly and her needs than to him. She admitted this was probably true, even though the three of them did a lot of things together. But caring for Molly and selling the studio were simply things she had to do.

"I told Harold that once Molly was more stable and independent, I wanted very much to turn my attention to him and to us, and work on improving our communication and our intimacy," recalled Mom. "But Molly was my immediate concern and focus. She had to be."

Also, that November, Amy came to visit Molly in Denver for a weekend. It was the first time they'd seen each other since Amy's wedding. Mom said the house was filled with laughter as they chatted, teased, and played with Mom's cats.

It turned out to be the last time the two friends would spend time together. "Over time, Amy might have withdrawn a little; she and Steve had children, she has a career," Mom said. "But Molly was not a good pal to her. She didn't reach out—even to Amy. She just doesn't nurture her friendships."

"No, she really doesn't," I said, feeling sad.

"But Molly remembers her own wedding anniversary and Amy's the day after, every year without fail," said Mom. "She also remembers Amy's birthday, and she has photos of her and Amy together everywhere."

Later that month, Molly and Mom flew to New Haven to attend the Yale-Harvard football game. The weekend of events functions as a de facto homecoming for many students. Back in February, Mom had written a short notice about Molly's accident for the class updates section in the Yale alumni magazine. Many Yale students sent cards and encouraged Molly to come back to Yale to visit. Mom organized with Molly's Yale roommates and several other close friends to meet at a tailgate party before the game.

"She had great success remembering names and people and places at Yale, even all the fight songs during the game," said Mom. "Her friends were amazed to see her looking great and doing so well."

A highlight for Molly was visiting with her long time friend, Susie. Molly and Susie attended the same high school and were on swim teams together. One year after Molly went to Yale, Susie followed. They swam together on Yale's team and were both Yale cheerleaders. In a photo Mom took that weekend, Molly is wearing her cheerleader sweater with the big blue "Y," and she and Susie have their arms around each other as Susie's young daughter stands between them looking up at them and smiling.

Brian and I drove to New Haven on Sunday and spent the afternoon with Mom and Molly and had a pizza dinner with them. Happy and comfortable at Yale with her friends, Molly was glowing in her moment.

Soon, Molly's progress and growing confidence were manifesting in her determination for more independence, just as they had at Loma Linda. And like that time, a result was often an angry outburst hurled at the family caregiver closest to her.

By early 1996, Molly was part of a singles social group that met occasionally. Mom would drive her to the meeting location and pick her up. One Saturday, the group went skiing, which Molly could still do quite well, although she now always wore a helmet on the slopes. Mom had dropped Molly off in the morning at a large parking lot in front of a hotel where her group boarded a charter bus.

When Molly called later from the ski area and said they'd be back in about an hour, Mom said she'd be there and told her to wait where she'd dropped her off that morning. Mom arrived, went to the same spot in the parking lot and waited and waited. As it got dark, Mom decided to drive up to the hotel building, just as Molly came walking across the parking lot in back.

"She had been waiting in an entirely different area, where she couldn't see me," Mom said. "She was embarrassed that she can't drive, and because others in the group waited with her while she waited for me. She was trying to fit in, I think. But she didn't know where I was and I doubt she remembered where she'd been dropped off that morning."

Mom was still learning then, herself. "We didn't have cell phones back then," she said. "But now I'd know to look around for her rather than waiting in the place we were supposed to meet. Now I know she forgets and gets lost easily. Now I'd call her cell phone, or she'd call me."

But on that night, Molly got into Mom's car and started screaming about having to wait and that everyone was wondering what was wrong with her and why her Mom wasn't there to give her a ride home. Mom took a wrong turn in the parking lot and had to do a U-turn to get out and Molly screamed at Mom about that, too.

"I couldn't drive to suit Molly at all no matter what I was doing. She was completely stuck in her super frustrated, anger mode—she was just furious," Mom told me. "'Fuck you! Fuck! Fuck! Fuck! Fucking stupid! Fuck you!' She was flailing her arms around. I was gripping the steering wheel just trying to drive home."

At one point, as Molly kept at it, Mom pulled over and slapped Molly with the back of her hand.

"It was the only time I ever hit her. Then she started slapping at me. It was crazy," Mom said, quietly. "Finally, I told her she'd be walking home if she didn't stop. I told her to shut up and not say another word. She stormed upstairs once we got home. We went on the next day as if nothing had happened."

But Mom was derailed. She called Dr. Schraa. "I said, 'I don't know if I can go on.' I told him how I wished I hadn't hit her. He said sometimes it's the only way to get through. He was very encouraging and tried to help me understand it wasn't me—it was an attack on me, but it wasn't intended to be that. It was Molly's frustration. I told him I didn't believe him, I wasn't buying it."

Mom was seriously considering finding another arrangement for Molly, feeling that she couldn't continue to be responsible for her. The situation felt beyond her capabilities; she was almost overcome by Molly's anger and hostility.

Mom took a deep breath and continued. "Eventually, I said to Dr. Schraa, 'If I'm going to carry on, I need someone to talk to.' And he said, 'Then talk to me.'

"I spoke with him on the phone and at his office several times, too. He was very helpful. He told me about how the brain's frontal lobes regulate impulse control, judgment, and emotion, and he gave me a book about frontal lobe injuries and how they result in a lack of awareness. I certainly identified with the difficulties it described," Mom said. "Dr. Schraa said he was specifically working on Molly's self-awareness and anger issues."

Mom wondered if she should join a support group, she felt at her wit's end, but Dr. Schraa warned her not to. He said that Molly was 100 times better than most people with brain injuries. He felt a group's members would not be helpful to her. "You need to be receiving—not giving—to others in a support group," he told Mom.

When Mom told me about the slapping fight in the car, her voice still cracking weeks after it happened, I felt like I'd been slammed in the stomach with a shovel. My insides turned over, learning what Mom was dealing with. A putrid but not unfamiliar gust blew over me—was I right to have wished so much for Molly to live? It's not easier on Mom. Is it ruining her life? Is it even fair? I'm not there, Mom is.

I felt horrible for my mother. I felt wretched about my doubts. I doubled over in my chair with guilt.

Mom had admitted that Molly could be testy and unpredictable at times, but this was far beyond what I'd imagined, or what Mom had let on. I felt selfish and naïve for not having been more aware. Right from the start, just like at Loma Linda, Mom was protective of her other daughters' lives. She didn't want our worlds to be any more impacted by Molly's brain injury and her needs than they already were.

"We haven't had any more slapping fights, thank goodness," Mom said, at the end of our call. "Really, I'm managing OK."

Molly's outbursts continued to occur from time to time, but they were never physical again, and Mom eventually stopped calling Dr. Schraa as Molly stabilized.

In fact, a sure sign of Molly's cognitive gains was her yearning for greater autonomy. Dr. Cilo agreed in December that Molly could be taught to drive again by the therapists at Craig. He prescribed a new series of HBO treatments, which he felt would help her get through the process and sharpen her skills. In mid-January, Molly passed her driving test. On February 5, exactly one year to the day of her accident, Molly got a car—a Honda SUV—and she was driving again.

I spoke with Mom the very next day. She said she was still nervous about Molly's driving, but they'd both get used to it. We reminisced about "one year ago..." and I realized how reintegrated into my life I'd become. The "anniversary" date had sneaked up on me. I wasn't focused on Molly day in and day out anymore. I was focused on Brian and my life. I had a lot of writing work. We were plugging away on our renovation, visiting friends, going to hear music, seeing movies, and making meals together. I was moving on. I had more notes in my calendar about upcoming Valentine's Day and gifts for Brian than about Molly's injury "anniversary."

It bothered me, and I told Mom that I felt very selfish. She said she wanted her daughters to lead their own lives. She said she was managing and doing fine. I chose to believe her.

Through the spring, Molly's therapy schedule at Craig was reduced and she began working with an independent occupational therapist that Craig had recommended. Lis became a key contact for Molly with the rest of the world, carefully coordinating activities and ideas with Mom. This took some pressure off Mom as both mother and therapist. Now she could focus more on being Molly's mother and friend. Our family had been advised about this more than a year earlier at Loma Linda: Family is support and love, and should not be the therapists and trainers. Let the professionals do this.

Once Lis came on the scene, we tried to address and correct Molly's problems through her and the other therapists and doctors. We'd report our observations of Molly's behavior, explaining any changes that had occurred, and collectively figure out how to make adjustments for improvement. Lis quickly became a vital partner to Mom in helping Molly live the best quality of life possible. Still, the reality is that Mom often has to deal with Molly in the moment as her "therapist," because she is her caregiver.

That summer, Lis began working with Molly on a variety of "community re-entry skills." In addition to helping her learn to navigate the streets of Denver and drive safely, Lis made inroads toward Molly possibly having a job again by suggesting she do some volunteer work. They began exploring places Molly might enjoy helping out. Lis also tried to coach Molly on her social skills—for volunteering and also because Molly wanted to start dating.

With more time away from Craig and therapies, and with her driving and feeling more independent, Molly's new interest in men made her seem for all the world like an awkward, ardent teenager. Also, I think when she looked around, women like her had a man in their lives. She wanted that piece of normalcy, too, to feel all together, acceptable, even desirable. It didn't take long. Once Lis helped Molly learn where the singles' groups hung out and how to drive there, she was dating once or twice a week. Through the summer, Molly became more convinced—and more vocal—about being ready to move out of Mom's upstairs bedroom and into a place of her own.

"The doctors at Craig said she'd never live alone," Mom recalled. "When the time came, I made the decision to give it a go. No decision is final, is the attitude I took. Molly needs a challenge; she always does her best when she has one."

In mid-August, Molly was so excited about getting her own place, she actually called me. It knocked me off my feet to pick up the phone and hear her voice. It was only about the third time she'd called me in the year and a half since her accident.

"I'm going to move out of Mom's house, Smith, and move in to my own place! Real soon. Really, really soon," exclaimed Molly. "And then I'll have a house and a boyfriend, too."

"Molly, that's fantastic. Mom told me you'd be moving to your own place once you guys found a good house," I said. "And what's this about a boyfriend? Tell all, Smith. Do you have a special guy in your life?"

"Well, I don't know. We'll see. Maybe," Molly said. "There's Gary and maybe Steve. I don't know. Maybe. Hell, maybe nobody!"

"It's great you've got some new friends, Smith. I just want to be sure that all these guys are really nice to my big sister," I said.

"It's OK, Lyrysa. I'm still your big sister, but these guys are nice, too. They're OK," she said, pausing. "And I'm OK, you know?"

"Yes, you are OK, Molly. Absolutely A-OK," I chimed back.

By the end of August, Mom had found a house less than two miles away, similar to her own house, but smaller.

"I knew I needed to find a place that I'd be comfortable with her living in. Something safe and nearby. Things like an attached garage. Drive in, put the door down, and walk into the house unobserved. And if it doesn't work out, I'll sell the house, bring her back home, and make another choice," Mom said. I smiled to myself, hearing her philosophy again.

I emphasized to Mom that I thought Molly living on her own nearby would not only help her to be better, but would also give Mom some relief and the opportunity to focus on Harold and their relationship. She'd said it was something she wanted to do when she had more time for herself. I knew it had been a trying episode; a happy marriage was something I wanted Mom to have. I figured they would work it out.

"When I told Dr. Schraa and Dr. Cilo that Molly would live with me after leaving Craig, I think they were seriously worried about me," recalled Mom. "But I've been pleasantly surprised how easy it's been to have her here. Molly has been compliant, for the most part. Really, her rebellions have been minor."

Mom admitted that in the beginning she didn't know enough about taking care of a severely brain-injured person to be concerned. "It took diving in. And I learned fast how hard it could be and sometimes it felt like going down a hellhole around here. But it's brain injury, not Molly. This is brain injury," Mom said, repeating our chorus for coping with Molly.

However, Mom was not comprehending the impact of her own piece of the family brain injury. The doctors were not just worried about Mom when Molly came to live with her, but about Mom's relationships with others. They knew that caring for Molly would be consuming and sometimes overwhelming, and that her well-being was not the only thing Mom needed to be concerned about. The hellhole was wider than Mom knew, and would take down more than she could rescue.

Harold helped Mom move Molly into her new house. He also had planned on his own what was next for him. At the end of the day, just after they'd unloaded the last boxes, he told Mom he was leaving, too.

I was stunned to hear this news—and with Mom's calmness when she told me.

"I was terribly shocked in that moment," Mom confessed. "But I said, 'OK, Harold,' very calmly. He said he had his stuff together and was moving into his rented art studio temporarily."

"Wow, Mom, I'm so surprised—and sad. I mean, it's just ironic. I thought he wanted more of your attention. Didn't he realize you would be more free from Molly now and could focus more on him?" I asked.

"I think he knew that precisely, and he didn't want that—at least, not now," Mom said. "With Molly out of the house, he knew I wanted to turn to our relationship and work on us."

She said she thought he'd had at least one girlfriend during their marriage—another surprise to me—and those relationships must have seemed more attractive and easier to him. "I'm not the jealous type who'll chase a man around. I'd rather just get out of it," she said.

I didn't get this call from Mom until a week later. Molly's moving day also happened to have been her birthday, September 4th. Earlier that day, I'd called and sang "Happy Birthday" to Molly on Mom's answering machine, and I'd sent a card and faxed her a birthday greeting, too. I had no idea what else had happened.

It turns out that Mom had made a reservation for Molly's birthday at a nice restaurant. "I asked Harold after he'd loaded his boxes into his van if he was coming to our birthday dinner that night," Mom said. "And he said he didn't feel he should be there. I said, 'I'm not angry, you might as well join us.' So he came and the three of us actually had a wonderful time."

At this point, relating this to me, Mom was composed, but I was shaken. I felt this weird mix of relief and concern for her. Mom concluded saying that Molly was adjusting well to living on her own, with a lot of help from her, and that she was adjusting to living alone again, too.

Harold and Mom's divorce was handled simply without contention within a few months. Mom told me after it was done that she didn't want to move her clothes and shoes to one side again; she didn't want to share her closet anytime soon.

However, whether under the same roof or not, Mom found that life with Molly continued to be consuming, demanding both her attention and energy. Molly in her own home was easier on Mom in some respects but more difficult in others. Mom enjoyed having a few more minutes to herself, to savor her morning coffee and listen to NPR. But it was harder to get Molly to appointments on time and to keep track of where she was and if she was safe. In fact, being Molly's caregiver was tough in ways Mom wouldn't think of until they were on top of her, or swallowing her whole.

Nonetheless, each of us was starting to take more definitive steps in our lives. In the spring, Sara passed the oral exams for her PhD and only needed to complete her dissertation to earn her doctorate in Spanish. She began thinking about getting a teaching position at a college or university. I had no doubt she'd succeed. Her Spanish language skills are so much a part of her that she sometimes forgets the English word she wants to say but has the Spanish word on her tongue instead.

Looking at Sara's accomplishments at that time had a huge impact on me. I decided that I would write Molly's story. I began to take notes on everything I could remember of the past year and a half and also did my first interviews with Dr. Lo and Dr. Cilo. It was sketchy, fragments here and there, but it felt good to take action on what I knew in my gut was the right thing.

In the autumn of 1996, Mary K. and Stephen sold their home in suburban Castle Rock and moved to downtown Denver. Stephen had resigned from his position as Lieutenant Commander with the Navy and enrolled in divinity school. Stephen called it a "sobering" decision to leave the Navy halfway to a 20-year retirement. His decision to become a pastor meant a change of lifestyle and life plan for him and Mary K., and Abi and Jacob, too. However, Stephen and Mary K.'s religious beliefs had become their primary focus and Stephen felt called to his decision.

Mary K. supported his choice, but it wasn't easy for her. She often confided in Mom, who had challenging experiences as a minister's wife. Stephen had a goal, though, that he and Mary K. would have a specialty together— to minister to young married couples, a group Mary K. felt particularly effective with. Despite their concerns and deliberations, together they had faith. And it had proven for them many times to be a powerful bond.

They moved into the student housing at the Denver Seminary, which was filled with other seminary students and their families from around the world. When I visited a couple of years later and heard their neighbors chatting while their children frolicked, a dozen languages were being spoken at once. Happily, Mary K. got to use her excellent Spanish, which she'd studied while living and traveling in South America right after college, as well as the Japanese she'd learned when she and Stephen were stationed in Japan before Abi was born. I even got the opportunity to try a bit of Shona, which I'd learned while living and working in Zimbabwe four years before Molly's accident. That experience felt like another world, far, far away.

I sensed changes taking place between me and Brian during that autumn. They were hard to discern, like a gnawing sound in the background. There would be tension between us whenever we were apart, working in New York City, or any job away from home. Once we were together again, we'd bounce back and carry on with a lot of affection, sexiness, and joy. But I was bothered by what I felt was an erosion of the ease between us.

In late September, Brian was working his carpentry jobs and also frequently assisting a professional photographer. He traveled to day and night photo shoots. He didn't talk about his work much when he got home. He'd say he was tired and he'd be out the door early the next morning to his next carpentry or photo job. I wanted to be helpful to him but I didn't feel he wanted me involved.

In the fall of that year, 1996, I discovered that Brian had had an affair while working on a photo shoot on a cruise ship. He sort of admitted it. Maybe there were others. He was not forthcoming. I was gut-driven. I found photos on his contact pages, notes from strangers, condom wrappers at the bottom of the trash. I strained to pull information out of him, strand by strand. It was like pulling weeds and not getting the whole plant on the first yank. A lousy conversation, an odd behavior, a look in his eyes—my instincts were screaming. Then, he'd silence my concerns with a bouquet of what I wanted to hear, what I wanted to feel.

But I was distracted again and found it difficult to write and work. My self-esteem was trashed and I was moody, imagining the other women. Finally, he said he wanted to love me and be with only me. We decided to work on reconnecting and he agreed to help me trust him again. I stretched to a place of distortion to put what I wanted to believe together with my reality. I didn't know how long I could endure the posture.

I told my family what Brian and I were going through, but not my friends. We began couple's counseling with a therapist. Around friends, we hid our problems well. I often felt like such a fake, pretending that we were OK. But I wanted to remember what it felt like when things were good. I leaned on my family members. It was one gift from Molly's accident; we were all very close. Our bonds had been tested, verified, and strengthened. My parents and my sisters were there for me time and again.

Even Molly wanted to talk to me on the phone. She even sent a "feel better soon" card and I knew she was doing her best to reach out. It was my first big, personal crisis without the Molly I had known. It was a hole I felt deeply, but my family members filled in. Molly wasn't the confidante I'd relied on for so many years, but she understood that I was hurting.

"Oh, Smith, I'm so sad for you. It'll be OK. You'll be OK. I wish Walt was here to help you," Molly said, startling me. "If he were here, Walt would help you and you wouldn't be crying still."

"You may be right, Smith," I said. "He helped me before. Remember when he insisted that I go skiing with the two of you when Chris dumped me over the phone when I was in Denver?"

"Yeah, Chris was a liar—and a jerk," Molly said. "I remember that day. You were crying and you didn't want to go but Walt made you get dressed and go cross-country skiing while we were doing downhill. He said you had to get outside in the snow and the sun."

"I felt a lot better being out with you guys, even just taking the drive in the car with you to the mountains," I said. "So Walt was right, wasn't he?"

"Smith, Walt was *almost* always right," Molly said, matter-of-factly. Every now and then, Molly would ring up a crystal clear memory. It was astonishing. And beautiful. And a relief. A reality check for me about who Molly was and still is.

Molly was encountering some hard realities of her own, however, as she embarked on her more independent life. Not long after she'd moved in to her new house, she pulled into her garage at the wrong angle and scraped the entire side of her new car. She was also getting lost a lot when driving. She'd eventually find her way back home, but often without ever getting to her original destination. She'd tell Mom out of sheer frustration, and Mom would do her best to explain what the best route might have been and where she probably made a wrong turn. Sometimes Molly's pride would take over and she'd get angry and wouldn't listen, other times she'd be yielding and want to learn. We were learning that Molly's road to autonomy would not be traveled alone.

Molly had qualified for social security disability benefits that summer, following testing, evaluations, and recommendations from Dr. Cilo and Dr. Schraa. In their report, they described that Molly's cognitive deficits, frontal lobe dysfunction, and diminished capacity for her brain to regulate her behavior and emotional expression were significant enough to have altered her personality and also had a major impact on her ability to function independently.

So even though Molly was living in her own home, she was fairly dependent on Mom for her life's structure—certainly in the management of her finances, but also some of her daily activities and interpersonal issues that she wasn't able to cope with on her own. Mom would check in on Molly each day and ask about her schedule and help her to plan. And Molly would usually turn to Mom for help when problems arose—if she needed directions to drive somewhere, wanted to make a dentist appointment, or how to tell a guy she didn't want to date him anymore. Molly felt comfortable with Mom's assistance. Mom created a certain freedom *and* a safety net that Molly liked and were essential to her building her autonomy.

Lis, her OT, still wanted to help Molly get out and into the community, so she arranged a volunteer position at a non-profit organization's gift shop. But Molly struggled with the math required to make change for purchases, and claimed the job was boring. Lis's next idea worked out much better; Molly enjoyed volunteering for several months at the Dumb Friend's League, one of Denver's oldest animal shelters. Her lifelong love of animals shown brightly, whether she was playing with the kittens or cleaning cat boxes, especially with these animals that needed so much attention. Eventually, Molly adopted two of the cats to live with her.

Meanwhile, Brian and I, reconciled and better, went on a road trip with Dad and Martha to camp in the Everglades over the Christmas and New Year's holidays. We visited Brian's sister and parents in Florida and spent hours in the car talking with Dad and Martha.

In February 1997, Mom decided she and Molly would go on the annual vacation to her timeshare in Puerto Vallarta, Mexico. Since she and Harold had divorced by this time, she invited Jo, her dear friend of more than 25 years, to go along. Jo lived in our old neighborhood when we were kids, had children our ages, and helped watch us when Mom was at work.

For what we called our "reuniting vacation," Brian and I flew to Mexico City, traveled through central Mexico for two weeks, and met up with Mom, Jo, and Molly in Puerto Vallarta for a few days of relaxation. However, an episode of "reality of life with Molly" crashed our party.

Molly had gone to Puerto Vallarta for the first time the year before and hung pretty close to Mom and Harold at the resort hotel. A year later, with her quest for greater independence underway, Molly was anxious to do more with me and Brian. We went on an all-day horseback trek in the mountains and villages surrounding the town. We also went on a whale-watching boat ride that Mom and Jo came on, too. On the way back from the whales, our tour boat made a short stop on a small island so passengers could enjoy a swim or take a walk on the beach. When it was time to head back to Puerto Vallarta, Molly stepped by mistake onto another small tour boat that was boarding at the dock. Mom and Jo thought Molly was with me and Brian; we thought she was in our group and would follow us. We had no idea she'd gotten on the wrong boat until our boat was underway and Mom looked at me and said, "Where's Molly?"

My eyes darted around and then I looked back toward the island and saw her standing on the deck of the other boat that was just departing. It was a dreadful feeling. We tried yelling to her, but we were too far away and the engine noise was too loud. My blood curdled with guilt. Molly had stayed so close to me in our other excursions that week. But I remembered that after a nice walk on the island's beach, the three of us looking in the tide pools for little crabs, I was focused on Brian as he and I walked to the dock, our arms wrapped around each other. I was feeling happy about us, and I was trying to be romantic. I was not paying attention to Molly. Maybe she felt left out and wandered away from me in retaliation.

There are no words for how wretched I felt when I saw the look on Mom's face. We knew that Molly would play it cool with the crew and the passengers on the other boat, not letting on that she had a brain injury, had gotten separated from her family, and had no idea where she was, where to get off, or where she needed to go.

Although we asked our boat's crew, there wasn't a way to reach the other boat until ours docked about 20 minutes later. It was the longest boat ride of my life. With the help of the boat company workers, hotel staff, and their landline telephones, within a panicked half-hour we'd tracked down the place where the other boat docked and Molly had likely disembarked. It was several miles away, north of town, where she'd never been before. We called the police and gave them a description. It was getting dark. Molly was alone with no Spanish language skills and she was lost. It would have been difficult for any tourist.

Mom jumped into a taxi to search the road that led to the other docking site. Brian walked around the hotel then on the road north. Jo went to their room in case Molly showed up there, and I stayed put in the hotel lobby, looking, waiting for a call from the police, and agonizing. Mom returned about 20 minutes later in the taxi with Molly. Mom had found her walking south, the right direction, along a deserted section of the road.

It was a mind-boggling and frustrating experience for Molly, and a terrifying time for Mom and us. I apologized to Molly and to Mom. Mom gently instructed Molly to stick close to her family, and we quickly set aside the incident. Brian and I had to catch a public bus the next day to travel east towards Mexico City. Mom, Jo, and Molly had another five days in Puerto Vallarta, which they spent reading, strolling, and relaxing around the resort.

What lingered were the lessons we all learned, loud and clear, from a distressing wake-up call. We needed to literally hold Molly by the hand sometimes. It was a sharp reminder that she was not as independent or as able as we imagined, she pretended, or she wished to be.

Molly was never one to shrink away after a setback, however, and was usually at her best when she had a challenge at hand. In April, she began classes at the Bel-Rea Institute, a veterinary technician school. Lis introduced Molly to the staff at Bel-Rea and got her schedule arranged. The idea to become a vet tech came from a man Molly had a few dates with who noticed the school almost directly across the street from her house.

Dr. Schraa at Craig, who Molly still saw a few times a month, was delighted with the plan. He emphasized that people with brain injuries, especially, need learning opportunities to make new connections in their brains so they can function even better.

"Vet tech school is a terrific way to get her brain constructing new pathways," Dr. Schraa told Mom. "Whether she's involved in a hospital rehab program or not, years of rehab are ahead of her. Learning and relearning are vitally important."

Mom told me after Molly's classes began about another positive aspect. "It's given Molly a purpose. She has meaningful work to do to help animals, which she's done her whole life," said Mom. "She has a schedule, she has to study, take tests. A regimen is really good for her. She has to focus and plan and think ahead."

None of this was easy for Molly to do. While she was happy going to school, it revealed her sizable cognitive deficits. Mom and Lis soon discovered that Molly had a very different capacity for learning and managing the work than other students. She went to class and read the books, but she failed assignments and tests and she had to repeat courses. Her instructors at Bel-Rea weren't sure she could learn the material.

So Mom found a tutor at the school and she also coached Molly and it helped; she began to pass her courses. Then the tutor from Bel-Rea found that Molly did better if the tutor read a test's multiple choice answers to her, otherwise, on her own, she'd choose the first answer she read rather than evaluating all the choices, one by one.

Later, with Lis' assistance in negotiations with the school, Molly was given permission to take tests in a separate room because she found the stress of a whole classroom of students taking a test around her very distracting.

The two-year vet tech program would eventually take Molly four years to complete. It was an ongoing and valuable experiment in how Molly learned. The teachers came to understand her challenges. Her effort was worthy of respect and everyone really tried to help her along.

In the autumn of 1997, about a year into our "reuniting," Brian came home one typical afternoon and made the most extraordinary declaration. After his usual, joyful bear hug greeting, he sat me down in a chair and sat across from me. Then he looked me right in the eyes and said, "I've decided that in order to be *truly* happy in my life, I have to live non-monogamously. And if you're OK with that, we can continue to be together in our house."

Everything went silent. My eyes blurred. I'd been blindsided. I went into a tailspin.

"What? What are you talking about?"

He said his lines again, perfectly, as if he'd been practicing his script for days.

My brain was reeling. Whatever I thought I knew exploded. Right then, and for weeks after, I tried to get Brian to explain himself. He'd repeat his declaration firmly, holding it up like a shield. Sometimes he'd add, "I've given this a lot of thought." He asked me to consider it.

I'd thought with all my heart that after our drive to the Everglades with Dad and Martha, our "reunited" trip to Mexico, the counseling, the dozens of discussions—things weren't perfect, but we were back on track. I was trusting him again. He seemed very devoted.

Now, I felt more than angst, I was scared. How could I have been so off? So out of it? So warped in my head?

I wrote in my journal, sobbed when Brian wasn't home, screamed in my car driving alone. And I was still trying to reason with him, thinking if I could understand what he needed, I could work on it. He must have hated that. I'd worked through his infidelity. Now he'd found something I couldn't fix and couldn't do. What he wanted was out. And still, I didn't let go.

I remember raking leaves with him in early December, on a beautiful sunny afternoon. He was chatting casually about some ordinary thing and I came undone. I went berserk. "What are you talking about? You're acting like everything is la-di-da. Like it's all OK with us. Nothing is OK with us. Nothing!" I threw my rake like a spear across the yard and stormed away.

I tried to ignore everything else blaring in my head and wonder, genuinely, if I could possibly live with him while he lived "non-monogamously." I studiously considered it. He thought it was possible. I thought it might be a phase. How would it work? Split the house? Share our bed? Different nights of the week? Honestly? I was beside myself with unanswerable questions.

It was a couple of weeks before I told my parents and sisters. Then they called me frequently; they knew I was teetering on the edge.

In one of the life lessons that came from that terrible time, each parent tried to lovingly counsel me. In separate conversations, Mom and Dad each shared their own truth about what happened in their marriage. The truths were not the same. I learned it doesn't matter. The rights and wrongs, who did what first or more, floated somewhere, but I learned that they each had their own truth, and it was OK. Sometimes, there's more than one truth.

Mary K. and Sara were incredibly attentive and helpful to me. Mary K. sent caring notes and cards that I read over and over again. Sara called me several times a week and patiently allowed me to unload on her, always offering gentle, loving encouragement.

I missed conversations with the old Molly more than ever, and the wounds of her injury gaped open all over again, oozing with new loss for me. Molly did return my phone call one day when I'd left her a message saying I needed a big-sister hug by telephone. But she couldn't focus on what was going on with me. She would shrink away and distract herself with something in her immediate world—her mail, a magazine, her cat. This highly sensitive stuff was too much for her. I couldn't blame her. I could barely get my own head around it. For Molly, I believe, it overwhelmed those places in the brain that wrestle with emotionally charged topics. Instead she told me that Janet Reno had called Mom's house to check up on her.

"Mom told her that I'm living nearby and going to vet tech school. Mom says she was impressed and delighted," Molly said, cheerfully.

I shifted fast to get into Molly's path of thought. I was amazed I could do it and also amazed by Janet Reno's attention a full three years after the accident. "Wow. Janet Reno is really great. That is so cool she called," I said.

"That's because I'm so cool, Smith," Molly said.

When I finally told my friends about Brian's declaration, their responses ricocheted around in my head. One of my best friends said to throw all his stuff out into the street and hit him over the head with my biggest frying pan. It took me a long time to get to anger, though.

Another friend I've known since high school found Brian's declaration so incredible, she based a short story for her MFA in fiction around it. She said my true story was truly stranger than fiction. I was a character in my own life that I didn't recognize.

Over sandwiches at a café, a writer and colleague, asked why I shouldn't have a little fun, too, "like the Europeans?" I left our lunch meeting and tried to imagine that maybe I could indulge in *un peu d'amour*, but instead I went home and vomited.

One of the carpenters Brian had worked with, a nice guy with a wife and kids, heard about it and said, "He's crazy! Does he realize he's just created the most eligible bachelorette in the tri-state region?" I didn't feel any of it.

I wished to have Molly and Walt swoop in and rescue me again. To push me, embrace me, and set me gently on my feet. I missed them both terribly.

During the Christmas holidays, my face erupted in cystic acne boils, nearly covering my forehead. My skin was a horror movie of stress. I hid behind huge Band-Aids. My hair was falling out again. I couldn't eat. I looked a fright. I was scraping bottom.

Some part of me was still refusing, still looking for a cure, still believing I was going to work out the dilemma. Brian and I had been together six and a half years, after all.

At my request, Brian agreed to visit our counselor. After explaining our situation, she asked if we were each willing to work on our relationship. I said yes. Brian said no, he wasn't willing. I had no words. She asked if there was any reason the two of us should continue to come see her. He said, "No, I guess not." I cried quietly, and said, "So be it."

Our counselor saw it clearly and she was right to put it out there point blank. I learned about willingness that day. I was wrong to be so slow. He'd been gone, really, for a long time.

When we got home, he asked what my decision was about us. I told him with a certainty that surprised me, that I could not live with him while he lived his chosen way. I realized later that night, lying alone on the futon in the guest bedroom, that he'd managed to get me to deliver the final blow. I was the one who said no.

I had had hope. I'm a problem solver. We'd saved a deserted old house. I'd managed to keep finding good-paying writing work. I'd worked with my family to help my sister—a miracle. What couldn't be repaired, restored, or rejuvenated?

Brian delivered an impasse I couldn't fix. He let me try. For weeks. Then he let me kill it.

We split up stuff. I cried like a banshee. I was in a daze. I made him take our new mattress, which I felt certain he'd "tarnished" when I was away. He didn't object. He'd been planning his departure a long time and knew what to do. I was a bungled mess of emotions and wouldn't realize my poor decisions until years later when I finally got angry. My thinking was wrecked; I stumbled along with my trauma and my piece of the family brain injury.

Brian moved out of town into his new place. I was left in a vacuum, in our half-empty house without "us." My heart pounded like a fist on a door each time I entered a room.

Around the same time, early 1998, Sara was looking for a teaching position to start in the autumn. She had offers from colleges in Michigan, but they weren't nearby and she would have to move out of Walter's house. Sara asked him if it was possible, when his sons were older, that he'd ever be willing to move. He said no. He had no interest in living anywhere else.

His resolve stung Sara. She realized she would never be a priority for him. Walter was an excellent father to his sons. Sara loved that about him, and she adored the two boys. "But I need to take care of my needs and my career and I need more from him than he's willing to offer—ever, I guess," said Sara, on the phone one night.

In March, she accepted a position as Spanish professor at Southern Utah University and Sara and Walter's relationship ended. Walter's anger was awful, Sara told me, and it made their final month under the same roof, in separate rooms, miserable.

The day Sara's classes ended at Michigan State, Dad and Martha arrived, packed her boxes into their van, and they drove to Utah. Sara and Walter had been together about five years.

"I'll always be grateful for his help while we were at Loma Linda," she said. "He held me and my world together a lot. He was amazing. And he was so helpful to us with his research about DNS." She said she'd never planned it would end the way it did. They simply had life choices that were incompatible.

It became apparent to me some years later that parts of my relationship with Brian, and perhaps parts of Sara's with Walter, were driven to the edge by the brain injury ripple effect. I suspect everyone in my family dealt with brain injury-soaked contention in their relationships. Some survived, some did not.

Molly sat at her kitchen table one night with textbooks, pens, and a stack of index cards scattered before her.

I was visiting Denver for a week and sat across from her so I could help her study for a test she had the next day. She needed to know the names and uses for about 40 pieces of vet medical equipment, such as examination tools and surgical instruments. She'd been in vet tech school about a year.

Molly had made photocopies of the illustrations of tools from her book, glued each one to an index card, and written the correct term and use for it on the other side. We worked with her flash cards for a couple of hours and she not only kept her focus on the task, but also became quite proficient at naming the tools and their uses. In our final rounds, she was probably getting 70 percent or more correct. This type of rote learning seemed to suit her and gave her confidence; important strategies for the future, I thought. I had no idea if she'd be able to retrieve what she'd learned during the test the next day, or if she'd even be aware that she was or wasn't remembering. However, I thought that for Molly reassurance was as useful as memorization.

"Smith, I am so impressed!" I said, after we finished our last round. "You've really got these figured out now and, look at me, I still can't even pronounce these names. Lar... rine... nos... scoop thingimigigees..."

I'd found that self-deprecating humor raised Molly's comfort with me and made her laugh, which seem to help her connect and communicate.

"Laryngoscopes," she rattled back. "Thanks, Smith. I need a good grade or I'll flunk and be in trouble again."

"You're not in trouble, Molly, it's just a bit harder for you, but you'll get through this. I know how motivated you are. You've always loved animals."

"Yes, kitties the most," she said, stacking her cards and books. "I don't want to be a dumb brain the rest of my life. And I can say the names better than you, at least."

"Darn right. I'll have to borrow your flash cards one day and practice."

"No, I don't think so, Smith. It's me. I'm going to be the vet tech."

I hugged and kissed her and told her to get to bed because a good night's sleep would help during the test. I had a flight home the next morning but I told her I'd call to find out how it went. She thanked me several times and was very sweet; smiling and sure of herself. A glimpse, like a photograph held up for a moment, of the Molly I had once known.

When I called a couple days later, she was excited to tell me she got an A. I felt great.

Unfortunately, Molly's efforts to volunteer at a veterinarian clinic while going to vet tech school were not working out. She simply didn't have the social skills and etiquette in a service setting to deal with pet owners.

She was often unpleasant and grouchy to the people who worked at the office, too, including the veterinarian in charge. She'd also forget to show up, or simply not bother to tell the clinic staff when she decided she wasn't coming in. Even with coaching from Lis and Mom, and second and third tries, Molly couldn't maintain appropriate behavior and her volunteering at vet clinics had to stop.

For us, this side of Molly's behavior and personality was just becoming evident. We didn't know Molly would act this way—it took a different placement and exposure of her to find out how her deficits were revealed in a new situation. We discovered she wasn't capable in situations where others were coming to her needing understanding and assistance. It seemed to overwhelm her and she became irritable and defensive.

Around the same time, we were also observing that the more independent Molly became the less compliant she was. I theorized to Mom that it might be because she was out in the world now, going to singles' parties, having a few dates, attending classes at school, shopping for groceries—trying to fit in. Although we didn't know exactly how she behaved in these settings, we knew she wasn't constantly grouchy and had to be pleasant enough to continue. But maybe the new interactions made her more aware of how different she was, so she was pushing the boundaries, trying to overcome them, but not realizing she was making things worse sometimes.

For example, she began to interject a pointed "yes" or emphatic "no," when someone else was speaking, whether she knew anything about the topic or not. She also began to interrupt someone by repeating the words they had just said. It seemed, perhaps, that she wanted to own the other person's words herself, to get credit, too, for saying them as if they were her idea. She'd often do this in a group conversation to "join in," to seem with it, to know already what the speaker was saying, and to seem like she was smart and contributing, like everyone else.

I could understand why it happened; she wasn't trying to be obnoxious. She didn't realize her conversation style was rude and made her stand out more, not less, as someone with a problem. I couldn't blame her. It was brain injury. I tried suggesting to her that she just listen and speak when someone else wasn't, but it really pissed her off. It was discouraging and made her difficult to be around.

As a family, we were still learning that a brain injury continues to evolve and manifest in new ways. Unlike any other injury, brain injury is unending; it has no pattern to follow, no moment of completed healing to strive for, and there's no way to anticipate what might come next. I do believe our own pieces of our family brain injury stunted us from comprehending this reality sooner. But we weren't in denial about Molly, even the therapists and doctors didn't know what to expect from her. It took wading in to the stream—a steady flow, a trickle, or a torrent. But to make progress meant getting in, going through it, step by step, being uneasy, getting knocked over, and not knowing if we'd ever reach the other side.

We'd always believed in Molly and didn't doubt her abilities until we were forced to. Now, we know *more* what to expect—what she is *likely* to be able to do or not, but back then, and even today, it is a process of discovery.

Dr. Schraa would explain that Molly's diminished frontal lobe function left her with little insight or judgment, which led to impatience, agitation, and impulsivity—and almost no awareness of her effect on others. Her ability to have an important task to do and focus on it in a busy or changing environment, with other people doing various activities and speaking around her, was nearly nil. Rote learning was more effective for Molly than deduction and reasoning in a shifting situation where she'd also need to react responsibly and with control. And so, without consistent judgment and social skills, Dr. Schraa thought it was unlikely Molly would be capable of holding any type of job again.

This was not what Molly or her family had hoped for. Her dreams and plans were wiped out, her story altered; a blank page. Her ideas, the very stuff we believe makes us individuals, were disrupted, tattered, and many were dumped. Molly was struggling to be in her brain-injured present, while often aware of who she was in the past.

She was going to earn a pilot's license and a law degree or MBA, and become financially independent through her own business. She was going to write books, learn karate, and achieve success, she wrote, with "a simple belief in self, by forever perceiving setbacks as new opportunities," and through "the unbelievable energy" she'd put into everything she does and cares about.

Pieces of that remained—her energy and determination. The rest of the picture had receded and faded away.

Back in New York, I put our almost renovated, beautiful old house on the market, unfinished. Brian had to return to work on it for weeks so it would be more salable. We worked on it in between our paying jobs. We hung the kitchen cabinets, installed wood flooring in the living room, put a door here, molding there. It was excruciating to be around him and surreal working together side-by-side again on a home that would never be. I never set foot in his new place. He was in my space a lot, which had been our space. It was a nightmare.

I went through the rest of that year, 1998, in a deep fog. Pain, confusion, sadness; barely holding it together. I remember telling Sara that despite her heartache at the end of her relationship with Walter, she was fortunate to have moved far away from him and started fresh in a new community at a new job in a whole new place.

It was hellish trying to write well and keep up with deadlines. I was schizoid at times, I'm sure, but I knew maintaining my work was good for me. My attitude about myself was crushed and I buckled in my grief too often. But over time, I managed to push myself to my feet, thanks to having work to do, wonderful friends, and especially, a great family. We were standing together despite the fallout from the pandemonium we'd gone through and the upheaval we were still in.

Mom, at the epicenter with Molly, was contending with becoming a full-time caregiver, a mother raising her eldest child again; halting her own career; and being divorced from Harold. Sara, Mary K., and I were scrambling in new situations in our relationships, too—some positive and of our own choosing, some not what we wanted at all. We all had decisions to make, and make again.

I reconciled myself that I had lived my priorities, which included Brian, Molly, my family, and my career, too. I had been settling in to it all, and perhaps my comfort level ignited Brian's fear of stasis.

Still, with his declaration of non-monogamy, he was no longer in the relationship I'd agreed to. And I thought, also, that because of Molly's brain injury, my expanded priorities, and my part of our collective family brain injury, I was no longer the deal he'd signed up for either.

There's no training for the family of a brain-injured person. We were muddling along in new territory. Years before, Tony Benjamin at Loma Linda had acted for a few short weeks as our family therapist. He was really treating Molly, but he helped us cope with our stress. He told us that because Molly had a brain injury, we all had a brain injury. He knew this was true even when we didn't, and couldn't, understand. There's no prescribed rehab for collective family brain injury. We simply wanted to do our best to help Molly, each other, and ourselves. Figure it out and keep going.

And there was Mom, at the forefront of caring for Molly. She said it was never a question; it was all she knew how to do. So Mom's new full-time job became helping Molly to be as independent as possible, with an excellent quality of life, at home. And Mom said, and still says all these years later, she made the right choices, again and again.

I wondered if in the future, I'd have the strength and bravery to pursue the choices I thought were right. To make my best decisions, like Mom had told me to when I was a teenager. I'd been badly burned. My stamina, self-esteem, and courage had turned and flown away. I wished that, like Mom, I could know my choices were right.

E l e v e n

IN addition to everything else, Mom was wrangling with the personal injury lawsuit that had been filed on Molly's behalf. Meetings with her lawyers and the defendants' lawyers, depositions of her and Molly and many others, including expert witnesses, went on and on for months. Luckily, Mom had been given good advice from the start. The day after Molly arrived at Loma Linda, an FBI agent who knew Walt and who had been to the hotel room where Walt and Molly were found, took Mom aside. "I didn't say this to you in case they ask, but get an attorney, today or tomorrow," he said. "It's a disturbing crime scene and you need someone right away."

Mom quickly secured a legal team. The case was heard in the Sacramento federal court. In addition to Molly, with Mom as her legal guardian, Walt's daughter, Kristen, was also a plaintiff in the case, with her mother as guardian. The defendants included the owners of the hotel, their heating contractor company, their propane company, and the company that manufactured the heaters used in the hotel rooms.

The fact that Walt had died next to Molly in the same bed was a strong element for our case. But a clear depiction of who Molly was, and who she became due to her injury, was also essential. Doctors stated that Molly's change of personality, loss of cognitive abilities, and impaired intellect and memory were more severe and more of burden on her and her family than most physical injuries would be. Molly's former existence was gone. After her rehabilitation, Molly could walk, hug, and read; but she does not accept, interpret, express, react, contemplate, decide, or love like she used to. She does all these things to a degree, but not in the ways she once did. Moreover she can't fully comprehend that, either.

Molly's deposition extended over two days. She was charming and lively; she spoke confidently and answered each question with authority. Molly has always done her very best to minimize her deficits.

"She was often accurate, especially about her more distant history and experiences, but some of her answers weren't correct at all," Mom said. "She would just say what came to mind first, or repeat what she'd heard someone else say, or she'd say what she thought the attorney wanted to hear. To a stranger, she probably seemed OK, but she was confused at times."

Mom had to backtrack and set the record straight on a number of points. Molly did speak knowledgeably about each of her sisters and our lives. She detailed Walt's life before she'd met him, and through their meeting and their marriage. On the second day of her deposition, she told the lawyer that she missed Walt a lot and was thinking of him especially because the following day was his birthday. This was true. She rattled off the names of the last books she'd read and the last film she'd seen. She said she'd thought about becoming a lawyer (true) and now planned to get a PhD and become a veterinarian (not true). She talked about being in vet tech school, but not about her struggle to pass classes. She also said she didn't take the fact that she was alive for granted. Molly was doing what she's done her whole life—her determined best to be strong, accomplished, and victorious.

Using Walt and Molly's more than 10 years of photo albums and vacation videos, as well as greeting cards and love letters to each other, Mom and her lawyers compiled a full and poignant representation of Molly's life pre-brain injury, Molly and Walt's life together, and the two of them with Kristen. They also described, as much as possible, what Molly lost when Walt died and she lost her healthy brain. They calculated lost careers, incomes, and pensions, but most of all, they expressed what Walt and Molly's situation would have been had they been able to live out their lives together.

In the end, our lawyers presented to the judge two accomplished and dynamic individuals with exciting careers. An energetic father and step-mother very much involved with caring for and raising their daughter. A passionate couple who were very much in love.

But the marriage was over, the husband gone, the wife displaced, the daughter removed, the dreams lost. No law degree, no two careers, no dual incomes. No house in Jackson Hole, no pilot's license, no horses. No more traveling together, no more pillow talk. No chosen companion, no best friend, no lover, no soul mate.

It was also important to establish the level of Molly's disability. She was approved for social security disability benefits a year and a half after her brain injury when her doctors determined that she was "totally and permanently disabled." They wrote that due to her cognitive deficits she was unable to regulate her actions or appropriately express her emotions, rendering her unemployable and not able to produce an income. Molly's adverse experience at the vet clinic had shown this analysis to be correct.

At the time, this judgment felt to me like marching into a wall. So defeating. Smashing another part of the Molly I knew—the Molly with an impressive career. How would Molly cope with it? It turned out she didn't mind; the identity loss was more my problem than Molly's.

Mom seemed relieved at the assessment. "If we're successful with this case, Molly doesn't ever have to worry about working," said Mom. "She could see her doctors and therapists, go to classes, do volunteer work she likes, play with her cats, exercise, read, go to the theater with me. I'd love for her to just enjoy a full, happy life."

The case's depositions were lengthy and often contentious, explanations of the evidence were very detailed and not easy to hear. It was exhausting and troubling for Mom to sit through.

"I expected the pressure and the excruciating process of poring over sometimes painful details," she said. "I knew it would be hard. But this is really tough."

"I can come and do some of this, give you a break, or just come be with you," I said.

"Thanks, darlin', but I'm OK. You have important things to do there in New York. And really, my lawyers are great," she said. "I will call you when I need you, I promise."

Ultimately, it was determined that the propane heater in Walt and Molly's hotel room did not vent properly, which allowed lethal levels of carbon monoxide to accumulate in their room. How this malfunction occurred was part of a multitude of management, maintenance, and repair problems. A bizarre array of fluky twists and turns had led to disaster.

The owner of the hotel had decided to repair the heater in "unit 4" himself—the last available room—so it could be rented. He thought he was competent to make the repair, even though he'd never done it before. He had watched others do it.

He replaced the heater's exchange burner assembly himself on Friday morning. He used incorrect parts and caused a misalignment of the heater exchange configuration, which caused incorrect and inadequate venting and combustion, among other mechanical problems. It was an unskilled repair, by an untrained and unqualified person with a total lack of experience. He didn't know he'd violated California law by working on the furnace without being licensed to do so. He thought he had no reason not to rent unit 4. Before he left town for the weekend, he asked the hotel's manager to just check unit 4 for heat before she rented it. She never did.

When Walt and Molly arrived late Friday evening, the credit card machine wasn't working and it had also run out of paper, so the hotel manager could not run their credit card and did not obtain a signature from them. She wrote down the card number and expiration date and asked them to come to the front office the next morning to sign the receipt. No one ever attempted to contact them about the matter. This was one of several of the hotel's standard protocols that were not followed in Walt and Molly's situation.

It was strict hotel policy that hotel staff should enter each room each day. This did not happen on Saturday or Sunday in unit 4. The couple had locked the deadbolt lock from the inside; the cleaner only had keys to the doorknob lock. The cleaner did not tell the manager she couldn't enter the room.

When the hotel owner returned late on Sunday, he was told by a police officer on the scene that the likely cause of the accident was carbon monoxide from the room's heater. An FBI investigator added, "It was not a survivable environment."

In their depositions, the hotel owner and the manager stated that at the time they were not clear on the difference between smoke detectors, which each room had, and carbon monoxide detectors, which no room at the hotel had.

By August 1998, the lawsuit was coming to a head. It was determined that "gross negligence" on the part of the hotel owner had caused Walt's death and Molly's injuries. Mom's lawyers also made strong liability claims against the other defendants, identifying a lack of inspections and a disregard of testing by the hotel's propane supply company and heating contractor company, and a failure to service, repair, maintain, and ensure the safety of the hotel rooms' propane heaters. These derelictions were deemed additional causes of the accident.

Finally, dogged research by Mom's attorneys revealed that the company that had manufactured the wall heater was found to have omitted a vent safety shut-off switch; an item costing a few dollars, which would have, according to expert witnesses, saved Walt's life and prevented Molly's injuries. The shut-off switch was not mandatory, but such switches were widely used in the industry as a built-in safety feature.

Just as Mom and her lawyers were thinking the case would have to go to trial, the defendants' attorneys offered to settle.

In the end, the settlement included the maximum amount available from the hotel owner, which was the top limit of the hotel's liability insurance policy. At the time of their depositions, the husband and wife who owned the hotel had sold it, had another property lost to foreclosure, had moved in with relatives elsewhere, and were both unemployed. They had a small IRA retirement account, which Mom and her lawyers chose not to pursue.

The other defendants—two businesses and a large corporation—paid over two-thirds of the total settlement amount.

A portion of the settlement funds, as well as part of Walt's FBI pension benefits, went to Kristen via her mother. Our lawyers were paid their well-earned percentage. And Molly's portion went into an account managed by Mom's longtime financial advisor.

The amount of the settlement was not excessive; it was "just enough," said Mom. If the money was wisely managed over time and if Molly never earned an income again, it was a "rough approximation" of what Mom and her financial advisor believed Molly would need to cover her living expenses and medical care for the rest of her life without ever burdening her sisters. These were Mom's priorities. As always, Mom was protecting all of her daughters' lives.

During the last days of the lawsuit, my dad suffered a stroke. Fortunately, it was a small one and fortunately, he was at home with Martha as his speech slurred, his body slumped, and the left side of his face melted. Martha knew exactly what was happening and quickly got him to a nearby hospital. She called me from the hospital once Dad was stabilized and I called my sisters. I told them I'd go visit him and report back. I compressed a week of freelance work into a couple of days and jumped on a train to northern Virginia.

Dad spent only one night in the hospital, and then was sent home to rest. By the time I got there, he looked OK and sounded surprisingly good, just sort of weary. His words came out slowly, but he seemed so happy to be sitting in his wooded backyard, with the birds singing, on a summer afternoon. He had turned 66 a couple of weeks before.

It was clear, however, seeing Martha's face, that she'd been through a horrible scare. The three of us had deep conversations into the night. Dad had confessions and amends to make about his smoking habit that he'd kept hidden for years, and had only revealed once he landed in the hospital with a stroke. We shouted and cried in confusion and frustration. We cried, too, glad we were all alive and could be together.

Two days later, Mom called me at Dad's house. "Molly is in the hospital. She has a burst appendix and needs emergency surgery." Mom's voice was serious. "She's stable now and they're working to clean up the damage before they can operate, probably day after tomorrow, but I have to go to Sacramento to be in court for the final negotiations on the settlement amount. This is it; I have to be there."

Sara said she wasn't available to come to Denver and Mary K. said she was tied up taking care of Abi and Jacob, so I told Mom I'd come to be with Molly. Martha and Dad assured me they'd be OK. I took the train home to New York, repacked my bag, explained everything to my neighbor who was taking care of my cats, and went to the airport.

The sequence: urgent phone call when I'm away from home, quick turnaround at home, hurry to the airport, fly to Molly—was eerily reminiscent of three and a half years before. So much of the tune had changed now; but it still plucked a scary chord.

Mom handed off her car in the Denver airport parking lot without our ever seeing each other. She had flown out in the morning and left a hidden key and a phone message telling me where I could find her car. I arrived in the afternoon and drove directly to the hospital. Molly had had her surgery the day before.

From what her doctor could figure, Molly had walked around with appendicitis for three or four days. This was astounding to them because a swollen, then burst, appendix is sharply painful, debilitating for most people. Molly finally did complain about a "bad stomachache," but by then, her appendix and surrounding tissue were so far gone they were gangrenous.

Molly seemed glad to see me and remembered Mom had gone to Sacramento. I spent the day with her, and just before "lights out," a nurse came to check her incision.

"I guess my bikini days are done, huh, Smith?" Molly said.

"Well, the scar will get smaller," I said. "But right now it looks like one of those big 'ol zippers on a sleeping bag, except it's on your belly." The nurse chuckled.

"Eewwwww, that sounds gross," Molly snickered.

"Some people think scars are cool and sexy, Smith," I said. "Like me, since I have so many. Signs of life experience, you know."

"No way. Not me. Only scary, scarry types would say that," laughed Molly.

The next day was Molly's 41st birthday. I arrived early and hung out in her room all day chatting and reading magazines with her. In the afternoon, Mary K., Stephen, Abi, and Jacob came for a little party. They brought balloons, funny cards, crayon pictures, and some cake and ice cream. Molly seemed to really enjoy the kids, the attention, and the festivities. I stayed with her until after she'd finished her dinner and brushed her teeth. But just before I left, she got glum and then she began to cry.

"It's not what I wanted, Smith," Molly said.

"You mean the birthday party?" I asked.

"No, no. This life. It's not what I expected to have."

I sat on the edge of her bed. "I know, Molly. I know." I held her hand and tears ran down my cheeks.

"Smith, you can't cry. Don't cry. It's..." She was exhausted; she squinted her eyes closed and fell asleep in moments. I stayed until her face smoothed into deep slumber.

When I arrived in the morning, Molly was cheerful and eating Cream of Wheat. That afternoon she was discharged and I brought her to Mom's house to stay until Mom returned. For the next couple of days, I helped Molly move around, gingerly, and prepared meals. She slept a lot and recovered quickly.

Midweek, the day Mom would fly in from California and I'd fly to New York, I kissed Molly good-bye, said I'd see her soon, and told her that Mom would be home in a couple of hours. She promised to stay put in Mom's guest bed and rest. I reversed the key arrangement with Mom's car at the airport, and once I arrived home, I checked in with Dad and he was doing better each day, too.

The next day I congratulated Mom on the successful conclusion of the legal case. She was so relieved it was over and that Molly was recuperating quickly. I also told her that I'd been thinking about Molly's medical emergency.

"I mean, in this situation, was her brain not *receiving* pain signals, or was her brain not *perceiving* pain signals? Or maybe parts of both?"

"I don't know. I know we have high thresholds for pain in this family," Mom said. "It's something for us to be aware of with Molly, though. Any complaint of pain should be taken very seriously—I'll be more careful the next time she says her tummy hurts."

"She just hates to admit any physical weakness these days; I think my big sister is still determined to be superwoman, you know—one way or another. And I guess that's OK by me."

"Me too," said Mom. "It keeps her motivated."

Indeed, from having nearly died almost four years before, to living with a severe brain injury, Molly was pretty capable and independent. Well, she was and she wasn't. But she believed she could be. And Mom, as her guardian and caregiver, did all she could to support Molly's resolute spirit.

In a lovely piece of cosmic timing at the end of that year, 1998, Mom met a wonderful man. Glen was a perfect balance for my mother. She was dynamic, fun, and active. Glen was soft-spoken, kind, but also gung-ho. She was generous and giving. Glen was skillful and thoughtful. They liked to get out and do things together, to be involved in the arts and to travel.

Glen, whose wife had Alzheimer's disease, helped Mom through the ordeals she confronted in caring for Molly. His humor and gentle, loving ways smoothed the sharp edges, brought calm, and provided a refreshing refuge when Mom needed to unwind or simply get away without leaving home.

However, no matter where Mom was, Molly was tethered to her, whether or not either of them wanted it that way. Trying episodes strained their connection, sometimes nearly strangling them both. But their bonds also strengthened as Molly learned and evolved, and she and Mom—and all of us—learned her limitations again and again.

Mom was able to flow with and manage the ever-shifting composite of her oldest daughter; sometimes familiar, other times almost unrecognizable. Molly eventually, especially on her good days, came to trust and genuinely value how Mom enhanced her day-to-day existence and made her good life possible. Our goal of a "normal life" was still present.

I wanted a close relationship with my older sister. Maybe not what it was before, but still substantial and meaningful to us both. But, as Molly once wrote, I'm an optimist to a fault.

In May 1999, Molly wanted to attend her 20th class reunion at Yale. She had happy memories of previous reunions and homecomings prior to her injury. Molly and Mom's experience at Yale, just months after Molly came out of a coma, was very positive. Now her roommates, fellow swimmers, and cheerleading buddies wrote and encouraged her to come to the reunion.

Mom put her on her flight in Denver, then a good friend from Yale picked her up at the airport and got her to the hotel near campus. Molly's weekend was filled with brunches, dinners, and get-togethers. She had a schedule, and probably with help from friends, got to the activities.

Then I got a call on Sunday, late morning. Mom said that Molly's friend could no longer take her to the airport early Monday morning, Memorial Day, for her flight home. Mom asked if I could meet Molly at Yale and get her to Bradley International Airport near Hartford.

Four of my New York City friends had arrived Friday evening and were staying with me in Copake for the long holiday weekend. I hung up, turned to them and said, "Enjoy the house, here's a key and a map, eat and drink anything you want. I've got to go to Yale and be with Molly—right now."

My friends were wonderful. They said they'd miss me but would be fine, and sent me on my way.

I met Molly at her hotel in New Haven Sunday afternoon. Her roommates had made sure she was ready to go. Molly was in high spirits and had clearly had a great weekend. It was heartwarming to see her with her friends, enthusiastic and beaming. It reminded me of the Molly I knew when I was in high school. I'd take the train to Yale and stay with my big sister and her roommates in their dorm room. The friends and the setting were the same; Molly and I were not.

Molly and I had pizza in New Haven, with lots of laughter, with the friend who was to have taken her to the airport the next morning. Then I drove us north to spend the night at a hotel near the airport. The moment Molly and I were alone, there was a dramatic mood shift. She yelled and swore at me. She was bitchy and mean. I don't remember what she was complaining about—everything—the way I was driving, the sound of my car's direction signal, the card key for the hotel door, the soap in the bathroom, the bed pillows, the closet, the desk lamp—anything. The more I tried to solve whatever was wrong or soothe her, the angrier she became.

We finally went to bed and I hoped that in the morning she'd be over it. I had to wake her very early and nudge her to get ready quickly so we could catch her flight. It was as if the fever never broke. She was in an extended temper tantrum. No screaming and kicking like a 3-year-old, but she sure was cantankerous. She didn't let up unless someone else was nearby—a bellhop in the elevator, a desk clerk, a parking lot attendant. She would smile sweetly to them until we were alone again.

I drove as calmly as I could while she fumed in the passenger seat, bitching about my driving and making harsh statements about anything she saw out the window.

"I hate that truck. I hate that sign. You drive like a jerk. Your driving is so jerky."

When I tried to change her channel and make pleasant conversation, she nearly bit my head off. We finally got to her gate. (In the days before the 9/11 security changes, it was useful to be able to take her right to the plane.)

I gave her a hug and a kiss, but she stood stiffly, barely looking at me.

"Bye Molly. Be safe. I really love you," I said.

"Bye Smith. Love you, too," she said perfunctorily. "See you later, or whatever."

I watched her walk into the ramp hallway that led to the plane. I waved and smiled in case she turned around, but she didn't.

I had never been so glad to get rid of her. I despised feeling that way, but it was such a relief to be on my own and have United Airlines take over responsibility for the next few hours. I sat in my car in the parking lot and cried. Then I drove home singing to music on the radio. My friends had left me ice cream in the freezer and a sweet note describing what I missed—kayaking and swimming and making a big dinner in my kitchen—and thanking me.

I had no idea why Molly was so hard on me. As often as I tried to console myself that this was about brain injury, I couldn't shake how deeply it hurt to have my beloved older sister, the Yalie, shred me. I theorized that she was tired after a nonstop weekend of reunion activities and being "on" for her friends. We had only gotten four hours of sleep. I also thought she was angry because, here I was, her little sister, the one her Yale friends remembered from my many visits, arriving to "rescue" her. I never told anyone I was there because Molly couldn't get to the airport by herself. But she knew why I was there. I was part of her entire weekend of reminders—of her years at Yale as a bright and busy student; of her friends, who now had husbands and families and interesting careers—and then, there I was. She needed me to help her get home, and she must have hated that. I could understand.

Molly infuriated and mystified me. But I finally realized that I never stopped being in awe of her. Inspired by her willingness to try, her zeal to go on, her determination.

Certainly, Molly's brain injury interferes with her ability to cooperate; and my piece of brain injury with my ability to cope. Once I could focus on this reality, I was more at ease with this person, who was at once intimate and a stranger to me.

About 10 days later, a package arrived. Inside was a little card—a short thank you note in Molly's ever-shrinking scrawl, and a classic, grey hooded sweatshirt with YALE across the front. I hugged it like a long-lost best friend. Had it occurred to her that I had been trying to help her? Had she realized she'd been difficult? Was it a moment of etiquette training from our youth kicking in? I'll never know. I called and thanked her and we had a fun, warm, and typically lighthearted chat; that is, typical for us now.

That summer, Molly started using a computer-dating service and was meeting up more often with a singles' group at happy hours around town. Mom and I agreed that it was good she was motivated to practice her computer skills and good, too, that she was reaching out and trying to build a social life. It made sense that Molly wanted to make friends and go on dates, especially now that she could drive and had her own home. But, this phase also presented hard challenges.

Mom called on a Monday afternoon in late June. Her voice was taut.

"Hi, Mom, what's up? You're home, right?" She and Glen had been on a four-day trip to Iowa over the weekend to visit Glen's family.

"Yes, we got in last night. Molly picked us up at the airport. She'd had a rough time, though," Mom said. "Turns out she spent Saturday night in the 'drunk tank.'"

"What? What do you mean? What happened?"

"Apparently she went to a wine tasting party late Saturday afternoon, downtown. She might have met up with her singles' group there, I don't know," Mom said. "It was sponsored by the city and they were probably concerned about their liability and they had police around."

"Did she drive?" I asked.

"Yes, she drove herself. But as she was walking out, she was wobbly, and she tripped and fell. The police were watching and they took her in. She never had a chance to get to her car."

"Thank goodness. I mean, that's probably good news, right? So they took her to the police station?"

"No, they took her to the 'drunk tank.' It's at Denver General, the city hospital. They test you and keep you overnight or until you're sobered up enough to get picked up," said Mom. "It's a large ward with beds, and Molly said they leave the lights on all night, which she hated."

"That must have been awful," I said.

Mom explained that on Sunday, when Molly needed to be picked up, she racked her brain trying to think who to call.

"At least she remembered that we were out of town," Mom said. "You know how she has a pretty fantastic memory for numbers and dates? She thought of Jimmy, a relatively new friend, and she remembered his phone number! He came and got her, they found her car, which had been ticketed but not towed, and he followed her home to be sure she got there OK."

"Wow," I couldn't think. "What a story. What a situation for her to be in!"

"I know," Mom said, quietly. "And there she was on time at the airport to pick us up last night. When she told me what happened, I was stunned." Mom sounded both exasperated and tearful—somewhere between wanting to ground Molly like a teenager for her bad choices and hug her out of real concern for her safety.

It was a distressing scene to imagine—poor Molly trying to have a typical social outing, but spending the night in Denver's facility for public inebriates. She must have been embarrassed and frightened, too. And yet, I was relieved she didn't get the chance to try to drive home.

It was a critical lesson in our ongoing education. We learned that everything, absolutely everything, affects brain chemistry. And in a brain that's already compromised, the effects can be surprising to unsettling to downright dangerous. We'd had glimpses already of the impact on Molly of tiredness, stress, even hunger. Now, we added alcohol.

We learned Molly was drinking too much. In fact, she really shouldn't have been drinking at all, much less drinking and driving. The prescription drugs she was taking to help her were serious and complex. She was trying to be like the others in the singles' group and be liked by them, too. But if this group was about drinking, then Molly needed a different group. Lis, Molly's OT, and Mom helped Molly get started with Alcoholics Anonymous. Molly stopped drinking on the spot and became very connected to her AA group. She wasn't an alcoholic, but she liked the support and needed to belong in a new way.

For the next five years Molly went to AA meetings. At the beginning, Molly went to meetings seven days a week. Soon after, she'd go a couple

times a week. It became part of her schedule, an important piece of structure, along with her classes at the vet tech school. I'm sure she felt welcomed
and on an equal footing with everyone in the group. With lots of mutual
support, her brain injury probably didn't matter to anyone.

The lessons to learn with Molly were endless. She had become quite
proficient on her computer, including using her credit card. Mom kept an
eye on Molly's spending and managed her finances, but Molly had her own
purchasing power.

She signed up for an additional computer dating service that cost
$2,000 and then told Mom it was a "rip-off." Mom looked into canceling
the service, but couldn't get the money back without a lawsuit, so they just
cancelled it. The one computer dating service that Molly did use, we were
to learn soon, was full of potential and pitfalls. But this was an early lesson
about Molly's spending choices and her credit cards, which remain caution-
ary and prickly issues.

That summer, Mary K. and her family moved to Hillsboro, Kansas,
so Stephen could take a ministerial position. Instead of being across town,
the Humbers were now an eight-hour drive away. It was a huge transition
for everyone, not least of all for Mom. Her grandkids would no longer be
within arms' reach, and Mom braced herself for the hole in her world. Mom
was also sad to lose the significant support Mary K. offered. The delight,
perspective, and balance offered by the Humber family were a lot less accessible in Kansas.

I went on alert. Sara was living in southwestern Utah, and even though
I was in New York, I knew I needed to step up even more for Mom, to truly
become her long distance supporter as she coped with Molly. Happily, Glen
was a short-distance supporter and a positive companion to my mother, as
they grew ever closer.

My life was changing, too. I got an offer for the Copake house, and I
met Larry and we began a sporadic, tentative relationship. Both of us were
bruised and wary; Larry and his wife had divorced several years before, and
I was simply uncertain about any of it, and had been for almost two years.
Still, I felt warm and good with Larry, sometimes.

The house sold, but at a sizable financial loss. It was like a fire sale, a get-
it-over-with divorce sale. Brian and I had never renovated it with the idea of
selling quickly—not until the very end. I'd thought we'd grow old in that
house together. Our financial investment, not to mention considerable sweat

equity, did not have anywhere near enough time to appreciate. The house was expertly and lovingly over-renovated.

This was another layer of loss for me. Five years of working on every square inch with Brian. Endless dust, drudgery, and unglamorous achievements. Visions of a future in our beautiful, eco-smart home, trashed. I'd never even unpacked my books or put anything on the walls. Or hung curtains. Or spread a rug on a floor.

Dad and Martha drove up to help me move out, which was simple because most of my stuff was still in boxes in the garage. They were rocks of support as I wobbled. They put their arms around me as I walked away from my house for the last time. We transferred my boxes to a small empty house nearby that I'd rented from a friend for two months while he sold it and I looked for a place to live. We slept in sleeping bags on the carpeted living room floor.

The last time I saw Brian was at the closing the next morning. Dad and Martha walked around the block of the lawyer's office while they waited for me. Their loving presence and calm heads meant the world to me.

When I called and told Molly about selling the house, she said, "Oh, poor Smith. How sad. How sad you must be."

She shared her memories of being at the house, both before and after her injury, which surprised me. She remembered the purple crystal doorknobs, the vegetable garden, and the large windows. She also reminded me of her transitions.

"I had to move, too, you know," Molly said. "And my house got sold."

"Yeah, I helped you move from California, and now you have your own really nice house," I said.

"Walt doesn't live here, though," said Molly, quietly. "But it is a good house, for a Denver house."

By the end of the year, I'd moved into an apartment in Valatie, a rural village about 20 miles south of New York's capital, Albany, and about three miles from Larry's rental cottage. Mom stopped by for an overnight visit a couple of weeks after I moved in and met Larry for the first time. She observed his quiet nature and he impressed her with his intellect.

Mom was on her way to Boston to settle up with Houghton Mifflin. They'd paid Molly's medical bills through their health insurance company's medical benefits trust fund. If Molly won a settlement, she had an obligation to repay them.

"We didn't want to pay any more than we had to because the amount was coming out of Molly's settlement, so it was a negotiation," Mom explained.

Once it was finalized, the medical bills were paid, and Molly separated from Houghton Mifflin, finally, and on amicable terms.

"We were very fortunate that they came through for her when we really needed them, especially for the HBO treatments," Mom said. "They've been really good to Molly."

Over the next months, Glen moved in with Mom as her partner. My relationship with Larry slowly solidified as we stretched to overcome the wounds of our previous relationships.

Molly's behavior, however, did not become more stable. Instead, she was often erratic, confounding Mom's efforts to develop a comfortable routine. Molly had her vet tech classes, occasional dates, AA meetings, and appointments with her therapists. But Mom had to oversee Molly every day, and took the brunt of her moodiness and frustration.

That was a lot, and Mom also became concerned about Molly's increasing road rage. She had experienced harrowing rides with Molly and feared she was a risk on the road to herself and others. With Lis's help, Mom enrolled Molly in a driving course that specifically dealt with road rage. Mom and Lis also asked Molly's doctors to re-examine her drug regimen. The challenge was to figure out what classification of drug was most suitable and which particular drugs worked best since they were affected by even tiny changes in Molly's world.

The doctors prescribed antidepressant medications. Each drug, alone or in combination with others, resulted in different behavior from Molly. Some medications seemed to make her hyper and silly, others seemed to spike her irritability and fury. A drug would be prescribed and then a period of time would need to pass, usually a month or more, to observe the impact on her behavior, like an ongoing experiment.

One of the drugs may have resulted in increased difficulties for Molly at Bel-Rea, the vet tech school, where she was botching tests or failing classes, in confusion and annoyance. She ended up having to take some classes a second or even third time in order to pass.

She also had more crabby sessions with Lis and tetchiness with Mom. She even hurled insults at soft-spoken Glen, who was always doing helpful tasks for her. Taken together, Molly could be really unpleasant to be around while her meds were being assessed.

Mom and Lis would report their observations of Molly's behavior to the doctors and new dosages or meds would be prescribed. It was an excruciating process, but brain injury is never the same twice and this troublesome tinkering with drugs to get the mix right for this particular patient was the only way, and utterly necessary, for everyone's sake.

I was elated when Mom and Glen decided to go on a three-week visit to China in the fall of 2000. It was important to me and my sisters that Mom be able to enjoy her love of travel and take trips when she wanted to. It was something she was supposed to be doing in her "retirement." I understood, too, that Mom needed to get away sometimes if she were to keep going with Molly at home.

So we tested the "it takes a village" philosophy, to collectively watch over and care for Molly while Mom was away. It was Mom's first extended time away since the accident more than five years before. Nearby, Lis and Mom's and Molly's neighbors and friends, and at a distance, me and my sisters, each did our part—visiting Molly at home, checking in by telephone daily, asking questions about her activities, reminding her of appointments. And Molly came through just fine. She seemed to enjoy all the attention. It was a victory for everyone.

That Christmas, we all gathered at Sara's home in southwest Utah. It was fun to cook meals together; play with the cats, Sugar and Pepper, again; and take walks amidst the gorgeous red rocks and canyons. Molly had her cranky times, but with all of us together, she was easily cheered up or could be left alone to stew when she became too ornery.

A couple of weeks later, in January 2001, Mom got call from Walt's mother. Ah Mee had bad news from Hawaii. Kristen, Walt's daughter, had died from an asthma attack. She was 20 years old. Mom told Molly about Ah Mee's call as they sat at the kitchen table that afternoon.

"She was stunned," Mom said. "She stared out the window a while, and then turned to me and said softly, with tears in her eyes, 'Some families die young.'"

Mom asked her what she was feeling and Molly said she was thinking about Walt; and his father and his brother-in-law, who were both young when they died, and now Kristen.

"It struck me as profound for Molly to say that, and to understand that," Mom said.

I thought Molly probably felt another wave of the loss of Walt wash over her, and perhaps, a moment of gratefulness to be alive. I did, on both counts.

Despite her drugs, Molly's moodiness and unpredictable behavior continued, I called often, but I felt useless. Molly was spacey and Mom seemed drained. I was as worried about her as I was about Molly.

By early spring, Lis concurred with Mom that one particular medicine seemed to be making Molly especially agitated and surly. Even one of Molly's occasional boyfriends told Mom he thought Molly was "more mellow" when she hadn't taken it yet.

The drug was one that Dr. Cilo had put Molly on, believing it would make her *less* irritable. Mom spoke to Dr. Cilo about it at a family medical meeting.

"I've observed that after Molly takes the antidepressant drug she's very fussy and hostile. Then, when it wears off, she gets better," said Mom, and added that she thought that drug was causing more harm than good.

"What did he say?" I asked. "Does he have something else he wants to try?"

"No. In fact, he said, 'So, where did you get your medical degree, Sally? I'm the doctor and she's staying on it!' Can you believe it? It made me so mad. So very calmly, I said, 'Dr. Cilo, I don't have a medical degree, but I spend more time with Molly than anyone else in the world. I know the patient.'"

"That's for sure. You do know her better than anyone else," I agreed.

"I see the differences in her behavior. I notice her personality and her reactions, every day, moment to moment," Mom paused. "Still, I was embarrassed."

The next day, Lis called Mom and said she thought Dr. Cilo's comment was rude, and that she wanted Molly to see another doctor she knew. She thought that a Dr. Carlson might offer another perspective on Molly's condition and her medicines. Lis said Dr. Carlson wasn't taking new patients, but that she would find a way to get Molly in. Eventually, Mom concluded that despite her tangle with Dr. Cilo, he and Dr. Schraa and the whole staff at Craig Hospital were great for Molly and had helped her tremendously.

We didn't know it at the time, but trying to solve the puzzle of the right drugs for Molly would be a perpetual quest—always searching to balance her brain chemistry to help her be stable and happy. New drugs come along. Molly, her brain, and her life evolve. The pieces keep changing, and each new grouping requires testing and fine-tuning.

Mom picks up the clues every day—Molly's attitude, energy level, even how she walks—and builds an overall picture. I get clues from a distance, something Molly writes in an email or says over the phone. Sometimes my perspective is advantageous, like noticing how much a child has grown in six months when you don't see her frequently.

In June 2001, Molly finished her vet tech coursework at Bel-Rea, at last. It took help from Mom and Lis and special accommodations from Molly's teachers. It was hard for her, but we all learned that Molly could learn.

However, completing the courses and actually working as a vet tech were very different skills. Molly tried one last time to work at a clinic to fulfill an internship requirement, but failed after just two weeks. Molly said she felt unappreciated, and that the clinic staff gave her less and less to do, particularly with pet owners and their animals.

Mom read me the letter the veterinarian wrote to Bel-Rea. She felt, unfortunately, that it was likely accurate.

The vet said they were aware of Molly's condition and knew that she tried really hard. But a simple suggestion on how to do something could make Molly argumentative. She was sometimes insensitive to staff and clients, and although they repeated instructions to Molly for her tasks, she made mistakes and got very frustrated when she was corrected. He explained they simply couldn't have her around the clinic because she wasn't nice to people, and in general, had a spiteful attitude. The vet was concerned about her negative impact on his staff and the animal owners, and worried, too, that she might harm an animal in one of her explosive moments.

Lis didn't want to show Molly the letter and Mom also felt that if Molly read the letter, she would either be devastated or just reject the entire assessment. But Mom felt that Molly did need to be informed of her shortcomings and hazards as a vet tech and understand how her behavior, in general, affects those around her so they could work on the problems.

"You know, we go along, day after day, thinking Molly is doing pretty well, when, in fact, she is *not* doing well, and we get this hard wake-up call," Mom said. "We honestly don't know how she is with different people or in different situations—I'm just really concerned."

"I know, Mom. I am, too. I also worry about how our 'family brain injury' impacts our own judgment," I said. "Look, we know that a lot of times Molly really is OK, but it seems to depend on what she's doing, who's around her, and whatever mood she happens to be in. Maybe, later on, she could volunteer at an animal shelter, someplace without medical tasks for her to do and less responsibility. It might help her feel productive."

"I'd be glad for her to volunteer at an animal shelter," Mom said. "But since she's all 'educated' now, her arrogance has increased; it could be a problem even in a volunteer situation. She loves to exhibit her knowledge and, of course, she's always right and always certain."

"Well, nobody will put up with that kind of help, even if it's volunteer," I said. "She makes it so hard to be around her sometimes, and it hurts *her* most of all. It's maddening.

"Yes, especially because she can be so pleasant at times. I just wish that somehow Molly could be happy just exercising, taking walks, going to movies, going on vacations," I could hear Mom deflating. "I'm just down on this stuff, honey. Tomorrow will be a better day."

Lis came to the rescue again and was able to work out a final compromise with Bel-Rea. Molly would graduate without the vet clinic internship requirement, but she had to agree to never work in the veterinarian field.

Mom and Lis decided that it was best to encourage Molly to focus on taking excellent care of her own two cats, each adopted from a shelter, and give them her love and attention. Lis said perhaps when Molly was ready and willing, she would look into other types of volunteer opportunities. To this day, Molly's cats are healthy, indulged, and happy.

Even though Molly cannot work as a vet tech, she attends continuing education conferences to maintain her certification. She will tell a new acquaintance that she worked in publishing, is a vet tech, and is retired. It's admirable and helps to define her. I like her commitment and the sense of authenticity she feels.

✿✿

Twelve

EVEN with vet tech school behind her, Molly's life did not settle into halcyon days, and it was not possible to predict potential storms. Years earlier, our family's total focus had been to keep her alive. Then our focus became to help her rehab and retrain her brain to be healthy and strong. Now, more than six years since her injury, we were encouraging Molly to live as independently as possible and feel content—normal. It's what she wanted, after all. But we could not have anticipated the difficulties—like falling in love.

Perry and Molly met in July 2001 through her computer dating service. In her profile, Molly posted an attractive photo and described her education, background, and interests. She presented herself honestly as having a brain injury due to CO poisoning and being a widow and retired. She and Perry quickly became very connected. In an email, Molly wrote, *"Hey Smith! Guess what? I'm in love! Whaddya know?!!!"*

It was a big deal—her first serious boyfriend and the first time she'd spoken about love since her injury. I emailed back, *"Hey, that's exciting news! How great, Smith – love! Wow! Who's the lucky guy? Can't wait to hear all about him."*

I called Mom. She'd met Perry, just briefly, and wasn't crazy about him, something about him rubbed her the wrong way. "A lot of bravado," she said. But, as always, Mom was supportive of her daughter. She said they'd been dating for a few weeks, were spending a lot of time together, and Molly was more upbeat than usual. Mom and I agreed that Perry didn't need to be perfect. It was great that Molly was happy.

When I called Molly to remind her about my upcoming trip with Larry to Denver, I told her that I was excited to see her and maybe meet her "new guy."

"We're coming next Friday, the 4th of August," I said.

"Well, I'm glad you're arriving on the 4th of August," Molly piped. "That day, by the way, is my 'rape date!' Did you know that?"

"Oh, gosh. No. I didn't…" I said, stumbling over my words. Molly knocked me flat with her astounding memory of dates, but I wished she could have forgotten some of them forever.

"… I'm sorry, Smith. That's a horrible thing," I said.

"Don't worry. It's OK," Molly said, sounding big sisterly. "It's OK, and I'm OK."

"That's for sure. You are definitely OK, Molly. Well, we'll be there soon and we'll have a fun time. It'll be great, I promise."

"OK, that's good you promise. It *will* be great," Molly said, cheerfully.

But it wasn't great. I met Perry only once; he was a jerk. We all had dinner together at a local Mexican restaurant. Perry was condescending and harsh to the restaurant's workers, especially a waitress who had dropped a drink. He seemed to relish an easy opportunity to pick on the person who was already down. I was astonished how mean he was, without a moment of hesitation or self-awareness. He was rude to me and boorish to Larry, Mom, and Glen, too. He didn't seem at all interested in creating a good impression.

I barely said a word throughout the dinner. I was flabbergasted. I watched Molly; she was beaming and delighted with him. I didn't get it.

Larry and I took a long walk after dinner to unwind and vent about Molly's new guy. I said that Molly dating over the past few years felt like a natural transition, a normal activity, but Perry was so bad I was sure she wouldn't put up with him for very long.

I was wrong. It would have been the case with pre-brain injury Molly, but not with Molly now. Instead, she would cling to him and her family would slog through many, *too* many months of Perry, the terrible, the conniving—and we didn't realize until later—the treacherous.

Early on, however, Mom recognized that Perry was trying to control Molly no matter where she was, but especially when she was with family. During our visit, he'd call her on her cell phone repeatedly, and then she'd become so negative and bitchy to Mom and us after talking with him that Mom told her not to speak with him when she was with us. Then Molly sulked like a sullen teenager, not allowed to be in contact with her boyfriend.

"My motherly instincts are flaring," Mom said. "I'm really trying to accept her choice of a boyfriend, especially since she may have limited options. But he's pushing me beyond a reasonable doubt."

I commented to Mom that I thought it was ironic that she got the cell phones so she and Molly could be in touch anytime, especially in an emergency. Instead, Molly's cell phone was driving a wedge between them.

Perry spent more and more time at Molly's house and wanted to go with her everywhere. And very quickly, he became a master of manipulation—continuously telling Molly what she wanted to hear—how beautiful and smart she was, how much he loved her, and that she was so good she didn't need a legal guardian at all and could be free and independent.

Perry's efforts went beyond wanting to be Molly's sole focus; he wanted to turn her away from her family. We sensed he was bad news, but we did not realize how dangerous he was. We couldn't have imagined at the beginning how their relationship and his influence over Molly would identify a major difficulty of her brain injury, and become a significant learning challenge for all of us.

A couple of weeks after I got home from Denver, the terrorist attacks of 9/11 occurred. My life as a New Yorker and as a journalist fell into chaos. I was busy working full time as a reporter for a newspaper and it took weeks for me to regain a sense of my own equilibrium. Along the way, like many other people, I spoke a lot with my family members—about how we loved each other and felt close even though we were spread all over the country. It was necessary affirmation for me.

I reached out to Molly, too, and reminded her that years earlier when I lived in Manhattan, she and I had been to the top of the World Trade Towers.

"I've been pretty shaken up by all this," I told her. "But I felt better when I thought about the two of us having fun when we went to the top and saw the view. It was so clear that day and we could see really far." I stopped and listened. Molly was quiet. "Anyway, I was just thinking about that and missing you, Molly."

"I miss you, too, Smith," she said. "It was windy that day up there, I remember that."

I was impressed. "You're right! We could feel the building swaying even when we held the railing." Molly was quiet again. I thought maybe I'd spooked her.

"I'm missing that protection, too," she said.

Does she mean the railing? I thought. I couldn't tell. "What do you mean, Smith?"

"I'm missing Walt," she said. "It would be good if he were here."

"Yes. That would be good. I miss him, too, Molly. A lot." I was glad Molly still thought of Walt as her protector. That was a Molly I knew and understood.

Sometime in September, Perry moved into Molly's house without Mom's knowledge. Molly probably knew Mom wouldn't approve. Lis, Molly's OT, had a morning meeting scheduled with Molly and found Perry there. Molly told her that Perry is "perfect," and that he wants to marry her. They'd been dating for three months. Mom told me that Perry had been talking marriage to Molly from their first weeks together, and, of course, Molly loved it. At that time, Mom thought it was silly, not serious. Now she felt concerned.

I asked, "Do you think he understands that as Molly's legal guardian she can't get married without your approval and consent?"

"Yes, I suspect he knows that and I'm sure he doesn't like it. I think he'd like Molly and what she's worth financially all to himself. I have to imagine she's told him about her settlement," Mom said. "The problem is he's got her figured out. She's told me he says all the time how in love with her he is, and maybe he is, but I *know* Molly sure loves to it."

"He's truly awful and Molly's completely smitten," I said. "I want her to have love in her life. It just stinks that this guy is her first serious relationship since Walt."

"And Molly wants to be married again, too—to have that piece of a normal life," Mom said. "But there's just something strange about Perry."

Mom's instincts weren't the only ones screaming caution about Perry. Lis suggested Mom hire a private investigator she knew to check Perry's background. Mom hesitated at first; it seemed a dramatic step to take. She'd never kept track of who came and went from Molly's house. She wanted Molly to make her own choices. And that had been fine, so far.

The private investigator came back with a report at the beginning of October. Mom already knew from Molly that Perry had a son who was in jail for drugs. The report also noted Perry's coming and going from jobs and a few minor traffic violations. However, what startled Mom was that two restraining orders had been placed on Perry and he had violated them.

Perry had brought a civil lawsuit against a woman he'd met through a computer dating service and who received social security disability checks as her income. She had ended the relationship and told him she didn't want to see him anymore, but she had to place a restraining order on Perry to keep him from showing up at her house. He had violated the order at least once. He claimed the woman defamed him; filed false accusations; and had caused the loss of his job and income, emotional distress, and depression. He acted as his own attorney and asked for a settlement of nearly three million dollars. Eventually, the judge threw out his entire suit.

And now this *same* guy was dating Molly and wanted to marry her. Mom said, "Now we know what we're dealing with."

Perhaps it should have been even more alarming to us. I'll never know if it was our family brain injury clouding our perceptions or our sincere effort to balance our concern about Perry with our fervent desire to allow Molly, a 44-year-old woman, to lead her own life. But we simply didn't know how questionable her emotions and judgments were. We believed in her abilities too much and we hadn't had the opportunity to discover how vulnerable she was. We heard a ringing bell; we should have heard a blaring siren. But we didn't realize how much rescuing Molly needed.

Mom sent a letter to all of her daughters and to Dad saying that Molly's boyfriend seemed to want to isolate Molly from her and that he was doing a good job of it. She said it was hard to rein in Molly without feeling like she was too commandeering, but every person other than Molly who'd met Perry had serious reservations about him. Then she detailed what she'd learned about Perry from the court documents. She did not discuss ending their relationship; she just wanted us to know what his agenda might be.

I didn't like Perry, but I'd given him the benefit of the doubt because he was making Molly feel so happy and loved. But he was worming his way into her life, skulking, with what might be an ulterior motive. I couldn't shake my wariness about him anymore than I could ignore a splinter in my foot. But I was far away and I *wanted* to believe it was OK for Molly to make her own choices *and* that she was well enough to do so.

A few days later, Molly sent an email to me, Sara, and Mary K. I read it in utter disbelief. It was obviously written by Perry. None of the language was Molly's; it rambled along with big words and strange phrases she never used. I conferred with my sisters and we knew it was Perry through and through, even if Molly had agreed to send it as her own. I was astounded that Perry had such gall he thought we wouldn't know our sister's "voice" and language, *especially* since her brain injury.

The gist of the Molly/Perry email was that Molly no longer wanted Mom to be her legal guardian. It stated that Mom (weirdly called *"Sally A. Shuler"* throughout the email) and her lawyer were planning to issue a restraining order against Perry, which would *"destroy my life as I know it and our plans for my future."* The email said that Molly would prove she was completely competent and able to manage her own affairs, and would be declared fully independent and become her own guardian.

Mom had not mentioned getting a restraining order, but now I knew Perry knew the rules. With Mom no longer legal guardian, Molly could say, "I do," and Perry would be her husband—and have access to half of everything she owned, including her settlement funds.

This could occur without Molly's sisters' support. I couldn't fathom why he bothered to blather all his propaganda to us. On top of the impudence that Perry thought Molly's sisters would actually think she wrote the letter, did he imagine we would think removing Mom as Molly's legal guardian would be a good idea? I wondered, too, if Molly had expressed any concern to him about pushing away her entire family.

Perry's ulterior motive, however, was no longer in doubt. His control of Molly was now clear and disturbing. My heart twisted in knots as I began to recognize how vulnerable she was.

When I read the email to Mom she said it made her incredibly sad. "We've all worked hard to help Molly be as independent as possible, but with her brain injury she is a perfect victim," Mom said, her voice somber. "She wants so badly to be adored, and we want her to have love—even be married to a wonderful man again. But she would believe anyone even remotely convincing, even if he's attacking me and her family."

Mom said she understood now that Molly's vulnerability would always be a danger.

"And with this whole legal guardian thing," I added, "he's proving he would willingly jeopardize her well-being."

"I need to talk to Molly," Mom said. "I want to guide her and help her understand. I think she can solve this."

A few days later, she sat down with Molly and asked her how she really felt about Perry.

"I love him," Molly said. Mom asked if she thought Perry treated her and her family fairly. Molly got antsy. "Yes! Maybe. Well, maybe not always," Molly faltered. "He wants my freedom."

"Do you feel trapped?" Mom asked.

"No. But, maybe. I need… Perry says I could be free," Molly blurted,

"Perry is trying to separate you from your family," Mom said. "If he loves you, why would he want to do that?" Molly didn't respond. Mom said she should think about it.

I also tried to point out Perry's fallacy in my reply to the Molly/Perry email. I wrote to Molly that we loved her and supported her and that she shouldn't allow Perry to push her mother and sisters away. I said that love was good, but a man who wanted to isolate her from her family was not good. I wrote that I *knew* her life was better thanks to Mom being her caring guardian.

However, I wasn't having a one-to-one correspondence with my sister. No matter what I wrote in an email to Molly, Perry's words, as supposedly Molly's, came back in reply. It creeped me out. Molly seemed to believe whatever he told her and would do whatever he wanted her to, even against her family. And still, I kept believing I could reach her and reason with her. I didn't yet know that the limitations of Molly's brain injury would not allow logic or even love of family to trump Perry's cult-like control of her.

That Christmas, Molly and Perry sent out a card that featured a photo of them, arms wrapped around each other, standing in front of a Christmas tree. Their lengthy pre-printed text was about creating long-lasting holiday traditions together. Molly looked lovely in the photo and totally joyful, but I knew it was all wrong. I stared at Perry's face; I couldn't decipher his ill intent from his small eyes.

It was a thorny place for the family. We didn't like Perry and we'd told Molly why. Mom would never allow them to marry, but she still felt Molly should and could make her own relationship decisions. We believed in positive, persistent teaching efforts with Molly, rather than to dictate all control over her. And she seemed so capable so often. We wanted for her to be happy and in love. It's hard to take that away from anyone, and harder still to take away our faith in Molly. I believe our family brain injury hindered our comprehension of just how defenseless she was in Perry's clutches. We only learned the lesson slowly, by going through it. We had no other way.

Regrettably, the ordeal with Perry dragged on. At least we refused to be isolated from Molly; we knew better than that. As the months went by, the problems would ease off, then swell up, then ease off again. But always, we stood by, aware, alert, and responsive. Mom gave Molly room to her exercise her own judgment as much as possible, for the time being. Mom had never treated Molly like a person who needed constant monitoring and to be told what to do or not to do. Mom knew it might come to that, but she wanted to hold off until that became a necessity.

Fortunately, Lis finally got an appointment with Dr. Carlson, the psychiatrist she believed could help Molly by managing her medications more effectively. By the end of their first session, Dr. Carlson had diagnosed Molly as bipolar, resulting from or amplified by her CO poisoning brain injury because of the loss of limiters and self-control. He took Molly off an antidepressant medicine and focused on treating her as brain injured and bipolar with a combination of drugs designed to achieve a more balanced disposition. Within weeks, Mom, Lis, and I agreed that Molly seemed more calm and thoughtful. And even though she and Perry were still together, I felt a better connection to my sister.

Meanwhile, Mom continued to take precautions. She asked Dr. Carlson after he'd been treating Molly for several months, to write his opinion of her status and situation. Mom sent his letter to her lawyer, just in case.

Dr. Carlson wrote in his report that Molly spoke freely about Perry and admitted he wanted to get Mom's guardianship dissolved. *"I think this is a bad idea and will endanger my patient... Molly's mother is her greatest advocate,"* Dr. Carlson wrote.

Molly had also told Dr. Carlson there were times she felt uncertain about Perry and felt he wasn't good for her. *"But, Molly has never said she feels her mother or Lis do not have her best interests at heart,"* wrote Dr. Carlson. *"I believe Molly is vulnerable and suggestible and subject to manipulation, persuasion, and coercion."*

Dr. Carlson confirmed what we were learning ourselves. That Perry had made use of the fact that Molly strongly desires to be told she is loved romantically and that she can be independent and doesn't need any special assistance from anyone. And that for Molly, having a boyfriend, or even better, a husband, would put her in a "normal" category in her mind.

Dr. Carlson's letter was affirming, but gave us a new measure of concern about the vindictive situation Perry had created, with Molly going along—the insane leading the brain injured, I called it. Mom was ready to push Molly to make a decision—one we thought she was capable of making.

In early spring, over mugs of green tea, Mom told Molly, "I want to be with you, Molly, but I don't want to be around Perry at all. You've made a choice to be with him, and now I'm making my choice." She said it hurt her that their choices were not compatible, but that she would always be there for Molly and loved her with all her heart.

Molly said she loved Mom very much, too, but that Perry was hostile about Mom. She said she loved Perry and was afraid of losing him because he was making her choose, too, between her family and him.

Again, Mom asked Molly what she thought about a guy who wanted to separate her from her family and why he would want to do that. Molly said she didn't know.

Then Mom invited Molly to join her and Glen for their traditional Easter Chinese take-out dinner that Sunday, and Molly agreed to come on her own, but Mom could tell she struggled with the choice.

A few days later, Molly told Mom and Lis that Perry was putting pressure on her to do what he wanted. She told them it really bothered her that he would get into her email account when she was asleep and read emails sent to her from Mom and her sisters. She said she didn't want Perry in her house anymore and that she'd tried to tell him to leave, but she wasn't strong enough and couldn't do it. She said she needed help. It was all Mom had to hear.

The next day, Mom went to Molly's house with a police officer to tell Perry to leave. She told the officer she didn't know how Perry would react and wanted the force of the law with her.

Mom stood in the doorway of Molly's house with the officer and told Perry, who'd come to the door, that Molly had talked to her about getting him out and they were in agreement. "I told him he had 48 hours to take all his stuff and leave and that Molly was coming with me," Mom said. "And that's when we went to the mountains."

Mom and Molly spent several days in Vail at a hotel—like a mini intervention, Mom hoped. But Perry continued to call Molly on her cell phone without Mom knowing it. She only discovered they'd been in contact when she became suspicious of Molly's grumpiness and examined her cell phone. Mom yelled, "No more calls!" Molly said he just wanted to say he missed her and loved her. Mom patiently explained his game of pitting his control over her against Mom and how any response from her only encouraged him. It seemed to Mom, though, that Molly wasn't fully ready to let go.

Perry did leave Molly's house in 48 hours, but left a letter for Molly that she showed to Mom. He wrote that Molly should resist and fight Mom at all costs or they'd never have their freedom together. Mom told me Perry wanted to rally Molly for their grand cause but she seemed disinterested.

One afternoon in June 2002, Mom called with good news. A house on Mom's cul-de-sac, just a few doors from her's, was for sale and she'd decided to buy it for Molly.

"I wasn't thinking about moving Molly, but I realize this Perry problem isn't going away," Mom said. "I never thought I'd have to watch over Molly like I have been. It never felt necessary before, but now it does."

"I think it'll be great to have her just down the street, Mom. Anyone will have to pass by your house to get to hers. It'll make it so much easier for you to keep track of her," I said. "And it will be easier for her, too, when she needs help."

"It's what we need; I know that now," Mom said, quietly.

It was painful to keep realizing that Molly was not as capable as we'd hoped. "It's best for Molly and you—for all of us, Mom. It's the right thing to do."

Molly's house sold quickly and she really liked her new house *and* being Mom's neighbor. Perry and Molly still saw each other, but less frequently, and Mom kept track of his comings and goings. However, when she and Glen went on a weeklong trip that summer to visit Glen's family, Perry used Mom's absence to pounce again.

Perry got Molly to give an attorney a $5,000 retainer to work on having Mom removed as Molly's legal guardian. It was a brash move. But if Molly's brain injury made her unguarded against predators like Perry, it also made her brag to Lis about the money, the attorney, and what they were up to without realizing she was letting Perry's cat out of the bag.

With Mom out of town, Lis called me, and I called Sara and Mary K. Lis contacted the attorney and explained Molly's brain injury. I called him and said my mother and her attorney would be in touch immediately upon her return, and he offered to return Molly's check.

I spoke with Molly and did my best to explain what Perry was getting her to do and what it meant. She did not argue or defend Perry, and it seemed she hadn't realized what the money was actually for. When I said the check would be returned to her, she was surprisingly grateful.

"Oh, that's good, Smith. Thanks," she said. "I'll put that money back into my account."

Finally, I told Molly I thought it was really sneaky and not nice of Perry to do this when Mom was out of town. "Yeah, I guess," she mumbled.

I said I knew she cared about Perry, but his actions were not loving or caring about her. I told her that she could always rely on Mom and her sisters and Lis to do what's best for her. "Think about it; we've always been here to help you and we always will be. OK, Smith? I love you so much."

"I know," Molly said. "Thanks, Smith. I love you, too."

By the time Mom and Glen returned, we had retrieved Molly's money from the attorney and thwarted Perry's latest scheme. Lis told Mom that when Perry tried to pull a fast one, he greatly underestimated "Team Molly."

I was in New York—working, dating Larry, and doing my life, but it felt good to have helped manage a Molly problem when Mom wasn't there. She needed to get away sometimes and know things would be OK. And yet, it was so annoying that Molly continued to see Perry. I didn't blame Molly for wanting to hear his proclamations of love. He touched her susceptible heart and his tactics worked on her like brainwashing. When I'd call her, I could hear Perry sometimes in the background barking out commands. I despised his takeover of my sister.

"Hey, Smith, you know what? I'm going to call you back sometime when Perry isn't there so you and I can talk," I said.

"OK, Smith. Whatever," she replied. My stomach roiled. His control, her willingness, and my disappointment meant less relationship between Molly and me.

We determined to keep up our tactic of giving Molly opportunities away from Perry. In July, I convinced her to fly to Virginia to celebrate Dad's 70th birthday with my sisters and me. In October, Mom organized for Molly to go on a three-week wildlife safari in Africa with one of her friends from Rotary. After she returned, I really wanted to hear about her trip. But the gorillas of Uganda and cheetahs of South Africa did not completely dispel Perry's influence—however, he seemed to be fading. In our emails and phone calls there were fewer of his intrusions. Still, it was so tiresome and draining to deal with.

Finally, I wrote Molly and simply said that I wanted her to have love in her life, but not from someone who shoved her family away. I told her, again, to remember that her family loved her and had always been there for her. I told her to remember the values she grew up with and to trust her good instincts.

That Christmas, there was no photo card of Perry and Molly in front of a decorated tree. By the second week of January 2003, Molly's relationship with Perry was finally over.

"Amazing. What happened? What did she say?" I asked Mom.

"He was spending more time at her house and I think she really wanted him and all his junk out of there," Mom said. "She'd told me she might need a restraining order to get him out, and she probably said that to him, too. Anyway, it was enough for him to finally go."

"How is Molly doing? Does she seem OK?"

"Molly is great," Mom said. "She did it, and she seems utterly relieved."

"It probably feels good to take back her life," I said. "I hope she feels empowered."

When I spoke with Molly a couple of days later, I told her that I supported her choice to end it with Perry and I was sure it would be a positive thing for her.

"It already is, Smith!" she said. "I don't have to eat all that bad food he had, and move his stuff out of my way in the bathroom. And I can use my computer whenever I want to by myself."

"That's wonderful, Smith. I'm so glad you're feeling good about it all."

"Yep, all done," she said. "Ta da! He'll be fine and I'll be better."

Was it the new drug regime Dr. Carlson had prescribed for Molly? Perhaps Lis's persistent coaching? Mom's unwavering presence and support? Maybe enough time for it to sink in? Whatever had worked, Molly took charge of her life and her decision; she was happy and we were, too.

After some months passed, Mom mentioned that Molly was just starting to check out a computer dating service again.

"I hope she's not in a hurry," I said. "I'm still digesting what we learned from the Perry fiasco."

"And what are you thinking?" Mom asked.

"Just how incredibly vulnerable she is," I said. "It was scary to realize how susceptible she can be if someone wants to take advantage of her."

"It's really hit me recently, too," Mom said. "As a mother, you have to teach a child, usually a young child, to be afraid. To *not* trust. I had to reteach Molly that lesson."

About six months after Perry left, Molly received an invitation from him for her and a guest to attend his wedding. When she showed it to Mom, Mom said, brightly, "Oh, let's go!"

They looked at each other for a second and then both cracked up laughing. Once she caught her breath, Molly took the invitation from Mom and threw it in the trash.

"Thank God that's over and out of my life," she said.

Molly did return to the computer dating service, but with Mom's help she learned to be more cautious. The two of them developed a list of safety checks: meet a new date in a public place during the day, do not meet at a man's house, do not give anyone her phone number via email, and so on. They decided, too, that Molly should introduce to Mom a man she's thinking she might date beyond the initial "Starbucks meetings." Molly agreed to the "dating ground rules" and didn't seem to mind the extra scrutiny.

For my part, I wanted to offer sister-support to Molly. She emailed me about a guy she wanted to be more involved with but he wasn't giving her the attention she wanted. He'd passed the "Mom test" and they'd been dating several weeks. I encouraged her to stay busy with her own activities and let him come around on his own. I wrote, *"Time is on your side, Molly. You don't want to scare him away by being too intense before he's ready."*

Later Molly emailed me back: *"Well, I wish I'd received your email before I called him. He said he really liked me, but that he didn't see any 'long-term prospects.' I had to hang up and disconnect our relationship. Not a good thing, Smith!"*

It's always interesting to me how Molly's brain puts words together. *"Did you 'disconnect,' like you hung up the phone or you ended the relationship?"* I emailed to her. *"Did he call you again or did you call him back?"*

"No, nothing like that, Smith. It's done," she replied. *"I must be in a hurry because I keep rushing everything with perfect seeming men. Can't even live with myself. What a prospect I must seem to everyone I meet. Always in a hurry for everything. Not too attractive, I fear. Oh well, I love you, Smith!"*

Her email was touching. What a joy to have her back without Perry typing over her shoulder! Just her words in an email to me. The moment I thought this, though, I knew I was being selfish. It was bittersweet to read her recognition of how difficult she can be, the romantic obstacles she faces, and how tricky even casual dating can be. For any of us, really, but I knew, especially for her. I began to see how her cognitive deficits brought about such stark beauty and sad truths.

Mom asked if she could see Molly's online profile one afternoon when they were working at Molly's computer. In it, she mentioned her former publishing career and the fact she was a widow and retired. She posted some nice photos and wrote that she enjoys doing all kinds of sports and outdoorsy things. But she did not mention her brain injury.

"I suggested she tone down the athletic stuff and I said it was important to say she has a brain injury; that it's a key part of her and people need to understand that," Mom said. "I also got her to add that she has degrees from Yale and Stanford."

"Oh, good," I said. "I'm surprised she didn't have her education in it already."

"I think she wrote it quickly and just focused on all the sports she used to do," Mom said. "Once we got those things added, I told her that if someone read about her and decided to get in touch, they'd be amazed by her, and she liked that idea."

"Well, that's true. I guess I only wonder if putting her brain injury out there attracts another creepy predator like Perry."

"I know, I thought of that, too," Mom said, "but I decided—and I really believe—that Perry was not typical."

"God, I hope you're right," I said.

I knew Molly wanted to be in a relationship, and I imagined she didn't think to mention her brain injury when she was trying to write an appealing description of herself. I don't mention my most "challenging" characteristics when I'm meeting someone new. Whether she forgot to put it in or was avoiding it, I understood.

Besides, Molly had reasons all around her to believe love was possible via cyberspace. Larry and I met through a mutual friend, but Mom and Glen met through a computer dating service as did several of Mom's friends and their significant others. Sara and her boyfriend met through computer dating, too, and Sara was in the process at that time of moving from southwestern Utah to Glenwood Springs, Colorado, to live with Jonathan.

After about a year of computer dating, Molly had met some frogs and some average guys. Then she met Dave. A great guy. A prince.

It would not be a fairy tale, however, with a happy-ever-after ending. They shared some good times; and we gained new insights about Molly. The lessons learned through Molly's dating, especially the Perry debacle and the Dave romance, taught Mom and me and my sisters, volumes about post-brain injury Molly's abilities in relationships of all kinds; how she interacts with people she cares about, other than her family.

Dave was nice looking, had a professional job, and lived in downtown Denver, in the hip LoDo district. He and Molly emailed several times and decided to meet for coffee. His first image was her profile, wearing a baseball cap, looking across the street, looking for him.

"She was very pretty. We had coffee, then an early dinner, then we strolled around downtown," Dave recalled. "She was in a great mood, very happy. She never took off her baseball cap, and I came to learn she was crazy about wearing it almost always. But we had a wonderful time together."

Underneath the baseball cap, Molly had luxurious hair the color of honey. Her figure was still athletic and slim; she looked terrific in jeans and a casual sweater. Her angular face was clear and beautiful and, best of all, her bright spirit was always evident when she was meeting someone new. Her sparkling eyes and smile were captivating.

Molly told Dave about her brain injury on that first date and, like others, he was amazed by her story and by her. "She told me about her family, and that her mom is really a hero," Dave said. "I discovered she was national title swimmer and a cheerleader at Yale. She was open about her whole life story. We walked and started holding hands. It was very easy."

Dave met Mom a few days later and liked her and Glen immediately. He understood that Mom was instrumental to Molly's well-being and Mom was impressed by Dave, too. Soon after, the four of them began to meet for dinner or go to a play or movie. They enjoyed being together.

It didn't take long for Dave to see the impact of Molly's brain injury, though. A couple of weeks after they met, Molly's purse was stolen at the gym. She'd left it in an unlocked locker, and in it were her credit cards, checkbook, cash, passport, everything. "It was so frustrating for her to cancel and replace all the stuff," Dave said. "And it was the first signal to me of her real deficits."

Two weeks later her purse was found in a trash can and only the cash was missing. Mom had to instruct Molly not to carry everything she owns in her purse—only what needs. And at the gym, lock it in the trunk of her car.

Dave learned that Molly had trouble thinking things through some-times, but she knew she adored Dave. She wrote, *"I love you so much it hurts"* in an email to him several weeks after their first date. It surprised Dave, but he also really cared for her.

"Everyone thought she was incredible, and I liked that," said Dave. "People were very loving to her and that was great to be around. We had really good times in the early days."

Molly frequently stayed at Dave's apartment and they became a familiar couple in LoDo's restaurants and shops. They could walk to theaters, where they often met Mom and Glen, and to sports venues where they cheered for Denver's professional hockey and football teams.

Molly's bull's-eye memory for sports scores impressed Dave and first demonstrated to him her uncanny ability to remember certain numbers and dates. "One night, she said, 'Is everything OK with us?' I said, 'Yes, of course. What do you mean?' And she said, 'Well, this is the 19th and it's been three months and bad things happen on anniversaries.' I tried to reas-sure her—it was kind of touching in a way—and we went to bed."

Dave got Molly doing activities again that she used to enjoy and that he also liked—travel, cycling, downhill skiing, and charity events. They even went to church on Sunday mornings sometimes. Molly and Dave spent time with both their families and friends, too, celebrating birthdays and holidays. When I was visiting, I noticed they laughed together and just seemed to have a lot of fun.

Dave also sought ways to enrich Molly's life. She'd recently started vol-unteering at a cat shelter and Dave arranged for them to volunteer in a program with Big Brothers/Big Sisters. They would tutor Hispanic stu-dents who spoke English as a second language, after school once a week. Dave worked with a boy student and Molly was paired up with a 5th grade girl, who she'd help with reading, math, and homework. Molly took a lot of pride tutoring the girls who looked up to her and appreciated her help. They didn't know or care about her brain injury; it was not evident to them. They valued her English speaking and reading abilities and her one-on-one attention. She told me she liked being a big sister to someone other than her *real* little sisters.

Dave accompanied Molly to Mexico with Mom and Glen for their annual winter trip, and also went to her 25-year reunion at Yale in late May. Larry and I met them in New Haven and the four of us spent part of the weekend together. Molly loved showing off Yale to Dave and showing off Dave to her Yale friends. I'm sure it was a solid piece of normalcy for her to attend her reunion this time with such a nice boyfriend, especially since the majority of her Yale friends brought along their spouses and families.

In June 2004, we all celebrated Mom's 70th birthday by gathering in Crested Butte, Colorado for a three-day weekend. Mom had proclaimed that what she really wanted as a gift was a weekend with her grandchildren and daughters and their significant others. I learned afterward, however, that it had been a very trying time for Molly. Dave told me that she had been despondent when they returned to their hotel room after our family dinner the first night.

"She started crying, and she almost never cried," said Dave. "She said, 'When I was growing up I was the oldest, but now it's like I'm the baby.' It was one of those times she was very cognizant of her situation; that she was the one most needing help and not the one most able to help."

Dave said she felt "reduced" by her sisters, that we were all "so normal and accomplished," he said, using Molly's words. "In a group situation like that, she sometimes doesn't feel like she's really able to join in."

My heart sank to hear how she'd felt. I'd been thrilled to see her so happy; she seemed delighted to be with Dave and her extended family. Even though the revelation made me sad, I was impressed she felt safe enough with Dave to share her feelings with him and that he was able to get her to talk about them. *That* was positive.

I know Mom and I both told Dave whenever we could how much we appreciated his kindness and patience with Molly, because we knew it wasn't always easy for him. Dave took it in stride and was remarkably steady. He said she had a lovely sweet side, but the challenge was that her brain worked in such inconsistent ways. "She'll be clever and witty," he said, "then a minute later, she can't be reasoned with."

They'd recently visited some of Dave's friends at their lakeside house. "Molly was pretty crabby and refused to go swimming with everyone else or even wade in the shallow water," Dave said. "She said she didn't like swimming!"

I told him that when I'd suggested to Molly a year before that she start sketching again, she told me she hated doing art. "But during her rehab, Molly swam well and also did some good drawing," I said. "My theory is that she fears not doing these things like she used to. She doesn't want to know any more of what she's lost. This way she remains in her pre-injury 'before' life, where she'll always be a great swimmer and an excellent artist."

My guesswork about Molly, however, wasn't helpful to her. About a week later, she told me that she wasn't doing her volunteer work at the cat shelter anymore, but wouldn't say why. I was afraid she'd been unkind to the shelter's staff and customers, as she'd done at the vet clinic a couple of years before.

"No, that wasn't it," Mom told me. "Dave and I compared notes on this one. When she'd go to the clinic, she'd do a good job. But then she'd forget to go again, or she'd do something else instead, and she'd never call to let them know."

Dave said as discouraged as Molly was about being told by the shelter not to return to volunteer, she was also quite lucid about her situation. She told Dave, "This really sucks. I got fired from a volunteer job."

Meanwhile, Mom continued to work with Dr. Carlson to fine-tune Molly's drugs to help her be more consistent and get along better in the world. She'd make notes about Molly's behavior and any problems, and then she'd share them, along with Dave's, Lis's, and even my "long distance" observations with Dr. Carlson when she and Molly would go for appointments every couple of months. The complexity of brain chemistry and Molly's evolving ways make delicate tinkering of her medicines a necessary and ongoing balancing act.

We've learned there can be serious consequences when Molly's brain chemistry falls out of whack. In the autumn of 2004, Molly found herself in a courtroom in front of a judge. In a burst of anger, she'd scraped her keys along the length of a shiny new pick-up truck because she didn't like the fact that the vehicle was not in a parking space at the gym and she had to walk around it. The owner of the truck happened to be in the driver's seat and saw Molly "key gouge" his truck. He jumped out and confronted her. Molly was instantly contrite saying, "I'm sorry, I'm so sorry. I'll pay for it." But the man had already called the police. A report was filed and Molly had to go to court.

Molly's lawyer explained to the judge that Molly was severely brain injured and also bipolar and stated that with one of her medicines, if she got too much it made her irritable and unstable. The judge accepted the explanation but the incident became part of the court record. Several months later, Molly presented a letter showing she'd paid to repair the man's truck and the record was cleared.

When Dr. Carlson asked Molly how she felt just before she scraped the truck, she said, "I felt like my head was going to explode." Such descriptions help him make appropriate modifications to her drug regime.

That autumn, I began to write this book. Molly was flattered when I told her I was going to write her story. My family and friends were extremely supportive. And I had no idea what I was getting myself into, but I dove in.

It was also around this time, too, that Dave was putting up with a lot more crankiness from Molly. It is, unfortunately, typical human behavior that over time we often take a situation or a person for granted. On top of that, it is brain-injured behavior that Molly wasn't aware of her increasing grouchiness toward Dave or how it was tainting their time together.

I happened to call her at home soon after they'd had an argument. She said she'd "really messed up" and was "very sad because Dave may not like me anymore." I suggested she talk with Dave in a day or two and apologize. Molly shifted. "I didn't do anything, Smith!" she snapped. "I don't need to apologize. I didn't do anything wrong!"

Mom said Molly was very clingy with Dave; she was almost always at his house and with him nearly every evening. Mom noticed, too, she'd become fretful and insecure about her self-image and was acting out by being bossy and bitchy to her, but especially to Dave.

Eventually, Dave suggested it would be good for both of them if Molly spent some time away from him and did things with other friends. The problem was that Molly had not made other friends. Even after years of Mom's help, Molly did very little to create or nurture any friendships. I was getting used to the one-sidedness of my relationship with post-brain injury Molly even though I still missed pre-brain injury Molly, my close sister and go-to friend. I figured it was the lopsidedness of a relationship with Molly, in addition to her testy attitude, that was troubling Dave. Molly needed to have her own interests apart from him.

On a suggestion from Lis, and some encouragement from Mom and Dave, Molly was convinced that she could become a docent at the Denver Zoo.

"She's always been interested in wild animals, especially big cats," Mom said. "And she enjoys being a student, and directed, rote learning is good for her."

"I think it's a great idea," I replied. "Besides, she loves a challenge."

Molly began the extensive, yearlong training in the summer of 2005. This project gave her a place to be a couple of days a week, and a lot of studying and memorization to do. It also gave her a mission and a goal.

It didn't solve Molly's behavior problems with Dave though. Larry and I visited Denver that summer and we spent some time with them—making lunch at Dave's house, going to a baseball game, dinner out in LoDo. Molly had cheerful moments, but overall she was snipping at Dave so much it made us cringe. Dave was unflappable. He'd just ignore her snide comments and continue the conversation with us, or he'd answer something she was crabby about very calmly, just to neutralize her. Larry said he didn't know how Dave could stand it sometimes. It was unpleasant to hear.

Finally, I tried to connect with her right after a barrage of her bitching at Dave. She and I were walking downtown behind Larry and Dave. "You know, Molly, you should take it easy on Dave. You're really griping at him and it makes you sound so mean. And I know you aren't a mean person, but when you talk like that, you sound pretty vicious."

"I'm not doing anything! I don't have to take it easy. What do you know anyway? I'm fine, Lyrysa, I'm fine!" she fired off. "So don't worry about it, OK?"

I told myself: This is brain injury. This is brain injury. I took a deep breath. "I just want you to know how you sound, Molly, so you're aware of how you come off to others, especially to Dave," I said, softly.

"Yeah, whatever, Smith. I am aware. I already know how I come off to Dave, so just don't worry about it," she snapped. Molly often grabs and reuses words she's just heard. They bounce back in your face like blinding lights in a rearview mirror.

"I do worry about it, Smith, I care about you," I said. But Molly stomped off.

I was reminded how uncomfortable it is to confront my sister about her behavior. Forget any notion of helping her. Forget having a rational discussion about how she might do better. Just mentioning something to her is an event to dread. Worst of all, I knew she truly loved Dave, but she didn't understand how damaging her grouchy behavior toward him was. Her anger was destructive and she didn't know it.

Mom continued to look for ways to involve Molly in activities that would broaden her world and not directly involve Dave. Mom was an active member of Rotary and she asked Molly if she wanted to become a Rotarian, too.

"Oh, Mom, do you think I could?" Molly said. Mom thought it'd probably never crossed her mind that she could be a Rotarian.

"I'm certain our group would be delighted to have you as a member," Mom replied.

Molly attended several luncheons as Mom's guest, got to know everyone, and in November, presented her vocational talk to the group. Dave had helped her put it together and she took the task seriously. Mom said Molly delivered her talk beautifully, describing her education, professional life, family, marriage, and the accident that changed everything. In closing, Molly said:

> "...Despite my brain injury, and with the love and support of my wonderful family, I am able to cherish each and every day. I wear a baseball cap that states, 'Life is good!' and I know that to be true. I am proud and honored to be a Rotarian and thank you for accepting me as a member."

"She had everyone in tears," Mom said. "And she was overwhelmed with compliments when she finished.

Being a Rotarian is great for Molly—the weekly meetings, charitable projects to participate in, a place of belonging, and the opportunity for actions that "build goodwill and friendships" and that are "beneficial to all," as the Rotary creed says.

Unfortunately, the erosion of Molly and Dave's relationship did not abate and their spats became more frequent. "We were walking to the Broncos game on a nice winter day and she was fuming because I'd put a new roll of toilet paper on backwards in my bathroom," Dave said. "I told her to change it anytime and I'd be fine. But she got stuck and it's hard to calm her down after something like that."

I told Dave that immovable anger is part of brain injury. "When she's driving, she'll yell at other drivers and won't let it go; or if I'm driving or Glen, she'll complain and seethe for hours," I said.

"It's just that most people respond to her so positively. She can be charming and funny—she can be spectacular," Dave said. "But if she's tired or frustrated, she breaks down and loses it so fast. It's very hard to get beyond it, and it takes a lot of energy out of me."

"I know it's exhausting for Mom, too." I told him. "You and Mom are closest to her and you get the worst of her. She's gotten used to you, Dave. So she lets down and isn't careful about being nice. It makes me sad to know she treats you as badly as she does her family sometimes."

Shortly after Christmas 2005, I learned from Dr. Lo that he was going to be at the Copper Mountain ski resort in Colorado in February for a ski vacation and conference about brain injury. I planned a visit to Denver with Larry so I could pick up Dr. Lo at the airport, drive him to Copper Mountain, and interview him. Mom hosted a celebration dinner at the resort for Dr. Lo and our family. Dave came with Molly and she was delightful. She looked beautiful and was on her best behavior. Dr. Lo was happy that his star patient was doing well. It was incredible to see Dr. Lo and Molly sitting together at the head of the table, chatting and laughing, a full 11 years after they'd first come together, with Molly in a coma and declared clinically dead.

During my conversation with Dr. Lo before dinner, I told him about Molly's difficulties and how they affect her daily life. He wasn't surprised by her erratic, moody behavior, her anger problems, and that she was most harsh to those she's closest to.

"It's that part of her brain, primarily her frontal lobe, that isn't functioning as a moderating influence as it did before," Dr. Lo reminded me. "So she has real trouble managing her frustration. Her anger comes out of that."

"It just makes her so hard to be around sometimes," I said. "And I don't know what to do or how to respond—even if I *want* to be helpful to her. Sometimes, I admit, I just walk away, and that's terrible, too."

"It may not matter anyway. She may just be mad for a while, until enough time goes by," Dr. Lo said. "Just try to remember her brain injury has let loose the limiters in the frontal lobe; they run wild, unrestrained. That's when her mean streaks come out."

I explained that Mom and Lis were working with Molly's psychiatrist to fine-tune her medications to find the best mix for her.

"It's a struggle, I'm sure, and it will always be a balancing act," he said. "But it's worthwhile because it really could improve her behavior. And that's what it's all about—for her, and all of you."

Molly and Dave had made arrangements to stay the weekend at Copper Mountain and ski, but Molly's behavior changed markedly. "It was awful," Dave said. "She was angry and complaining, and always mad at me.

"Finally, when we got back to my house, I said, 'Are you ever going to be happy with me again?' She yelled, 'No!' and stormed out." He called her the next day and said they had to spend some time apart.

Within a few days, he recognized that even with the occasional bright spots, his relationship with Molly was not right for him. "I always accepted the extra care and patience she required, but I was simply worn out by her mood swings and tantrums. I realized I couldn't be happy with her when she was more and more negative and angry—it was draining."

Only Mom, with her unshakable commitment as mother, had spent as much time with Molly and coping with her deficits. And Molly could not be what Dave ultimately wanted—the person he wanted to marry. Molly wanted to be married to him, but Dave knew he couldn't spend the rest of his life with her. I thought he had to have wondered for months, "Why am I putting up with this?" But for a long time, he did.

"Molly's a *good* person. She had an excuse for the problems I had with her," he said. "A terrible injury from that stupid heater. A stupid *heater.* It's heartbreaking. I want her life to be as good as it can be. She has it within her to be wonderful."

Dave broke up with Molly on February 19th, 2006. Two years and two months exactly to the day they met, Molly observed.

Although she loved Dave, I don't believe Molly ever understood how hard on him she was. Even before her brain injury, Molly could be harsh; I'd experienced her severe moods and it was always disconcerting. But Dave was her boyfriend, a relationship by choice, and he had choices to make. If I'd met post-brain injury Molly at a cocktail party in her negative mood, I wouldn't *choose* to be with her again. But she's my only big sister. I don't have another choice. I know we love each other, but our relationship is up to me.

Molly was hurt by the break-up and had a hard time letting go. For several weeks, she'd email Dave saying how much she missed him and she'd close her emails with *"I love you."* In one she wrote that she missed him even though he did not miss her. Then she added, *"Why do I sound so pathetic when I say that?"* I thought it was pretty brave self-awareness.

Mom had assured Dave that Molly would be OK and move on, but she expressed to me her concern that Molly might interpret it as another man "abandoning" her—Dad left, Walt died, and Dave broke up with her. But I never heard Molly talk about it that way. She did say to Larry, about a year later, after he described losing a great fish off his line on a recent fishing trip, "her big one got away, too."

Sadly, Molly did not stick with most of the activities she'd done with Dave. Her skis and bicycle hang on hooks in the garage, although it's probably best that she didn't do these sports by herself since her balance is a little dicey. But she didn't join a group or find a friend to go with.

She also stopped tutoring with Big Brothers/Big Sisters, which particularly disappointed me. I thought it was a perfect activity for her—to mentor and help others, be appreciated, feel valued for her intellect, and most of all, to have a purpose she could take pride in. I tried a few times to get her to tutor again, but she flatly refused. "I don't do that anymore," she said.

Molly did stay with the Rotary Club because Mom is very involved in it. She rides with Mom to the weekly lunch meetings, but will also drive herself, if necessary. She participates in Rotary service projects, many of which Mom has an organizational hand in, and Mom, Glen, and Molly even travel to attend some of the annual Rotary International meetings. Molly's fellow Rotarians are her friends, even if just at Rotary gatherings.

Molly also completed her zoo docent training in June 2006 and she volunteers at the zoo on Mondays. She has a "flexible" schedule, so she arrives sometime in the morning and usually stays the entire day. The zoo doesn't rely on her to be there, but appreciates her assistance when she is. And she takes pride in her work. She wears a khaki docent's uniform, a name tag, and a large button that says, "Ask Me." She happily answers visitors' questions about the animals, and also directs visitors to the nearest snack bar or bathroom, accurately, but a little less cheerfully.

Molly especially likes working in the areas for the large cats, and recently, I spent an afternoon with her at the snow leopard enclosure. The adult female had three romping kittens. They were a fabulous attraction at the zoo, and Molly reveled in answering the same questions over and over again for hours as the crowds moved through. How old are the kittens? Where is the father? What do they eat? Her answers were knowledgeable and her utter delight in the snow leopards was contagious. When I'm in Denver, I always try to spend time with Molly at the zoo.

Mom steadfastly looks for ways to help Molly engage with other people and make friends. But if she connects with someone, it's not for very long.

She can be excellent in the moment and very amiable. But she still doesn't give attention to her relationships, even the "built-in" ones with me or her other sisters.

I understand it's her brain injury, but I keep believing, right or wrong, she can learn to do better. Meanwhile, I try to shift my expectations. I don't look for a Christmas gift or birthday card from Molly anymore. They dwindled and then finally petered out over the years since her injury. I don't anticipate a call or email from her unless I call or email her first.

It's not possible to sit down and have a heart-to-heart with her either. It's just not who this Molly is. I can tell her what's on my mind and how I'm feeling, but she'll usually be distracted and won't focus, listen, or respond appropriately. She's not inclined or, more likely, not able to share her feelings very well or to be mindful or self-aware. What is it, I wonder, in the human brain that generates contemplation?

I think what's missing in her is empathy. It's not a regular part of her consciousness and this changes the type of sharing she's capable of. I still listen for a reflective moment from her. It feels like the ever-hopeful, quiet, aching waiting of trying to get a chickadee to eat sunflower seeds from my extended hand; she stays in view, watching you and chirping, but rarely alights.

However, the more Molly is out and about and interacting, the better. Mom loves movies and the theater and she, Glen, and Molly go frequently. These outings are excellent for Molly because she really enjoys them and for the length of the film or play, she will pay close attention. I believe this helps her with face-to-face conversations because she practices focusing, listening, and thinking about what someone else is expressing.

I learn a lot from Mom; and she's learned another language—the one Molly speaks, physically and verbally. Mom is adept at deciphering signals in Molly's behavior or in what she says. Is she unusually tired or grumpy? Is she using odd words? Is she stumbling when she walks? Is she missing her regular appointments? Is she making excuses or too quiet?

Mom is around Molly nearly every day. She knows which problems truly matter and must be dealt with. She's also pretty good at letting go of the relentless minor annoyances. She knows Molly's sulking and bad humor today will change to something brighter tomorrow.

For my part, I try to keep a good sense of humor with Molly, especially self-deprecating humor. This eases the way between us and seems to help

Molly feel comfortable with me; I think she hears me more. I point out the crazy things that happen to me, the mistakes I make, all my goof-ups. She'll laugh at me and with me and it makes us more alike.

I often say to Molly, "Well, Smith, that's just my part of our family brain injury messing me up."

"Yeah, I know how that goes," she'll say. "I got a big brain injury, Smith, a much bigger, badder, better one than yours."

"Maybe you do, Smith," I'll say, "but you're not alone. Maybe one day I'll catch up."

When it's especially hard for me with Molly, I repeat to myself, "this is brain injury, this is brain injury." Then I smile at myself—and my own piece of brain injury.

Coping with any personal relationship is just that—personal. It takes making adjustments and course corrections along the way that are distinct and geared precisely to the other person. This is just a very different journey than the one Molly and I started decades ago.

T h i r t e e n

IN July 2006, Mom was diagnosed with breast cancer. Her email to me, Sara, and Mary K. and was very composed. She wrote, *"I'm not as terrified as I probably should be."*

I didn't freak out, but I was scared and called her immediately. She explained she'd had an ultrasound and a needle biopsy because her doctor didn't like the look of something on her recent mammogram. Her cancer was a "1" on the scale of 1 to 4; it was caught early. Mom had been through melanoma in the mid-1970s, and after surgeries and treatment she'd come through it well.

"This is my second bout with cancer, and like before, I feel terrific and I can't believe I'm sick," she said.

"That's good," I said. "But I want to come be with you for whatever treatments you're going to need."

"Well, I'm optimistic that we'll nip this in the bud. And I'm hoping we can limit the treatment to radiation so I don't have to face hair loss from chemo," Mom said.

"It doesn't matter about your hair, Mom, I just want you healthy. Besides, you're beautiful no matter what," I said. "I'm concerned about the stress you have to contend with all the time. Have you talked with Molly yet?"

"I told her about it over cups of tea right here at the kitchen table last night," Mom said. "Just the two of us."

"How did she react?"

"She was excellent," Mom said. "I mean, I could see in her face that she was shocked and pretty concerned. After I told her everything, she was quiet for a minute. Then she asked, 'What does this mean?'"

"That's a thoughtful question," I said.

"I thought so, too," Mom said. "I told her, 'It means you'll have to help me some.' Then she sort of straightened up and she set her hands on the table and looked directly at me and said, 'Don't worry, Mom. I'll help you. You know I will. I'll help take care of you. I'll help you get better.'" Mom paused. "She meant it, I could tell. And it meant the world to me. She'll be OK."

"I *know* she will, Mom. I can help with that," I said. "I'm glad to hear she's sympathetic—and resolved. That's a powerful thing. Now, we need to focus on you."

"I plan to take this in stride and fight it with gusto," Mom said, "just like I did before."

Mom had a couple of surgeries that summer. Glen was helpful at home and Sara and Mary K. each drove to Denver several times to be with her for a few days. I flew to Denver in October and spent several weeks going with her to her daily radiation treatments and being with Molly at a time when Mom needed to rest and heal. It was important to me that Mom felt she could do that and I wanted to be sure she was relieved of as much stress as possible.

And Molly was good, especially with the little things—bringing Mom a book from upstairs, setting the table, getting the mail, and most of all by simply being sweet and attentive. "She really enjoyed having her sisters around more, too," Mom said. "Each of you came and helped take care of me, and that really helped Molly."

After a few months, Molly decided Mom needed a cat on her lap. "An important part of healing," Molly said. Mom's cats, Mama and Lil' Darlin' had died a year or so before; each had lived to be about 20. Mom had not gotten another cat mostly because Glen didn't like having cats in the house. As a farm boy from Iowa, he believed cats belonged in the barn.

But Molly convinced Mom and Glen to take a look at the animal shelter. They found Tally, a fluff ball of love. Even now, the moment Glen sits down, Tally is in his lap. She won him over early, and he pets her as if he's always been a cat-person. A couple weeks later, Molly and Mom went back to the shelter and chose Pepper to be a cat companion to Tally. Molly's idea really helped, and Mom's house is once again a cat-happy home.

After the surgeries and treatments were completed, Mom told me the worst part had been hearing the diagnosis. "'You have breast cancer.' That was horrible," she said. "But then I thought, OK, now how do I deal with it. I got a super medical team and I listened and did what they told me to. And I counted on all of you for your support and I got that 100 percent. The biggest thing was that you all helped with Molly. I didn't worry about her; I concentrated on me. And she was fine."

Once again, we all learned something new about Molly: She was able to cooperate when called upon (and reminded a few times). Again I witnessed Mom's great positiveness through another hard experience. Her courage and confidence are endlessly inspiring.

"I couldn't do what Mom's doing," Molly told me when I was visiting in October. Mom was napping and we were in the kitchen making dinner. "It's too icky and it takes too long. She's really tired a lot. *A lot!* I couldn't do it."

I stopped chopping carrots and looked at Molly. "But Smith, you already have. Look at you! You've also come through a really tough, huge problem, and you've done really well."

"Not like cancer. That's much scarier. It's growing. That cancer stuff—growing. Much worse than a stupid brain injury."

"Well, I think you're both amazing. Totally amazing," I said.

"No, not *totally*, Smith," she said. "I'm just a half-brain."

"You have a whole brain, Molly. And you do great," I said, cheerfully. At that moment, I missed the salad bowl and spilled my pile of chopped carrots. They slid off the cutting board, rolled across the counter, and scattered over the floor.

Molly burst into laughter. "Yeah, I'm totally better than you sometimes!"

We giggled, crawling around on our hands and knees picking up carrots, with Molly teasing me the whole time.

I'm always glad when Molly is playful. It's who she was—and is. She still has a great wit, so I try to find lighthearted paths through our conversations. Hers isn't the same clever humor she used to dish out; it's sillier. Her laughter is similar, but rowdier. But humor eases her way in social settings and helps her to engage with others. And people notice. When Molly is joyful, for just about any reason, she can be radiant.

She celebrates other people's good news, too, almost always without resentment or sullenness. Even other people's romances matter to her.

Sara and Jonathan were married in a small ceremony in May 2007. In June, at their home in Glenwood Springs, they hosted a dinner for their two families. The next afternoon, they held a big block party for family and friends. Through it all, Molly was genuinely happy for Sara and Jonathan and delighted in their marriage.

Over the long weekend, Molly also got to spend time with Dad and Martha, whom she hadn't been with in a while, and we all enjoyed being with Abi, age 16, and Jacob, age 11, getting to know Jonathan's family, and meeting many of Sara and Jonathan's friends. Molly had a few grumpy moments, but most of the time she was in high spirits.

"It's good to see so much love, isn't it?" I said, as we watched Sara and Jonathan together surrounded by friends at the block party.

"Yes, it is," Molly said. "I believe in love."

I turned and smiled at her. "That's great, Molly. Well said. There's power in that belief."

"That's right. I believe in that, too," she said, still looking at Sara and Jonathan.

It was such a hopeful quality coming from her—to believe in love. She loves Mom and tells her. She loves her family members and almost never closes a phone call or email without saying so. She showers love on her cats. It's painful to know what Molly has lost, but I'm grateful for what's present and possible.

In early July, I called Mom and told her that even though we'd all just been together for Sara and Jonathan's wedding party, I thought we needed to celebrate Molly's 50th birthday in September. I'd only just realized the milestone event was coming up.

"There were so many days, Mom, when we didn't think she'd make 38… or 40! And now she's turning 50 and I think we need to celebrate her getting there. It's an achievement."

"You're right, Lyrysa. Do you think we can get everyone in the family to come to Denver again for a party?"

"Oh, why not? After all, she's only going to turn 50 once and it's a biggie, especially for her. We can let her know we're looking forward to her *next* 50 years."

We called everyone, made flight reservations, and organized a 50th birthday celebration weekend in Molly's honor in Denver. It helped that her birthday, September 4th, happened to fall, as it often does, near the Labor Day holiday weekend.

Dad and Martha and Larry and I came in on the same flight, and Mom and Molly picked us up at the airport. In the car, Mom shared the news that Walt's mom, Ah Mee Weber had died. Mom had received a note from one of Walt's sisters the week before. Ah Mee had been sick with a heart ailment but was doing better and was at home where her daughters were taking care of her. She died unexpectedly after breakfast one morning. It must have hit Walt's sisters very hard. They'd experienced so much loss.

We were terribly sad to hear this news, and Molly, who had known of Ah Mee's death for several days, was still mournful. Her eyes were glassy as she looked out the car window. I imagined she felt an important connection to Walt was gone. Ah Mee was always so kind to her, and they had an easy-going comfortableness together. They'd shared a unique bond.

We had a cookout in Mom's backyard the first night and an official birthday dinner, complete with cake, candles, and singing, at Molly's favorite restaurant in Denver the next night. We spent the weekend hanging out, taking long walks, and talking and laughing together. We even got a personal tour of the Denver Zoo with Molly in her docent uniform as our guide, answering all of our questions and some from other visitors, too.

Molly did get confused a few times during the weekend. She put on her docent uniform on Sunday morning, the day before we'd planned to go to the zoo. When I reminded her that our plan for that morning was to do an exercise walk together, she got tetchy and refused to change and wore her uniform instead of workout clothes for the walk. And she was almost late to her own birthday party at the restaurant because she adamantly insisted she had plenty of time to shower and get dressed, even at the last minute, when she clearly did not.

Most of the time, though, she was cheerful and happy to be the center of attention, and we were happy to celebrate her 50th. When we had to leave, Molly was grateful and even cried a little as we hugged and said good bye.

The year 2007 continued to be monumental. As I was researching this book, I sought out experts in CO poisoning, brain injury, and HBO, and I came across Dr. Lin Weaver and his recently published study about CO deaths and injuries in hotel rooms. Several years before, Dr. Lo had suggested that I check out Dr. Weaver's work—research about the healing potential of HBO on brain injury, especially from CO poisoning.

I emailed a synopsis of Molly and Walt's accident to Dr. Weaver and asked if they'd been part of the data collected for his hotel CO study. Meanwhile, I gathered via the Internet Dr. Weaver's many articles about HBO and CO poisoning.

His email back confirmed that Molly and Walt were part of his study. I was surprised that I felt startled. The incident that had seemed only for our family and small circle of friends was, in fact, part of large research project to change CO detector policy nationwide and enlighten others to the dangers of CO.

In his email, Dr. Weaver said he was moved by Molly and Walt's story and was glad to hear about her remarkable rehabilitation. From their data, of course, he had no idea what had happened to that female subject in California since she'd been plucked barely alive from the hotel room where her husband had died.

He then asked me if Molly might be interested in being a subject in a feasibility study he'd just begun regarding HBO for people with "chronic stable brain injuries." He wanted to learn if HBO therapy for people who already had a brain injury might have an impact on, and might possibly improve, the individual's mental and physical functioning. Dr. Weaver stressed that he did not know if HBO would help the subjects or not, but he thought Molly would be an excellent candidate for his study.

I'd looked around many times over the years to find a clinical trial that Molly could be a part of—as a way for her to contribute, for all us to give back and to learn—to everyone's benefit. I'd never found any. I leapt at this opportunity. I told Dr. Weaver I was almost certain Molly would want to be a part of his study, and I felt sure my mother would want her to be, too.

He said the difficulty might be that Molly would need to be in Salt Lake City for over three months so that she could receive the 60 consecutive HBO treatments—once a day, five days a week. Also, Molly would undergo several days of testing of her cognitive, emotional, and physical abilities just before the HBO treatments began, just after the 60 treatments were finished, and then again six months after that. I told Dr. Weaver I understood the logistics and the commitment required and I'd call my family and get back to him.

Mom was thrilled about the study and the chance for more HBO, and Molly said, "I'd like to do more HBO and stuff. They can study me, if they want. Why, I'm fascinating!"

"Yes, you are, Smith," I said. "First of all, you're alive. And you're doing so well."

"Well, Walt didn't do so well," Molly's voice trailed off.

"No, but even though he died, Smith, he was part of Dr. Weaver's other study about CO poisoning in hotel rooms. You and Walt both were, so hopefully, you have both already helped other people not to get CO poisoning," I said, gently.

"I hope so," said Molly. "That would be good—to not have it happen to anyone else."

Once Molly got off the phone, Mom said she'd welcome more HBO for Molly, which might improve her cognitive abilities, and for Molly to be thoroughly evaluated again.

"It will be interesting to see what they discover," I said. "I feel pretty hopeful. And really, any bump up, any improvement at all would be great."

"You got that right," Mom said. "And as Dr. Lo once said, we have nothing to lose and everything to gain!"

Mom and I scrambled to pull everything together so that Molly's three-months could begin with the next available opening in the study's schedule, only a few weeks away.

Mom learned of an apartment complex that allowed for a short lease and was not too far from the hospital's HBO center where Molly would need to be every morning. I photocopied all of Molly's pertinent medical records, HBO reports, and medical and psychological evaluations over the past 12 years and sent them to Dr. Weaver's lead researcher, Sue Churchill. She conducted a telephone interview with Molly, Mom, and me to be sure Molly would be able to follow through and complete the study.

Mom and I both spoke with Molly to help her understand the commitment she was being asked to make, and she was a little nervous at first. But she was genuinely pleased about making a valuable contribution to medical research about brain injury and HBO. Mom helped her understand that the 60 HBO treatments could also be really good for her. I emphasized that she alone in our family could do this important work.

"I can't do it, Mom can't do it, none of your other sisters can do it," I said. "You are in a unique position to help other people for years to come by being in the study. I know you'd like that, Smith, and you'll be making a fantastic contribution to science."

"I like all of that," she said. "I'm going to bring Honey with me. That will be a fantastic contribution, too." Molly was convinced. As long as she could bring Honey, her elderly cat, with her, then she was willing to do it.

Mom worked out the finances—travel, the apartment, rented furniture, utilities, living expenses. We also had to pay for the 60 HBO treatments Molly would receive, which were offered at a substantial discount. But it was still a big check to write.

Sue Churchill asked if Molly would agree to be a part of a companion study, too, with a neurologist at a hospital in Las Vegas. Molly would receive two functional MRIs (or fMRIs), one before and one after her HBO treatments in Salt Lake City. The fMRIs and airfare to fly Molly and Mom back and forth to Las Vegas would be covered by the study.

The technology for fMRI was in development when we were at Loma Linda in 1995. The scan shows neural activity, allowing scientists to watch various parts of the brain fire up and perform in a full color display as a patient thinks or performs certain activities. Mom thought it would be fascinating to learn more about how Molly's brain was working and Molly agreed.

Finally, Mom and I worked out a schedule for Salt Lake City. Molly's HBO treatments were to begin in late September and conclude just before Christmas. Mom spent the first month with her, then I arrived and stayed for five weeks so Mom could go home to Denver. Then Mom returned to replace me and finish the project.

Overall, Molly was a trooper and went along with the tedious routine of being awoken early every morning, going to the hospital with Mom or me, and getting in an HBO chamber for two hours. But Mom and I both experienced days when it didn't matter what we did, Molly was going to be irritable.

Mom sent me an email one afternoon; it was the only way she could vent privately in the small one-bedroom apartment.

> "Molly is lying on her bed reading one of her Harry Potter books, which she seems to really enjoy, but she's very angry because the mail hasn't arrived with her repaired iPod in it. When I try to cheer her up, she snaps at me or mocks me. Ouch!" Mom wrote. "This is one of those days that I'd like to pawn her off on someone else."

Other days, Molly's mood was better and she'd be pleasant. I knew it wasn't easy for her to be away from her spacious home, her nice life, and her independence for three months. After all, Mom and I traded places in Salt

Lake City, while Molly stayed cooped up in the apartment. So we did our best to boost her spirits.

We kept up with emails on our laptops, including Molly, if we reminded her to. Mom and I also asked friends to send post cards and greeting cards to Molly, which we hung all over the apartment. Molly would go with great anticipation to our mailbox every afternoon. It was wonderful when there would be a card for her, especially one with a cat. I took to sending cards to her myself when I was home in New York and even when I was with her in Salt Lake City, knowing how important it was to her.

It helped, too, that Molly got into a routine, whether with Mom or me. Each morning after her HBO treatment, we would stop at Starbucks and she would get her favorite frappe coffee, just as she would nearly every day in Denver. At the apartment, Molly spent a lot of time listening to the iPod Sara had given her, loaded with thousands of songs she loved. Mom emailed me during the first month:

> *"Molly loves music. She sang herself to sleep last night listening to her iPod. We should never underestimate the impact of music in Molly's life. I forgot how soothing it is to her. I can now understand why she leaves her radio on all the time at home in Denver."*

My first week with Molly in Salt Lake City, I got the idea for a "chain of achievement"—a paper-loop chain of inspirational words—and I got Molly hooked on doing it. Each morning, after the hospital and Starbucks, over our breakfasts of fruit and yogurt, I'd ask her what she was thinking about and what her "word for the day" should be. Most mornings, she'd chat for a while and eventually arrive at her word; sometimes she'd just blurt one out. She'd write it on one of the paper strips I'd prepared, and I'd help her tape it in a loop onto the chain. *Intent. Create. Family. Energy. Courage. Kitties. Gratitude. Catitude. Joy. Accomplishment.*

Molly liked having a visual reference for her ongoing effort. I hung the chain from a ceiling corner and each day it got a little longer. Soon it stretched across the dining room. I used it to encourage her to talk about what she was feeling. She used it to count the links and count down her 60 days of HBO.

Meanwhile, we found ways to feel at home in Salt Lake City. Molly and Mom located some good restaurants, and Molly and I discovered the discount night at the movie theater. In the afternoons, Molly would read and nap while

I worked. I made vegetarian suppers and she came to love my wilted salads (she referred to them as "withered"). On weekends, when she didn't have HBO, we would explore the beautiful state parks and little towns in the mountains.

Honey was the perfect, cuddly companion for Molly. She was always on her lap and slept with her at night. Molly's daily routine also included taking care of Honey, which gave Molly a focus. And we all loved having a cat around to make the sparse apartment feel like a cozy home.

During the three months of HBO sessions, Mom noticed that Molly's balance seemed improved and thought her walking was smoother. I noticed that Molly's short-term memory seemed sharper and she was reading with more enthusiasm, although part of that credit may go to J.K. Rowling. Even though some days Molly was agitated and mean, she was often calm and bright. I reminded myself to be patient and realize that if there were improvements from the HBO sessions, they would probably surface later. I rooted for a positive accumulative effect—especially on her grouchy days.

Molly fulfilled her commitment and completed the 60 HBO treatments, all the testing and evaluations, and the fMRIs. After stopping to see Sara and Jonathan on their drive back to Denver, Mom and Molly got home on Christmas Eve.

I called Molly on Christmas and told her she was my hero for accomplishing the goal of finishing the study and for doing so much to help other people.

She laughed and said, "Oh, it wasn't hard. It took *forever*, but only *I* could do it. I was the only one in our family, anyway. I'm glad you and Mom took turns being with me and Honey."

Over the next months, I noticed Molly was more thoughtful and I felt she was also more willing to share. I realized these changes could have been a result of the bonding time we had in Salt Lake City, or just my relentless optimism, but I was glad to feel them no matter what.

From emails with Dr. Weaver, I learned his HBO study was complete. More than 50 people with brain injuries participated, analysis of the data is occurring, and results will be published in a journal. I'm looking forward to reading the report and Molly says she's proud to have contributed to the scientific research. She said she felt special to do something important. I told her that she's extraordinary and what she did will have a lasting positive impact.

Then, I thought to myself, the study was great for Molly because it gave her purpose.

F o u r t e e n

THOUGH I was far away in New York, I felt really connected to Molly and Mom. I was finally learning how to participate as a long distance caregiver, and our experience in Salt Lake City was good proving ground. Mom trusted me and Molly was getting used to me as I continued to figure out how to be helpful to both.

I was in touch with Mom frequently and persuaded her to delegate some tasks to me that I could do from home, such as research, emails, and phone calls to help keep my sister's logistics organized. I also started taking notes whenever I listen to Mom about her concerns about Molly. Then I'd email my notes to her so she could discuss those topics when she and Molly met with Molly's therapists and doctors.

Now, Mom turns to me as a sounding board and a good "ear." Anyone in Mom's position needs a place to download and vent, to discuss and dissect, to share victories and struggles. I'm learning not to offer ideas to solve problems unless Mom asks for my help; she needs me to listen, not fix things. Mom knows she can lean on me and that's a big step for us. I caregive the caregiver.

I also redoubled my efforts to connect with Molly, one-sided or not. I'm her second caregiver, but I'm always her sister first. I tell her I love her, always want to hear from her, and that I'm standing by for her.

I was far away, but I found ways to be close. I committed myself to offer care and comfort—to the one least likely to ask for it and to the one who didn't know to ask for it.

I'm also in training as I'm pulled along this path. Mom shares with me what she's learning, day-to-day, in all sorts of circumstances with Molly. It's essential preparation since I will stand in Mom's shoes one day.

Mom and I agreed that if I should outlive her or she is not able to help Molly anymore, then I would become Molly's primary caregiver and guardian. Next in line, potentially, would be Sara, then Mary K. Mom also arranged that whoever is caregiver will have ownership of Mom's house to live in, just a couple of doors away from Molly's. This established set-up works well in providing Molly as much independence as possible, but making caregiving and oversight easier and convenient, too.

Certainly, my life has seen many changes since my sister's accident. And there's more to come. I'll need to extricate myself from my life in New York and move to Denver in the not-too-distant future, find a job, and become an on-hand caregiver. It's possible that one day I may be living in Mom's house and taking care of Mom and Glen and Molly, even though as I write this Mom is healthy, vibrant, and strong.

It makes me sad to know I'll be farther away from Dad and Martha in Virginia, and from my friends in New York. I'll just have to get on a plane instead of a train to visit them, and I may need to bring Molly with me. It will be wonderful, though, to be closer to my younger sisters and their families.

It's also troubling that I don't know what will happen to my relationship with my boyfriend, Larry, who has his own home and his own life in New York. I don't know what will happen to my career, either, whether I'll be able to pursue the writing work I'd prefer to do.

Sometimes it's unnerving that none of this was my plan for my life. I never thought about caring for my older sister—my parents, yes, but Molly, no. I'll admit there are times when Mom calls and I wish I hadn't answered the phone. If I don't have the energy or the time, I'd rather not hear Mom's latest struggle with Molly, because, some days, I can't escape the discouragement and dread and fear that weigh down on me. It's hard to hear, hard to feel useful, and some days I just want to shove the millstone off my back.

Then I remember—Mom doesn't have that choice—and I snap out of it. I listen and I try to be positive. I take pride in being the best I can be for Mom and, therefore, for Molly. I have discovered the value of being present and responding.

I have always been a caregiver in my family—I recognize it is part of who I am. And Molly and I have been very close. Through the years, both before and after her brain injury, I've been there for her. But even so, this new role is not automatic for me; I'm growing into it. And I'll continue to shape it to work for me. It's more than destiny; it's what I can do.

It's been Mom's wish from the beginning that Molly's care not interrupt her sisters' lives. And Mom has worked diligently to master the situation. But it was never possible for any of us not to have our lives affected. And I have made the decision to be involved; to make Molly's well-being part of my life. An altered course by choice. I change my plans and my thinking all the time to accommodate my new priority—Molly's care. My choice influences how I spend my time, which jobs I go after, which career turns I take, where I live.

But Mom's selfless dedication to her oldest daughter has made it possible for her other daughters to live our lives without being constant caregivers, even if I am not totally carefree. I cannot overstate what Mom's sacrifice and devotion to Molly have meant, not just to my sister, but also to the opportunities and the choices I have in my own life today. Mom has been my biggest supporter in every way, in addition to everything else she does.

At times, I feel like I'm wearing a Janus mask, sad and happy at once. I miss the sister I once knew *and* I'm really interested in this unusual character who is my big sister. So, I stay connected. Emailing with Molly can be fascinating, especially when she flips my head around with an astute observation or sparkling comment. She says whatever's on her mind in her unique way. And she always closes with her characteristic line of x's and o's and her name.

To an email I wrote telling her about how good I always feel after exercising, she responded:

> *Yeah, I get it already. I know what you're trying to do, Smith, you're trying to make me exercise and feel good about me. Grrrrr.*
> *I like it when you're so much like me. I love you more than you can ever know. Extra immensely, I'm sure. I'm glad you're still my little sister. Life is surely rough, isn't it? Especially in my roughed up brain.*
> *xooxoxoxxxoooxsmith*

In an email I sent describing my efforts to find some good paying freelance jobs, I concluded by saying that she made my life wonderful. Molly responded:

> *Smith, you make my life confusing. I can tell ya', it does NOT pay to have a brain injury. I just read your nice email again. It*

brings to mind the effort I'll need to expend in simply responding to
you! I look forward to our next, future conversation, on whatever
topic it may be.

I love you anyway! xxooxoxooxoxxxxooxoxooxoxoxsmith

When I call Molly, I often end up leaving a message. She never calls me first, but every now and then she'll return a phone call. When I pick up the phone and hear her say, "Hi, Smith, what are you doing?" I feel like doing a victory dance.

I try to talk to her the way I used to, sister chat. I prompt her by yakking about my work or Larry, and then I'll ask her about her activities, people in her life, what's on her schedule, what she's thinking about, how she's feeling. She'll be pleasant, but give only short responses. I'll ask her opinion about something in my life, to give her an opportunity to advise me.

Most of the time, however, she doesn't discuss the topic I bring up. Instead, she'll talk about what her cats are doing at that moment, or what birds are on the feeders outside her window, or she'll read to me whatever is on the kitchen table in front of her. I listen, change gears, and ask questions about whatever she's focused on. She doesn't ask me questions, though, so the bonding feels thin; but we laugh and it's our time of sharing. And I'm realizing that this is OK. It's not an act, it's my relationship with Molly today. It's what we have.

It's true that sometimes staying in touch with Molly feels like just one more chore on my weekly to-do list. There's not an ongoing conversation or a strong feeling of connectedness between us. We do express a lot of genuine affection for each other, and that's no small thing.

For the first time in many years, she sent me a birthday card. I was stunned. I was thrilled! Mom says Molly remembers everyone's birthdays; she never forgets a date. She just doesn't plan ahead to send a card or take the initiative to call.

The birthday card arrived only a week late, in two envelopes, like a wedding invitation. It featured a picture of two kittens on the front, of course. Inside Molly had drawn hearts and written three distinct short messages. It appeared she might have started and stopped writing the card a few times. Sadly, I noticed her handwriting had shrunken and deteriorated badly since the last time I'd seen it, and she had trouble spelling "birthday" both times she wrote the word. Still, her "kitten kaboodle" birthday card, with its tiny messages of love, all with exclamation points, was the best gift she could have given me.

I used to think about changing my expectations about post-injury Molly, now I'm learning not to have any. I'm getting used to this Molly. She is, still, my only big sister.

Once people know even a little bit of Molly's story, they almost always ask, "How is Molly today? What is she like now?" I've formulated a quick description, but it's only a sketch. The full picture of Molly is manifold. I want to accurately represent her, the beauty and the beast. Her story, like many, has light and shadows. I won't reduce the magnitude of her injury or the severity of her disability and its impact. And because it's me describing her, I have to be optimistic, too. Molly is complex and constantly changing. But her story is always about life. A big, full life, which is what I want to say.

For what she's been through, Molly is astonishing. Just looking at her, you wouldn't know what had happened. You see a whole Molly, physically all there and apparently OK. It's not easy to grasp the profound injury at work. Molly almost always wears her pretty hair in a ponytail, topped with a baseball cap, no matter the occasion. She always carries a water bottle everywhere she goes even though she doesn't often sip. She chooses to wear casual clothes unless Mom works with her to dress up for an event. She is healthy and robust, keeps busy with a variety of activities, and has her own life. A very good life.

Molly endeavors to hide her brain injury, and she's often successful. She smiles, she's lively, and she can be charming. People don't know the severity of her disability because it isn't immediately obvious. The invisibility of her injury is partly where her self-reliance comes from, but also her frustration and anger. It's easy to overestimate her, and she's reluctant to ask for help when she needs it. She has a lot of autonomy, but she is not self-sufficient.

Since her injury, Molly has a different walk and body posture. Even after all these years, I'm still getting used to her changed physicality. No longer the smooth, strong athlete; but instead a determined, somewhat awkward, sometimes lopsided and teetering presence. She struggles with the steadiness of her gait. I have trouble recognizing her from a couple of blocks away walking toward me. It isn't the image of Molly that I remember.

Sometimes on a smooth surface and without interference, Molly trips and does a "face plant." Mom has learned that a rash of these forward stumbles or falls often signals a need to adjust her medications. The drugs that level her behavior can also warp her balance.

Molly has memory deficits that become conspicuous when she loses her words or thoughts mid-sentence, forgets what she's doing in the midst of doing it, or has scheduling mishaps. She needs lots of reminders and help with planning to remember where she's supposed to be when. Her hairdresser, Pilates instructor, and trainer at the gym have learned to call her before an appointment. Mom will also call her an hour or two before they are to go to a doctor appointment or Rotary function.

Molly lives alone in her own house with her two cats, but she is not independent. She needs help with her health care logistics (medical appointments, prescriptions, insurance paperwork), finances (balancing her check book, keeping track of credit card charges, doing taxes), and with home care (cleaning, maintenance, and repairs).

Heroically, Mom does much of this legwork herself and she hires and manages others for some tasks. It's a full-time job and then some. Glen is a tremendous help with Molly's home care; he's a very good handy man. He does it because he loves Mom, but it's irksome to me that Molly is not nearly grateful enough to Glen for all he does for her.

Molly employs the same house cleaner that Mom uses so her home is basically clean, but it isn't tidy because she isn't good about putting things away or prioritizing her belongings. Molly's brain injury contributes to the clutter strewn about—papers, magazines, and nearly anything that comes through the door lands on her kitchen table and stays there, usually until Mom comes through and puts most of it in the recycling bin. Similar pile-ups occur in her closet with clothes she no longer wears and in her bathroom where dozens of partially used toiletries cover the counter. None of this is a big deal. We all have quirky ways of living in our own spaces. It isn't how Molly used to be, but it's how she gets by now, and I think it's impressive that she functions as well as she does. It's better than some who don't have brain injuries!

Like most of us, Molly benefits from structure in her life and Mom has helped Molly establish a weekly routine. Usually she has one scheduled activity a day, sometimes two. They're good for her, and she enjoys them. Yoga and Pilates classes, Rotary meetings, volunteering at the zoo, working with a trainer at the gym, going to her hair stylist. She has appointments with a doctor or her PT, and she is invited sometimes for theater or movie dates with Mom and Glen. And every day, Molly goes to Starbucks. It's her thing, a rare initiative. Starbucks is an essential part of her daily routine, like a compass point.

Molly's weekly schedule helps her focus. It eases her way in the world—and eases Mom's mind. She generally knows where Molly is and what she's up to. Mom's burden is lighter when Molly has her own agenda. Sometimes, it's not easy to get her to keep up with it, but it provides a framework and gives Molly a specific place to be each day, a good reason to get up, get going, get out of the house, and go relate to others—not just her cats.

Most weeks, Molly gets to her appointments just fine and mostly on time. She'll deliver to Mom a stack of all of her receipts for the week, and she'll write a check for each of her bills and mail them promptly. She's reliable with certain tasks; she keeps her cell phone charged, puts gas in her car, and shops for groceries and cat supplies.

Some weeks, however, Molly doesn't show up, doesn't call, doesn't take care of her receipts and bills—and may not even realize it. Mom is ever vigilant. She has tried to teach Molly to check her calendar through the day for appointments and to be responsible with her money and respectful of others' time. This is useful coaching, but Molly needs many reminders.

Fortunately, Molly has better social conduct than she did the first few years after her injury. She may still become inappropriately emphatic and loud when expressing her opinion in a group, and she has a tendency to sing along or make comments out loud during a performance. Sometimes her expression freezes, usually in a strained smile. But she no longer mocks other people in restaurants when they cough or slurp their soup and she doesn't make grotesque faces when she's annoyed or upset.

Mom encourages Molly to make plans and ask someone to go along, but she doesn't. If Molly receives a notice about a vet tech conference, however, she'll register and drive herself—after checking the route with Mom. If Mom invites her to do an exercise walk with her, she will. If Mom suggests they go to a movie, she will. She simply doesn't initiate communication or plans with anyone, but she's glad to accept invitations, which mostly come from Mom, or from me or my sisters if we're visiting.

A few years ago, Molly, still a fervent Democrat, was invited to do door-to-door canvassing with the local Obama for President group. She'd made a donation and an Obama volunteer chatted with her on the phone, heard her enthusiasm, and asked her to join them. I was staying at Mom's house while she and Glen were away on a trip. Using the address Molly was given, I printed a Google map and some directions where she was to meet the group, about a mile or so away. We looked over the map together and she took off confident and excited. I believed her entirely.

She never found the location and returned an hour and a half later. She said, "The map didn't fit with the streets. The streets weren't there."

Apparently, the group had waited for a little while. Molly told me later they'd left a message on her home phone asking if she was coming. Unfortunately, when she was out driving, she did not call them or me on her cell phone, which she had with her. As gently as I could, I reminded her to pull over the next time and call me. She took her large Obama/Biden button off her sweater and said, "It doesn't matter, Smith."

I knew she was frustrated, but most of all she was disappointed. I felt terrible. I knew that Molly gets lost easily on foot or in her car, especially going to an unfamiliar location. If she sticks to her usual routes for the places she frequents— a favorite restaurant, the hairdresser, Starbucks— she's fine. But if she's walking or driving to a new destination, or if there's a road construction detour on her normal route, she can get lost for hours.

I had a deadline that afternoon for a freelance writing job, but I was kicking myself that I had not gone with her to make sure she met up with the Obama group. She'd really wanted to do the canvassing for a cause she very much believed in and I was crestfallen she didn't get the opportunity. She would have been with a good group of people, doing a constructive activity that she lined up for herself, and she probably would have been persuasive and felt successful. I suggested while I made dinner that evening that she call the volunteer and try again the next time the group went canvassing, but she never did.

These days, Molly is better about pulling over and calling Mom on her cell phone when she can't find the place she's looking for. I've even told Molly to call me in New York if she can't reach Mom because I might be able to help her using my computer. Mom believes, and I agree, that Molly is better about asking for help in general. That's important progress I can see.

Unfortunately, Molly still doesn't have friendships apart from family members and acquaintances at her activities, like Pilates or the gym. A while ago, she was still meeting for coffee occasionally with computer dating contacts, but she's stopped using those services now.

I *want* to develop a close bond with Molly, as best I can. But I often feel guilty because it's hard to be close to her, to feel like good friends.

I've thought it might help to involve Molly with the local brain injury group. It would be therapeutic not just for the supportive atmosphere and supervised outings and activities, but also because she'd be around some people with *more* and some people with *fewer* brain injury issues than she has. She'd benefit from the interaction with people who understand and accept her, and maybe even make some friends. And people in the group would benefit from knowing her.

It hasn't happened yet because Mom and Lis say she'll resist going, which is probably true. But I think I'll drag her to the brain injury group meeting with me one day. I honestly believe that once she goes, she'll decide she likes the group and will go on her own after that—just as she goes to yoga, the zoo, and Starbucks on her own, very happily.

But for now, Molly's social life and companionship depends on her mother. Molly has worthwhile opportunities with the Rotary group. However, she attends the weekly luncheons and will go to the outreach gatherings and charitable activities because Mom is involved. At least with Rotary, Molly learns about and gets the experience of helping others in her community and around the world through Rotary's projects.

Dad stays in touch with Molly mostly by emailing her, even though she may take a while to write him back and she doesn't usually respond to his questions; but at least it's interaction between them. He and I have chuckled about her reply emails and how off-track they can be. But I remind Dad that we should be thrilled that at least she uses her computer and writes email and almost always sends some kind of reply. He agrees and says her emails are usually a lot of fun because of her wit and honesty. And, in what's become a tradition, she finds a new way to express her love to him with almost every email. Here are a few examples he shared with me.

> *I love you, Dad! Millions and morillions and gazillions worth!*
> *xxxxoxooxooxoxoxoxxooxooxoxoxooxooxoxoxomolly*
>
> *Gotta be going soon, Dad! I love you! More than your imagi-*
> *nation can imagine! xoxoxoxoxoxoxoxoxoxoxoxoxoxoxxoooomolly*
>
> *Should be a pretty nice day today, then a crummy day*
> *tomorrow. Will go down to the 30's then. Bad day! But,*

I love you, Dad. More than any steam shovel can lift.
xoxoxoxooxooxooxooxooxooxooxoxooxooxoxoxoxoxoxooxoxoxomolly
    I have to go to my dentist this morning. I like going to my
dentist, because I floss regularly, and I brush also. Oh well, it
seems we will have to get along until we either die or whatever
else...sigh. I love you, Dad, until whenever you said and longer.
ooxoxooxooxooxoxoxoooxooxxoxoxoxoxooxoxoxoxomolly

In Molly's "life care plan report," which was created in 1996 at the end
of her daily outpatient rehab, the physicians and psychologists predicted
in their assessment that Molly would show increasing emotional frustration with people and situations and they expected this problem to worsen
over time. They wrote that she would need planning and assistance to be
more productive (such as volunteer activities) and for social interaction and
activities. Molly's frustration is often present, some days more than others.
But all along, Mom has provided Molly with a high level of support and
engagement.

The report also stated that Molly is *"at risk for further neurologic deterioration and early onset dementia and also depression due to her brain injury."*
This prospect is terrifying to me. The words dementia and depression swirl
around me like a cold autumn wind, a reminder that winter is coming,
sooner than I want or expect.

In the past year or so, Mom and I have discussed certain times when
she's observed what seems to be some dementia. Molly used to take care
of her meds herself—getting the prescriptions to the pharmacy for refills,
organizing the pills into the day-of-the-week boxes, with the correct number
of pills for the separate morning and night boxes—and did it just fine. But
when Molly became especially moody and irascible over a period of weeks
recently, Mom checked her pillboxes and discovered they were askew—the
wrong pills, wrong time of day, wrong dosages.

It has never been a simple drug regime, but she used to get it right,
almost as a point of pride. Molly gnashed her teeth when Mom explained
why she was going to take over the task, but it was too important to risk
and Molly resigned to Mom doing it. Now, Molly is often sweet and thanks
Mom when she sets up her pillboxes. And at least for now, she takes the
correct pills, correctly. But Mom is aware that may not last.

Even so, it will always be a challenge to set her medicines and dosages to balance the mental and emotional benefits with the physical side effects. All kinds of other changes in Molly's life have an impact; whether she takes ibuprofen for arthritis in her shoulder or her hormones shift in post-menopause, we will always need to be aware of her behavior and fine-tune her medicines accordingly.

After Mom straightened out Molly's pillboxes, Molly was happier and more pleasant, but she was tripping more and did several face plants. Mom contacted Dr. Carlson and they decided to cut back a bit on one of her medicines. Mom could tell the difference quickly. Molly remained cheerful but was no longer falling.

But even the delicate leveling of medicines cannot solve all the behavior issues. Molly surprised Mom by showing up early one winter morning recently, in her pajamas and without a coat. Luckily Mom was up making coffee. "Well, good morning, Molly. How are you?"

"I'm cold and I don't have any clothes to put on," Molly said.

"Why don't you have clothes to put on? You have lots of clothes," Mom said, studying Molly as she sat down at the table.

"I just... I don't have the clothes," Molly said. She didn't tell Mom why she was there or what had happened. Mom asked her if she got locked out.

"Then Molly got the strangest look on her face. Her mouth was open, her eyes were blank, but she couldn't get the words out," Mom said. "It seemed to be what I've feared—some level of dementia. It really scared me to see the awful hollow look on her face."

Eventually, Molly admitted she got locked out while picking up her newspaper from the driveway and they both walked over to unlock the door, using a spare key. But Mom was deeply disturbed by Molly's disorientation and bewildered expression.

"Do you think Molly might have been embarrassed or defensive about locking herself out so she didn't want to admit it?" I asked.

"No, it wasn't like that. I think she was truly lost in that situation," Mom replied.

Sometimes Molly is able to laugh about her brain injury and ask for help, but often, she desperately tries to hide her condition and despises admitting that she has a problem.

The next week, at their appointment with Dr. Carlson, he said he thought that Molly not being able to speak was due to an excess load of frustration and anger at herself. He added that locking yourself out is upsetting to any of us, but particularly so with a brain injury. He assured Mom that unless this type of incident became much more frequent, we shouldn't be alarmed.

Molly's lack of planning and forethought (unlock the door, it's cold outside, wear a coat) is the result of her brain injury. She becomes frustrated with increasing challenges so a problem snowballs (I closed the door, I can't get in, I'm only wearing pajamas).

These are the double-edged puzzle pieces—the better Molly's brain is working, the more she is aware of her cognitive deficits, and that's frustrating to her. Her heightened frustration can cause a backslide because she moves quickly into anger, which in turn diminishes her cognitive functions and disrupts her ability to understand and get along in the world and with others.

Without a doubt, the most constant and vexing problem with my sister is her anger. Since her injury, and increasingly in recent years, Molly can boil over with seething and explosive anger, which she most often hurls at those closest to her—her family.

This is especially disheartening because her anger and the errant behavior that typically accompanies it, drives away the very people she most *needs* to be with, like her long-time therapists, or most *wants* to be with, like Dave, her ex-boyfriend, or her sisters—even her mother. She can make it hard to want to be around her.

Molly's anger is fearsome to me. She feels out of control. I don't know what to do or say when she's lashing out. It's like trying to calm a cornered, snarling cat; anything you do—from reaching out or trying to soothe her or even leaving her alone—just makes her growling worse. My skin prickles with cold sweat.

From Dr. Lo at Loma Linda, to Dr. Schraa at Craig Hospital, to Dr. Carlson currently, we've been told that anger management is a frontal lobe behavior problem and it will likely always be a difficulty for Molly.

Damage to this area of the brain, located right behind the forehead, causes the most challenging and lasting problems for many brain-injured people. Often called "the brain's boss," the frontal lobe is a highly developed part of the brain that coordinates responses and activity among all the different regions of the brain, including conducting traffic for mental behavior.

The frontal lobe controls what's called executive thinking: use of language, short-term memory, organizing, problem solving, initiation, sequencing, insight, decision making, and, the biggie, judgment. The frontal lobe also manages impulses and emotions and governs personal reactions such as embarrassment, apathy, guilt, and compassion, all of which are critical to guiding proper social behavior. Understanding that future consequences result from current actions? That's frontal lobe, as is repressing or overriding social responses that are inappropriate. But it's not just what we do—our frontal lobes makes us who we are.

Dr. Lo had told us that Molly's personality change, which her family feels so keenly, stems from the severe damage to her frontal lobe resulting in the loss of emotional control, inhibitions, and limiters. These "limiters" balance our negative and positive impulses and help us behave in acceptable ways. This processing and the learned behaviors controlled by the frontal lobe are developed throughout a person's upbringing and with a tremendous amount of guidance. They help determine the type of person one is, and shape one's personality.

"Molly's outbursts are not unusual, even now, all these years since her injury," said Dr. Lo. "Brain-injured people often display lack of judgment and high levels of agitation. That fine balance between negative and positive feedback that keeps us from doing adverse things is missing for Molly, so she behaves without the usual controls."

"But so many of her brain functions are so good and keep getting better," I replied. "Her anger issues seem like they *never* get better."

"Yes, but the frontal lobe behaviors require *very* precise modification and refinement. Its thinking processes are of a much higher cognitive function and are extremely tenuous. Any kind of damage really screws it up," Dr. Lo explained. "Certain brain compartments can repair and go on very well, but the frontal lobe circuitry is delicate and complicated. It's the last area to develop in a child and the hardest area to rehab in a brain-injured person *because* the wiring for these processing and judgment skills is more elaborate and detailed, and really only gained over time. The frontal lobe does not heal easily."

"Well, it helps to be reminded of the brain physiology, Dr. Lo, but it's never easy to go through all the emotional incidents with her and not take her anger personally, even after all these years," I said.

"I understand," Dr. Lo said. "But remember, too, that Molly's anger is uncontrolled; it's not reasoned anger, it's *frustration* anger."

If something upsets her, Molly can be overwhelmed. With diminished insight and limiters run amok, it's nearly impossible for her to put a lid on her anger. In the brain of an immature teenager, the frontal lobe is not yet fully developed. And like that 13-year-old, Molly lacks control and judgment and is not *able* to think through the consequences of her actions, especially in the heat of the moment. Her deficits in memory and learning result in self-centeredness and a lack of self-awareness. This leads to impatience, irritation, impulsivity, and insolence.

That's the science of frontal lobe injury. The reality is that Molly's family, especially Mom, frequently feel the burn of Molly having little or no compassion. She doesn't seem to care. Her damaged frontal lobe reduces her comprehension of herself and her behavior, and she's often not conscious of her impact on others.

I have to remind myself regularly of these aspects of frontal lobe injury that Molly's therapists and doctors have taught us. She is not aware of her own shortcomings. And my wanting to help her have more self-awareness is tricky to do when her brain injury prevents her from understanding its very effects.

On occasion when I've told her that my feelings were hurt by something she said or did, she is genuinely surprised or just shrugs her shoulders. She is less able to learn from consequences because she doesn't realize she's caused a problem. It's not deliberate or spiteful. She lacks judgment, and therefore simply lacks the ability to empathize.

One time when Mom was receiving counseling from Dr. Schraa, she was distraught and said she was finding it nearly impossible to discuss any problem with Molly because she had no warmth or affection or any concern for her family members—not even her, her mother.

"I don't think I can do this. I've spent too many years of my life earning respect and getting admiration from my children," Mom told Dr. Schraa.

"The problem is, Sally, that with her frontal lobe injury, Molly thinks she's acting perfectly OK. She's been *taught* she has a brain injury, but she doesn't *perceive* it," Dr. Schraa said. "She can't manage her impulses; she has a broken filtering system. Her combative outbursts are immediate expressions of frustration and anger and show she feels out of control."

"But I can't..., I don't know, Dr. Schraa, if I can handle it," Mom said. "She's so hard, her anger..."

Dr. Schraa said, gently, "Sally, she's not even aware of it."

It is typical that the family of a brain-injured person receives the most abuse and anger from their loved one. True to form, Molly's family members get the largest dose of Molly's rage, especially Mom and Glen because she's around them the most. It's a function of time and comfort levels. Molly puts forth her best behavior and social self-control with people outside the family, but not with Mom and Glen, her sisters when we're around her for a few days, a longer-term boyfriend like Dave, or even her therapists once they become "like family." She doesn't think about being nice to family. She lets down her good manners, doesn't realize it, and doesn't consider the need to mind her behavior, ironically, because she is at ease with us. Instead, she reacts spontaneously without conscious thought and without the rigor of trying to get it right and put on a good face as she does with acquaintances and strangers. The paradox of her default behavior is painful for her family members, especially since we've all experienced how nice she can be to total strangers—who think she's utterly and always delightful.

These frontal lobe problems are hard, too, not just because we take the brunt of Molly's harshness, but because it's tough to feel that we can help her do any better. Mom helps Molly's frontal lobe functions a lot by keeping her busy and feeling productive as much as possible. But Molly's decreased ability to learn from experience or even from teaching harms her capacity for retention, even though she's able to absorb new information. Now we know she needs to learn the consequences of her behavior—and learn them again and again. And we, her family, and especially Mom, her primary caregiver, must expect this, and teach her—again and again.

During a visit to Denver, Larry and I brainstormed about how we could help Mom with this repetitive teaching. If only we could *train* Molly to be nice. Have her sit on her hands quietly if she starts to feel agitated. If she could just listen, if she could bite her tongue, even if she's beginning to fume inside, and just not say anything. But this is not the reality of her frontal lobe abilities. Instead, she fires off whatever contrary remark comes up, raucously proclaiming the opposite of anything anyone has said. Or annoyingly repeats what anyone says just after they say it. Or loudly spews a stream of callous criticisms. It's like a disturbed hive relentlessly buzzing, flaring, and stinging.

I believe part of what's happening is that Molly doesn't want to feel inferior to others because of her brain injury. I think she imagines her constant interjections as bolstering her place in a group and assuring that she's part of the conversation and participating just like everyone else. Unfortunately, she sometimes aims to position herself as better than someone else, especially someone she feels competitive with for attention and praise, like Glen, and she will bitterly disparage him. It doesn't help that Glen is by nature a quiet, soft-spoken person and I suspect Molly views him as an easy target.

Over the years, I've tried to calm Molly when she'd start in on Dave, Glen, or Mom, and she'd invariably get really pissed off at me. These days, my skin is tougher and I absorb her fury and let the smarting pass. I've learned from research that it's important not to let Molly get away with her angry behavior, no more than a parent should ignore a teenager's bad manners. Mom has been good about correcting Molly and can do so effectively because she's the mom. I have to caution myself, though, not to avoid the things that set Molly off, because then she may learn to manipulate her family members. If she senses that she's dominating a situation with her anger, then I fear she's likely to continue using this power, like a reign of terror. I'm working on a consistent response to break patterns of unacceptable behavior and remind her of consequences. So I try, even as her little sister, to step up as often as I can to remind her to be kind.

But when I'm around her, I sense Molly's anger as a constant hazard, ready to explode, even when she's unperturbed. She's a minefield that looks like a spring meadow. For me, it's exhausting to police her constantly, awful when she bursts, dangerous to let her get away with her wrath, and dreadful trying to ignore her mean grumbling. It upsets me to let her rage away, blurting out her cutting comments and griping under her breath. Or to call her out on her harshness, propelling her to fight back at me. Or to watch her storm out.

So I try to engage her, distract her, make her laugh; I try to be positive and keep the peace. But there's no escaping kicking the beehive sometimes no matter what I do.

One night when Molly and I were in Salt Lake City together, we had a pleasant dinner in a nice restaurant at a table in the middle of a crowded dining room. When we stood up to leave, I put my coat over my arm to walk to reception area, but Molly took her jacket from the back of her chair and swung it around her shoulders and punched her arms into the sleeves. As she moved, I instinctively reached over and slid several glasses to the center of the table. In the moment she realized what I'd done, her fury burst out. "Why did you do that, Smith?! Have you got a problem or something?! I'm not doing anything. What's your problem?!" she yelled and glared through me.

"No, Molly, it's not a problem, I was just afraid your jacket might knock over the glasses," I said in a hushed tone and moved toward the exit.

"I didn't do that, Smith!" she shouted. "I know what I'm doing and you don't!" She stormed passed me and out the door.

I would have moved the glasses away for anyone who was about to accidentally knock them off the table, but I could not convince Molly of that as I drove us home. "Whatever. Sure, Smith, whatever. It's *your* problem. Too bad for you, it's your problem," she repeated, staring out the window.

She did not acknowledge that I'd tried to protect her from an embarrassing situation in a public place. Instead, she created a big scene and I was thwarted. And she didn't give a damn one way or the other. She was completely unaware of others' perceptions, including mine. She didn't care. But actually, she couldn't care. I got a grip and counseled myself: This is brain injury, this is brain injury. I know Molly is typically more irritable at night because she's tired so she's quickly defensive. She also despises feeling patronized. Therefore, her frontal lobe deficits left her lashing out in frustrated anger, which for her probably felt like power and control.

I was left to wonder, though, if it was worth it. I spared the restaurant's glassware, but not the commotion and turned heads. If I hadn't reacted automatically, I could've just let her break all the glasses. Would that have been a better way for her to learn? She might have been surprised and apologetic. She might have been defiant, shrugged her shoulders, and walked out. I'll never know. As it was, she stayed mad and grouchy until the next morning. And then it was gone. For her.

But for the rest of the next day, I licked my wounds, I tried to recover.

I was feeling ashamed of feeling embarrassed about her, and ashamed that it wasn't the first time. I sheepishly wondered, again, if it would be easier if Molly were a quadriplegic and used a wheelchair. Then she would garner sympathy and understanding from others because of her obvious disability—and I'd get some leeway, too. But there's no consideration of Molly's disabilities; people can't see her severe injury. And I don't get any Brownie points.

Finally, I reconciled the event as a teaching moment for me.

Incidents like this occur all the time. I'm not around Molly every day, but Mom could probably list several "explosions" each month—in the grocery store, at a medical appointment, going to a movie, driving in the car, with Glen, and with her, even if she is the "mom."

Through our experiences, I'm learning that Molly doesn't register these episodes deeply. She forgets about them by the next day and will be as sweet and jovial as if nothing had happened. However, it's never easy for us to simply chalk up Molly's assaults to brain injury. When Molly got bitchy with Mom recently, Mom clamped down hard on her. The agitation remained between them, thorny and heavy, as they drove home. The next day, she and Molly had an appointment together. "I picked her up and she was fine—very cheerful, in fact," Mom told me. "I was still bleeding, but Molly had moved on her merry way."

In my mind, Mom has been remarkably steadfast at being empathic to Molly, recognizing that her mean comments aren't deliberate, and remaining an adoring mother. But my big sister still holds sway over me. After she blasts me, my aching doesn't disappear quickly, and I struggle to swallow my hurt. Earlier on, my self-protection mode made me wary around Molly, now I'm learning and I'm bolder when I deal with her. I figure I have only my own bruises to overcome. The sting lingers; I just know now to expect that.

But in recent years, Molly has become particularly belligerent with Glen. For no reason, she'll complain loudly from the backseat about his driving or spit tetchy remarks or mock him at the dinner table. Glen bristles, understandably, and sometimes fights back, which leads to all-out shouting matches. Arguing with a brain-injured person like Molly, who cannot be reasoned with when she's tilted into fully loaded anger mode, is a normal reaction, but it's also futile.

Worst of all, Mom ends up trapped between her bickering loved ones, and has to be the referee and break them apart. Often Mom has to quell the battle in public, at a restaurant or a theater, and sometimes she has to yell at them to stop, which works, but then the evening is ruined and everyone is upset. And Mom, stuck in the middle, is hurt most of all.

In separate conversations, Mom has told Molly that she must stop berating Glen, and she has told Glen to ignore Molly and remember it's because of her severe brain injury and nothing he says to defend himself will get her to stop. Mom has sought assistance from Lis and Dr. Carlson with the Molly and Glen problem, too, and Molly might behave better for a while, but too soon the ugly scenes repeat at the next dinner or drive in the car.

Molly's malicious anger toward Glen horrified all of us sisters, too, because we all love Glen and know how wonderful he is for Mom and how much she loves him. I was startled by Molly's hostility; Glen is a very kind man, and it was so agonizing for Mom.

During recent visits, I'd end up asking Molly to stop ragging on Glen, and she'd turn and lash out at me, which I actually preferred. I felt it wasn't fair to ask Glen to accept that this is Molly's brain injury and he should just ignore her. I'm her sister, I've had years of practice, and I still find it very difficult to not take it personally.

Like me, other family members also looked for ways to help. When Sara and Jonathan were in Denver for a visit not too long ago, Molly yelled out in their neighborhood restaurant that she wished Glen was already dead. Sara and Jonathan were shocked. "Finally, I said to Molly, 'Oh my god! I can't believe you just said that,'" Sara told me. "It was so terrible."

Sara had told Mom before that they had to do something to get Molly's nastiness toward Glen to stop. This time she said *she* would deal with Molly on it. Mom told Sara that anger management was really for Molly's psychologist to work on. She said she appreciated Sara taking up for Glen and shared her feelings about Molly's mistreatment of him, but said she always tries to remember what Molly is truly struggling with.

"At one of our visits soon after, Dr. Carlson talked to Molly about being competitive with Glen," Mom said. "And Molly pretty much admitted she didn't like Glen taking up my time."

"Do you think Molly understands how much she's hurting you when she tears into Glen?" I asked.

"I've begun telling her that more," Mom said. "But she so often interprets any little lesson or criticism I present as belittling to her. She hates to be reminded of her brain injury."

"But it *is* her brain injury that's causing this outrageous anger. I want her to understand that and that she's really hurting *you*—maybe that would help her get it under control," I said.

"When Molly's anger is out there, I don't feel I can help her control it," Mom said. "I just make her stop talking and send her home. It's embarrassing and infuriating, and I know Sara felt that. I certainly have. But, honestly, I don't know if this part of Molly's personality will ever improve."

Dr. Schraa had explained to us that Molly would always struggle to learn and retain refined behavior. "Her frontal lobe is very damaged and it's the least healed because it's the hardest to repair," Dr. Schraa said. "It's the loss of impulse control, etiquette, social behavior—and it regulates emotions and personality; how to be tactful and considerate. It's all the stuff your mother taught you last."

Mom paused, and then told him, "Well, I taught her once. And I can teach her again."

And again, and again.

Finally, after a particularly bad episode of Molly screaming at Glen, Mom was at the end of her rope. Mom sent Molly home, Glen went to another room, and Mom decided she had to stick up for herself; an act of self-preservation.

She went to Molly's house the next day, sat Molly down, and said they needed to have a hard talk. Mom told Molly that Glen was her partner and her choice, and that she loved him very much. She told Molly that she loves her very much, too, but she would not let her ruin her relationship with Glen. Mom said Molly would not be allowed at her house anymore unless she always treats Glen and her with respect and kindness. She must make the choice to be nice to Glen and to her or she will not have dinner or watch TV with them, or go with them to the movies or theater, or anything else. She can just stay home—period.

"When you're mean to Glen, it hurts me the most," Mom told Molly. "The pain I feel is terrible and I will no longer put up with such behavior from you.

"I've seen you be so kind and sweet to everyone else—Rotary friends, acquaintances at the hair salon, our Pilates instructors, even people at Starbucks—and it really hurts that you don't treat us the same pleasant way," Mom said. "I know you can do it because I see you do it all the time. You're going to have to think about it and work at it. But you *must* be pleasant with me and nice to Glen, too, or you will not spend any time with us at all."

The effect of this clarifying "hard talk" was that Molly's behavior improved significantly. She seemed to understand that there were real consequences to her behavior and that if she can't be nice, then she will be left alone. I believe it also helped for her to understand that it was not a given that she has dinner with Mom and Glen, which she used to do almost every night. Not any more and it's better for everyone—Mom gets a break and it helps Molly not to take them for granted. Mom says when Molly is invited to their house now, she has to make a decision to be on her best behavior.

This decree to Molly was a monumental accomplishment for Mom. She'd nibbled around the edges of it before but had not made the choices, requirements, and consequences patently clear to Molly.

During their hard talk, Mom also said aloud for the first time that if she can't manage Molly and her temper and behavior, then Molly might have to live somewhere else and have professional medical workers take care of her. I had mentioned this possibility to Mom many months before during another rough time and asked if she felt it was something that needed to be broached and explored. Mom said then she was not ready to "threaten" Molly with that yet. I'd said it wasn't a threat, but a repercussion Molly needed to be aware of.

Mom has held as a high priority that Molly be allowed to live in her own home as independently as possible. She's never wanted Molly to live in an institution. And I have always agreed with Mom on this priority, our whole family has. Molly needs as much autonomy as possible. We've always believed it helps her to be as good as she can be.

But I was becoming concerned that Molly was wrecking Mom's life, jeopardizing her health, and causing her too much stress for too long. I felt defensive for my mother and concerned she might be at her wit's end and might even collapse under the strain.

However, I think after Mom's "hard talk," Molly realized that her independent lifestyle was contingent on her behaving as nicely to those closest to her as she does to her occasional acquaintances; it struck a sharp chord in her that she needed to feel. Mom wasn't wielding it as a threat, but her pronouncement probably helped Molly grasp the gravity of the situation and that Mom was quite serious about the behavior improvement she expected to see. I told Mom it was essential that Molly recognize her independent living situation as a privilege, not a given and not a right. It's like a driver's license that has to be earned and maintained through proven good behavior—or else taken away.

We'd hoped that Molly could learn to be nicer to everyone and control her anger better; the trick would be finding how to reach her and have her understand. Mom did that successfully. She presented Molly a challenge to be met and she got to her viscerally. I'm convinced that's why this lesson from Mom has had more stickiness than others before it. At least for now.

I've always believed that Molly can still learn just about anything she is determined to. Anger control is the toughest yet—but don't we all struggle at times to express anger civilly and not blow our tops? Molly *can* learn to behave better just like she learned to swallow, walk, and drive again, and be a vet tech and a zoo docent. But because social behavior is frontal lobe circuitry, it will be difficult and she won't learn it just once. She'll make mistakes over and over, especially as her cognitive abilities decline as she ages.

I'll be on the lookout, along with Mom, because I want to be ready to intervene to help Molly learn, and relearn. It's a less comfortable position to be Molly's teacher as her sister, but I've never believed she can't learn, even from me.

Fifteen

MOLLY'S brain injury is severe, but her life is good. Yes, the petulant child remains in my adult sister. She is often self-absorbed but she has some sweetness, too. Luckily, Molly can have fun; she is not marked by melancholia. She has a wonderful sense of humor, even bawdy at times, and she's boisterous and laughs with gusto. At family gatherings, she wants to be involved with everyone. If her mood isn't sour, she engages in light conversation easily. She stops me in my tracks when she is thoughtful without prompting. And when she struggles to find a simple word she wants to say, I find it hard to breathe.

I've learned from Mom not to overlook the sadness and injustice of her situation. In the height of frustration with her or just the day-to-day annoyances, I turn to that place and remember. I realize again that simply her ability to be frustrated or joyful is utterly amazing. The fact of our relationship, as close as we are as sisters, is truly wonderful. Recognizing Molly for who she is today reminds me to be grateful.

In official terminology, traumatic brain injury (or TBI) is an injury after birth caused by an external force impacting the brain, such as a blow to the head from a fall, sporting accident, assault, or motor vehicle crash. Acquired brain injury (or ABI) includes all TBIs and also injuries after birth in which brain cells are damaged by cerebral vascular accidents, such as stroke or hemorrhage; direct infections, such as meningitis or encephalitis; toxic substances, such as drug or chemical poisoning; or loss of oxygen to the brain, such as carbon monoxide poisoning.

Recent events, such as the gun violence that wounded former Representative Gabrielle Giffords and the hundreds of thousands of veterans with brain injuries from the wars in Iraq and Afghanistan, have pushed TBI into the national consciousness. Happily, Ms. Giffords continues to work on her rehabilitation with gusto—and a helpful medical team and loving family.

Sadly, TBI is being called the "signature injury" of the wars in Iraq and Afghanistan. Explosive and blast attacks are more common in these wars, and advances in protective armor and medical triage mean many soldiers survive casualties that would have killed them in past conflicts. As a result, TBI is occurring among these wars' 2.4 million veterans at a significantly higher rate than from any previous wars; 30 percent or more are believed to suffer TBIs. In many cases, these TBIs lead to brain disease and cognitive problems, personality changes, and loss of impulse control—facets of brain injury my family knows well.

Other families do, too. More than 6.2 million individuals in the U.S. are living with brain injury-related disabilities. The number of people with brain injury who are not seen in an emergency department or receive no care is unknown.

Brain injuries are called the "invisible injury," and their invisibility makes them an under-recognized and difficult public health problem. Molly's brain injury is life altering—for her, me, our whole family, yet most people don't know. They see her, physically intact and attractive; her devastating injury invisible. I didn't know anything about brain injury until Molly's accident occurred. Now I know more; mostly I'm aware of the "invisible injury" as pervasive.

Clearly, the sheer number of people with the "invisible injury" should make apparent the need for attention and concern. And although people are becoming more aware of brain injury, there's still a lot of misunderstanding.

Having a brain injury isn't about being stupid, no more than losing a leg is. My sister was once a person with extremely high levels of intelligence, function, and ability. Her memory of that adds to her frustration. She remembers what she could once do and who she was, as would the person who's lost a leg. The difference is that Molly's brain injury prevents her from being able to fully understand her injury and recognize its impact.

I know it is nearly impossible for others to fathom what a person with a brain injury and her family struggle with because of its unusual nature. The severity of the disability is hidden, and even disguised as the person with the brain injury often does her best to cope and not appear disabled at all.

Molly's courage to try to not seem disabled, but still be willing to label herself out loud as a person with a brain injury is heartening. She'll put it out there, running the risk of being thought of as "damaged," and yet she manages it. It seems she knows her honesty helps others to not overly patronize her, and perhaps even feel admiration for her. It's one way she stakes her place in the world.

The ultimate hardship may be that there is not one type of brain injury and no single treatment. Each brain is unique, each brain injury is unique, and each rehabilitation is unique. Treatment is a crapshoot. Outcomes are unknowable. It is both hard news and good news that there is no predicting what a brain-injured patient's end result may be. It is only known that any effective rehab requires a determined patient with a strong support network and excellent medical care and rehab specialists.

And as I've learned first hand, the family of the brain-injured person should not only be involved in the rehab, but are similarly and permanently affected by the injury, too.

Still, there is tremendous hope for brain injury healing and improvement in brain function. In my family, we will always believe that HBO and Dr. Lo's aggressive use of it helped Molly dramatically, each treatment breathing new life into her brain cells and igniting activity.

Meanwhile the debates about such "alternative" uses for HBO and its effectiveness on brain injury continue. No clear consensus has emerged from recent studies even though scientific rationale, physiological indications, and anecdotal evidence for HBO grow; they don't yet translate into clear clinical benefit. Many believe, however, that controversy will inspire inquiry and that one day there will be an expansion of approved uses of HBO.

"Studies are coming along and we'll have to wait and see," Dr. Lo told me. "I'm a scientist and I have to rely on available data. But I believe HBO is amazing. And maybe in a few years, I hope we'll have protocol to treat brain injuries and other wounds with HBO."

In addition, new research points to the regenerative abilities of our brains, and that proper diagnoses and therapies may help unleash these rehabilitating powers. The brain has more than one hundred billion neurons, and scientists are discovering that with consistent therapy and training, and constant practice and stimulation, brain neurons *can* repair themselves. They may not align in the same pattern, but they can create new connections and paths, enabling them to rewire and renew functioning.

And so Molly is here, familiar and remarkably able, but not the same person she was. Her character isn't totally lost, but her presentation of it is changed. She holds her face and its expressions in a different way, reflecting a different personality, and so much more.

But Mom sometimes reminds me that a few days after Molly's accident, the neurologist at Loma Linda told her that Molly would likely remain in a "vegetative state" and that her "probability of a meaningful life is zero." When I remember those odds, I feel pretty damn good about Molly and her life today.

I am convinced that Molly's innate doggedness helped her to survive and contributes to her strong capabilities today. I try hard to remember that Molly's anger is usually conveying frustration, hurt, fear, or confusion. And since Mom's "hard talk" with her, Molly seems calmer. She's more cheery when she has a lot of alone time, doing her own thing. Mom still keeps track of Molly's whereabouts; she's not "out of sight, out of mind." But Molly's behavior is improved when she doesn't view time spent with Mom, or any-one, as a given. It's a lesson for me to follow when Molly's behavior slides out of whack again in the future. Her constant evolution is so challenging, but it's also hopeful. There will be more heart-to-heart talks with Molly when she needs reminding.

It's also useful to cope with Molly by taking a break from her. Everyone does, including her therapists, doctors, family members—everyone, that is, except Mom. She rarely takes even a day or two away from caregiving to Molly. It isn't that Molly is with Mom constantly; but the responsibility for Molly is almost always present for Mom.

As a long distance caregiver, I am attentive to Molly but also watchful of Mom's stress and exhaustion. I hope she doesn't feel a lot of drudgery, but the constancy of problems in caring for Molly does have a Sisyphus-like strain. Mom says Molly moves in only two directions—up and down. I add endless.

Mom pushes the boulder up the hill, and watches it roll down the other side, knowing that she will push it up the hill again. I know Mom doesn't jauntily whistle her way down, but I want there to be days when she at least strolls and feels some satisfaction, some hope, perhaps a touch of joy, before she faces the boulder again. Year after year, I've witnessed my mother, still willing and often smiling.

I feel uneasy, though, that Mom may take on too much. I don't want her to feel trapped, even though she is in many ways. I know one day I may feel that way, too. Mom is a great caregiver and a devoted mother. She says it's what she does and who she is. But sometimes she's exhausted and even says so, and I know she needs a boost.

I try to help by visiting in person and over the phone. I try to give Mom a break by taking on certain conversations with Molly, to reinforce what Mom told her already or get across something Mom needs her to understand and hopes she'll hear it better from me. From checking her appointments to conserving money to wearing sunscreen to taking a walk every day.

It's not easy for me to feel success with Molly, though, or to see improvement. One day, I'll need new measures of caregiving accomplishment. For instance, I'd like for her to have talk therapy weekly. Her psychiatrist, Dr. Carlson, sees Molly every few months, primarily to manage her medications. But with Molly, changes happen more than every six weeks and may be about her mood not her medicine. A psychotherapist who Molly was comfortable sharing her feelings with could provide rapid response, and might be able to guide her to feel less anger and more contentment.

Mom is led by her motherly instincts and her conscience. Sara says Mom can still see Molly as the pretty little girl with a ponytail. I realize that Mom's view from the past is valuable for her. She brings a lifetime of smart priorities and sharpened skills to her caregiving—from succeeding as an executive, to surviving divorces and cancers, to raising the four of us.

Today, lessons about Molly come from hard times, happy events, urgent problems, and everyday adventures. We learn, she learns, and then we do it all over again. Every episode is similar and unique—this is brain injury.

The ordeals of Molly's relationships are cases in point. Molly's vulnerability with someone like Perry and lack of anger control with Dave revealed her impaired perception and lack of self-awareness in ways we could not have imagined. These incidents became demonstrations of our family's ongoing high-wire act with Molly. The tight rope we walk is to allow Molly independence, freedom of choice, stimulating activities, friendships, and decision making as much as possible. But we also hold an unobtrusive but vigilant shield of protection—watching over her physical and mental health, guarding her home and belongings, taking care of her finances, and warding off anyone who may try to take advantage of her.

And even though Molly usually realizes the necessity of our interventions, we strive not to be heavy-handed. We don't like to remind her of her brain injury either. I appreciate how tricky it is for Molly, the former athlete, to cope with her physical limitations. And when she's aware of it, for Molly to accept her loss of mental capacity rightly causes her a lot of frustration, especially since she was always praised for her smarts. I understand why she doesn't like to think of herself as diminished in any way.

And even so, she gets around and does her life. Some of her former skills are compensated for, some have come back to a degree, and others will never be regained. She may deliver an incorrect answer to a visitor at the zoo or be sharp-tongued with her physical therapist, but most of the time, she behaves well enough to blend in.

In part, her ability to manage so well in the outside world makes her harsh behavior to her family members feel even worse. The upside is she can be very loving, especially around her family. Such irony. More elusive for Molly is an ability to express thoughtful or deeply felt emotions. I know it's a frontal lobe deficit but it feels like a gaping hole to me.

I want Molly to interact with me and her other family members because I want her to feel her presence in our family. I know she has authentic emotions even if she rarely articulates them. These days, her softness has become hesitant, her firmness has become harshness; she's sweet, not deep. Mom is really good at sensing what Molly might be feeling and I'm paying attention and learning the cues. I want to be able to give Molly the emotional support she needs to feel happy and have some inner peace.

As a family, we had the best intentions with Molly. Each of us sacrificed in unique ways to help her. But we didn't know anything. We were ill prepared to deal with brain-injured Molly; she'd changed so profoundly. But we learned to sail amidst the storms of our lives. We were determined and steadfast; we kept our goal in mind—a normal life—and managed to muck our way through.

And it makes my skin crawl, even now, to know that I wondered if I would have been so determined to help Molly live if I'd known what lay ahead for her and for me and my family, especially Mom. How impossibly hard will it be for Molly? How much stress and difficulty are we prepared to deal with? Is this fair to Mom? I'd wanted the same person I knew and loved to return, not this demanding look-alike. How could I have been so selfish and afraid?

In ignorance, humanity took over.

We were dealing with a life and we chose to do everything we could to save it. It's what most humans do. It's our first instinct, the natural thing—save a life. Whether it's a turtle crossing the road, a baby bird that falls from the nest, or a person with a brain injury that sends her hurtling into to an unfamiliar life. What's natural is to put the bird back in the nest and hope it will one day sing. It was a collective family gut reaction to go to extremes, whatever we could possibly do, to save Molly's life, and she gave us reasons; from her past, to hope, and in the moment, to believe.

And so, human instinct and love of family prevailed, took control of terrifying soul-stirring decisions, and guided us well. Saving a life was the right choice and still is. And now, our family has new meaning, a particular knowledge gained through adversity.

Mom has had the most vital role in giving Molly the best life possible—again. She provides so much more than comfort and safety. She enhances Molly's life with opportunities—to be with her family, take classes and go to school, travel, and live her own life. Mom helps her set goals and develop her ideas, which support Molly's sense of herself. It's hard work and I'm aware that what Mom does is fraught with the dilemma of balancing Molly's need for caregiving with her autonomy.

And yet, at the point when Mom had been independent from her children for many years and was nearing the time to enjoy her retirement, she found herself caring for her eldest daughter again, who is more like a teenager than an adult. Mom has admitted that going in reverse to take care of a child again is relentless, and at times, overwhelming.

"Your Mom did the most noble thing. To give up her career and much of her life to become a mother again and to be able to do it so well," Dr. Lo observed. "With all the HBO and the retraining she was able to get for Molly, she's helped her build a new life. Your mom told me once, 'I have the skills. I did it once and I can do it again.' And she has. It's incredible."

Molly underestimates her shortcomings and rarely, if ever, admits she's made a mistake. It probably feels like a weakness to her. I think Molly will always struggle between needing assistance and wanting independence, especially when I become her primary caregiver. I'm one of Molly's little sisters, not her mother. My caregiving will be different.

Mom and I are closer than ever with our focus on Molly and mine on Mom and Molly together. I look ahead and see my world blended with theirs. And I take to heart the lessons Mom has learned and shares, her gifts to me as I go forward. But I fear I won't be as effective with Molly. I need to find confidence. But, for now, my role is to support Mom and be a friend to Molly. It's my moment on tiptoe.

"You know, Molly has done pretty well," Mom said to reassure me. "She still needs supervision, and that might increase over time, but it's not minute-to-minute. It's not horrendous, but it is constant."

"You are always tuned in to her, Mom, I know you are," I responded.

"Look, I know full well we could have put Molly in an institution and we were encouraged to do that, but I also know if we had, she would not be here in the way she is now," Mom said. "My life would be simpler, but not necessarily better. In fact, I know my life would not be better. I have learned so much. So we keep her in her home and it makes a huge difference in her well-being and in all of our lives."

"I know it's better for all of us that she's as good as she is," I said. "But it starts with you, Mom. Then the rest of her family. And then all the people who help her get along in her world."

"That's right. Our neighbors on this street, our friends at Rotary, Pilates, the hair salon, the gym, her therapists, her doctors," Mom said.

"Don't forget Starbucks!" I added.

"Oh, Molly loves Starbucks," laughed Mom. "She can't do without Starbucks."

"And the truth is, we can't either," I said. "They're *all* part of the village that helps to take care of Molly."

During one of my visits, Molly took me to her local Starbucks and beamed as she introduced me to the barista who sees her almost every day. I told the young woman that I appreciated her taking such good care of my sister and making her coffee just right. The barista handed Molly her frappuccino and told me how much she enjoys seeing Molly's smile. As the barista poured my coffee, I told her I was grateful to her for being part of the network that comes together in little ways for Molly every day.

It does take a village, to put forth the cliché, but honestly, what it really takes, whenever possible, is a family. Brain injury is just so hard, so excruciating, really almost too much for "the village." Of course, the volunteers and paid professionals of "the village" are very important, and for some people with a brain injury, it's all they have. But for Molly to be as good as she is, she needed sustained advocacy and her family had to step up. We were galvanized; to huge effort and some sacrifices. The caregiving is just that consuming and demanding and unending. As I heard once, it requires the constancy of the sea and the patience of an old oak tree.

Molly's daily activities out and about place her in her culture and with people in her community and enable her to feel ordinary. This achievement is a reflection of Mom's ability to provide consistent structure, safety, and emotional support. Molly thrives today because of Mom's care and love.

Molly sometimes expresses gratitude to Mom, but more often Mom will hear it second-hand. Their hair stylist or Pilates instructor will tell Mom that Molly says how much she appreciates everything Mom does for her. Molly will also proudly attach herself to Mom with new acquaintances. She'll say, "I'm Molly. That's my mom; I'm Sally's daughter."

Of course, Mom loves to hear it. "It's like a reward to me, and I know it's genuine," Mom said. "Every now and then, she'll tell me how grateful she is to me for saving her life. I always remind her it was her entire family, Dr. Lo, and HBO that helped to save her life."

Still, it breaks Mom's heart when she sees Molly exhausted and grappling and down on herself. And although Molly is somewhat emotionally flat, Mom believes she feels more than she can express. I think she's right.

"A few days ago, Molly was really sad about something," Mom recalled. "I told her that often times, big disasters become blessings. I said, 'The best part of your injury, Molly, is that I get to spend a lot of time with you. I wish your brain injury didn't ever happen, but you and I have become so close.' And then, with tears in her eyes, Molly said she really misses me when I'm away, even for a day. I felt like I understood what she was really trying to say."

My relationship with Molly begins with respecting a new person in a familiar body. Molly did not come back, a new Molly appeared. Pieces of the old Molly exist in the new Molly. But even now, all these years since her accident, parts of the new Molly are unrecognizable to me. That narrow eye she gives me or the smile that's too squinty. I miss the depth of her imagination and passions, her curiosity and thoughtfulness. My interactions with my big sister are too shallow. I struggle to settle the old and the new Molly.

Mom has said that Molly's sisters got their oldest sister back, but not the one they adored. She is not the Molly I had known for 35 years. And yet, even with brain injury, our DNA, our family history and stories, our values and belief systems, our allegiance as sisters remain at our core.

But she is not my go-to sister and close friend as before, and that leaves part of me hollow. I've come to realize that my adoration of Molly before her brain injury and the priority I made our relationship was more on my part than hers. Now, Molly is a different person and I am learning to love her again even though I never stopped.

My becoming Molly's next caregiver was decided, in part, because of my availability, but also because I offered. Someone needed to be ready for this role and I perceive myself to be closest to Molly, after Mom. I suspect my whole family thinks of me this way. I don't know if Molly does. I've never asked. But it will be my responsibility to take care of her as she and I age. I don't know what form my caregiving will take; I know it will be different than Mom's. But I anticipate increased irritability and dementia with Molly and that her ability to take care of herself will diminish.

It's daunting. Yet, I can't imagine not being with her in the future. This responsibility—it feels like my destiny—stems from my belief that I can make a positive difference in Molly's life. What I can do to help Molly be happy may be limited, but I still need to try.

Mom says she would have done what she's done for Molly for any of her daughters. I feel the same way. I would take care of any of my sisters. Whoever needed me. People everywhere are taking care of a parent, child, sibling—someone in need. I know that I'm a caregiver. It's part of who I am; it always has been. But it isn't all I am.

Molly's CO poisoning was clearly the fundamental turning point for her and a pivot point for her family. One way we measure time now is by pre-brain injury and post-brain injury; the date, place, and what we were doing when we got the news forever emblazoned in our minds. And we each came to realize, each in our own way and time, that pre-brain injury Molly was not returning. Even the victory of her survival—that accomplishment was different from what we started out imagining it would be. I threw my entire being into urging Molly to live and then recoiled at the hardships once she was molding herself into a new life.

We were used to setting our expectations based on the fantastic "Before Molly," and we had to let go of that. The "After Molly" is not the same. She adapted and we had to adjust. Each family member deals with her differently now because each of our relationships with her had a history *and* was dramatically altered post-brain injury. Mom says Molly's brain injury shapes our family. I believe it colors our family; the way painting a room changes the atmosphere, the mood of it.

My memories of Before Molly are not tarnished by the challenges of After Molly. Just two separate lives, two lives connected. These days, I tell Molly that I miss her when I'm not with her. The next truth, which I do not say aloud, is that I also miss the pre-brain injury Molly, with her encouraging big-sister ways. But building our new relationship doesn't mean forgetting the old one. It's taken years of a persistent effort to cobble together a new sisterhood with her.

When I'm with Molly, I sometimes feel unmoored, unsure of what to say or do. When I'm not with her, I sometimes feel at sea; unable to be completely steady, largely because I know the next confounding dilemma about her is right around the corner to throw me off course. I will never know the answers to why Molly's CO poisoning accident and aftermath happened to her, but allowing some uncertainties to exist has battened down some of my turmoil.

So I press on and try to keep gratitude and creativity close at hand. Along the way, I have felt both tangled in and supported by the bonds of my family. I've wanted to shake them off and also, hug them so close. But my family is my place of certainty. We have each other as sources of perspective, humor, sanity checks, know-how, and strength.

Pre-brain injury Molly, at age 31, wrote in an autobiography exercise, "My heart and happiness, I realize now, have always rested with my family." I believe she likely feels the same way now, but she does not say so.

During a visit, I told Molly that I was always trying to learn more about her. "Do you remember yourself the way you were before your brain injury happened?" I asked.

"Sometimes. Some stuff. But not really that much," she said.

"I know you remember a lot—like when you were a kid, and later on, your work and your friends—and a lot about Walt," I said. "Your long-term memory is pretty good, Molly."

"I don't know, Smith. Sometimes I feel like a stranger to myself. That sucks. That's frustrating," she said, ringing with clarity.

"Yeah," I said, catching my breath. "That's got to be really hard."

"But I'm Molly," she said, and looked me sharp in the eye. "I'm still Molly."

When I shared this exchange with Dr. Lo, he offered sage perspective. "Molly did suffer some irreversible brain damage. You accept some loss," he said. "But there's also the second chance of enjoying her presence for some more years, even as a different personality. You can never appreciate her without remembering that she was almost lost, even though it's frustrating you did not get her back 100 percent. There is an essence of her. You can appreciate her even more knowing what she's come through."

I realized Molly knows the differences between the two eras of her life, but sees herself not before and after, but as a continuum. That's my epiphany. Molly was not recovered, she was transformed.

Molly proclaimed that all she wanted was "a normal life" about two weeks after she was declared clinically dead from CO poisoning. It was her early desire and our enduring inspiration.

Rehabilitation of her brain was required to reestablish emotional and thought processes as much as possible. The improvements and changes are lifelong developments. And when healing the mind, a new character emerges. It occurs to me to wonder if everyone should endeavor to live this way a little bit—with flexible results of who we are or might become.

The neuroplasticity of the brain, its capacity to create new pathways and grow and regenerate brain cells, is a vital part of rehab for anyone with a brain injury. Perhaps it should also be a part of everyday life for the rest of us.

Scientists have discovered that basic, simple exercise, like a daily walk, strengthens and revitalizes our bodies *and* our brains. Exercise creates new neurons and a greater capacity to learn. It boosts memory and recall and sharpens thinking and processing. Exercise makes a brain better.

Oliver Sacks, the neuroscientist and author, also suggests that every time we practice an old skill or even better, learn a new one, the brain's neural connections are strengthened and expanded. So if we stimulate and push our brains to grow—by studying a new language, learning to ballroom dance, play an instrument, even thinking of an old problem in a new way—it will challenge the brain, keeping it active, engaged, and adaptable. It may be that my helping to take care of Molly will mean better brain health for us both.

Mom reminded me recently that when the neurologist at Loma Linda told her that hope was gone, and suggested we pull the plug on Molly, "We wouldn't agree to do it because Molly was giving us too much, so much hope coming from her."

"Maybe, on some days, she's still giving a lot to us," I replied.

Mom nodded in agreement. "I think that's true."

Mom hopes that Molly will learn to relate to people better. "To love children as much as she loves cats; to have greater tolerance, better control, more graciousness," she said. "I hope for her to have good health, and, especially, to have a gentle, thoughtful life, full of love and caring."

Then, as she recognized she'd laid out a very tall order, Mom said, "I have learned, too, from Molly. I have learned patience."

My hope is that with a little encouragement, Molly might be willing to try some new ways to improve her abilities. I'd love for her to pull up her innate zeal and feel engaged in a goal; she's always responded so well to a challenge.

I just don't want her to get caught up in her losses—what she can't do anymore. I hope I can figure out what I can do to help her go forward and have a sense of purpose and feel successful. This is *my* purpose with her. Some healing is a function of the heart.

I read Joan Didion's, *Year of Magical Thinking*, a few years ago and connected deeply to her struggle with mourning and grief over the sudden death of her husband. I found myself in her passages, but other times standing very far apart.

Didion wrote about how grief just happened, but that mourning, the act of dealing with grief, required attention and had no time limit.

For me, my mourning is unfinished because my loss is incomplete; Molly is gone and she's still here. I needed to mourn, but there wasn't a clear way to do so, or a reason to. For here she is. And isn't.

Molly's situation removed all the standard rituals of mourning and silenced all expressions of sympathy and loss. I didn't put off or avoid grief. It came in waves; sometimes I could barely hold my head up. I had to convince myself to breathe, dragging air in across my teeth. I flailed against my sorrow to find buoyancy. And still, my grief is left floating, nearby, unsettled.

So, now I make a choice—a conscious, deliberate choice. I simultaneously mourn the loss of Molly while celebrating the life of Molly today. I can't substitute the new Molly for the old one. Molly did not recover. I'm not comfortable with that word and I don't use it for her. This is not a story of recovery.

For Molly, I like the word rehabilitate. Webster's Dictionary says: *to re-enable, to restore to good health or useful life.* I especially like the "useful life" part. It allows for differentness and intention.

A little more than a year after Molly's accident, she and Mom took a writing class together. In one paper, Molly wrote that being in a coma was *"a treacherous realm,"* and that for her family it must have been, *"a harrowing experience to witness a loved one is such a locked-in state, and the family left to wonder if the patient would ever recover to be the person she was before."*

The answer for me is that Molly's body recovered and she is not the same person she was before. When her presence was lost, and then recreated, it changed Molly. And me. Both of us. All of us.

I hear reports on NPR and read in newspapers about someone wanting "a normal life again" after a shooting in their neighborhood, or a town trying "to return to normal" after being flattened by a tornado. People who've been through traumatic events say they want "to recover, and go on like before;" they talk about "getting back to normal." These phrases make me wince, even though I empathize with wanting the familiarity and comfort of normal.

I had to throw out the almost quaint notion of Molly making a "complete recovery," her life "back to normal." I stopped looking for that stuff. No one returned to the "normal life" we had before Molly's CO poisoning. Molly's brain injury and our family's collective brain injury are wounds that never totally heal. You learn to live with them.

Today, Molly's presence with me and mine with her are reinvented. I look for new ways for us to connect. Sometimes it's kind of lonely, even when I'm with her. But I try to set aside the person I once knew and discover the person here now.

The bizarre dichotomy of still loving and mourning the old Molly, and trying to love just as much the similar, but vastly different new Molly is a struggle I expect will stay with me. Each problem, frustration, or sadness with Molly causes grieving for the losses all over again. It stays fresh. It's not wrapped up neatly. No tidy edges in this kind of grief. This grief is a big undone, messy pile in the corner of my eye, burrowing in my brain, rattling in my heart.

It's like litter on side of road. You don't want it there, you didn't put it there. You make attempts to clean up, but there's always more, and you always see it. You sort of get used to it, but it never fails to hurt. You still wish it wasn't there.

I read that closure is a state of grace many who suffer the loss of a loved one seek. I was once looking for closure; my friends expected that for me, too. But I learned not to yearn for closure. I live without that grace because Molly died and lived. Acceptance is my state of grace.

So, this is an unfinished story. It has the bristly discomfort of troubling events and thorny sentiments, strewn over an inherently complex terrain of brain science and bewildering behavior. I've felt remorse and utter joy in an instant. And there's Molly, my big sister who's so hard to comprehend. But, as Dr. Lo said, "she is here and that is miracle enough." And he's right.

"I have not had other patients like her, nobody else like her," Dr. Lo told me. "There was one lady, she was pretty healthy, too, and she had almost as much CO poisoning. She was trying to commit suicide. I did HBO like I did with Molly, but she died. She didn't have a will to live. Molly was amazing."

Molly fought for her life, and we fought for her life, too. "And we got a life," Mom said, "an imperfect life, but it's her life. She's a new person. And besides, what's a perfect life? Her life was never perfect anymore than mine has been. I have less judgment about it."

Molly was not restored to a normal life, but instead, she claimed what's popular to call a "new normal" life. This realm of a new normal Molly was beyond me for many years. It did not come naturally. It filled me with unease. Finding my rhythm with it was like staggering blindfolded. Finally, like an unseen slap in the face, I snapped to attention. Hey! This life is real. See it. Live it. It took convincing myself and determined practice. I faked it for a while, very clunky and awkward, but it slowly emerged and it's almost automatic now. I had to move past my anger. I'd believed in pure outcomes. I felt betrayed. I have to learn again and again that life is not fair.

And today, even as Molly declines in some areas, I am so grateful for Molly's resilient, imperfect, good life; she's alive to think, have ideas, feel sad or angry, and feel love. Our new normal is created by finding aspects of life that are meaningful. This is my rehab, my evolution. I know a bit about brain injury and its range of disability. I think I'm pretty good with Molly. I hope I'm becoming more compassionate.

If the loss of a mind is a loss of that self, then a new mind is a new self. Molly's new self is the one she's created, with a lot of help from Mom. And it's normal for her. More and more I don't think of Molly as she was before. I remember that person, but I perceive her as she is now.

When Sara told me years ago that she'd begun to dream in Spanish, I knew that her Spanish was no longer a "second" language. Sara and Spanish were fully integrated. More than a decade after Molly's CO poisoning accident, I first dreamed of Molly as brain injured, not as a comparison to her before or a nightmare (which I'd dreamed many times), but as an everyday reality.

In my dream, I'm visiting Denver and I'm in a liquor store on a Sunday morning buying a bottle of red wine. I'm dressed casually, but Molly walks in wearing a dressy outfit. I comment that we're both up early for a Sunday. Molly says with a big smile, "Yes, of course, we go to church early on Sunday mornings in Denver. We're very efficient." I pay for the wine and the store clerk slides a plate of cookies across the counter and offers them to us. Molly says, a bit loudly, "Look, Smith, he is also being efficient according to protocol and he is treating you exquisitely!" The clerk half-smiles and looks at me and my "funny" sister with a bit of confusion. I say, "Why, yes, he is! Very exquisitely. You're right, Smith." Molly takes a cookie and I say thanks.

There was no hiding, no explanations, everything was fine. It is how I know Molly now, even in a dream. The new normal.

I'm not wondering each morning what miseries await. There are bad days, good days, and better days. That is normal life. And now I know that normal is precarious. I live with that truth and I redefine normal almost every day.

A few years ago in my writing group, our exercise was to create a six-word memoir for that moment of our life. I wrote: *Getting worse, getting better, going on.* From that declared hope comes all kinds of possibilities, learning and growing, a continuum. It's one way Molly teaches me how to live.

And to be with Molly, to be present, is the best way I have to bond with her. To love her for who she is, now, and still.

Appendix:
A Primer on
Carbon Monoxide Poisoning

Carbon monoxide exposure sends an estimated 15,000 Americans to emergency departments each year, and causes 500 unintentional deaths, and this is likely an undercount. CO poisoning remains the leading cause of poisoning deaths in the U.S.

CO emissions are produced whenever a fuel, such as propane or natural gas, oil, kerosene, coal, wood, or charcoal, is burned. CO levels can become hazardous when the fuel-burning source is not functioning correctly, used correctly, or vented correctly.

At low levels of exposure, CO causes symptoms such as headache, dizziness, fatigue, and nausea, which might at first be mistaken for the flu. But beware. If symptoms get worse (confusion, drowsiness, chest pains, fast breathing or heart beats, vision problems) or more than one person in the same area has similar symptoms, get outside in fresh air immediately and get medical attention. Don't ignore the symptoms and go to bed. Continued exposure to CO can cause loss of consciousness and death.

Recent studies show that a large proportion of the public remains unaware of the risk of CO poisoning. Most people I've spoken with are astonished at the number of potential sources of CO. Gas- or oil fired furnaces and hot water heaters; gas stoves, kitchen ranges, and clothes dryers; wood stoves and fireplaces; fuel-burning generators, space heaters, lanterns, and barbecue grills; and internal combustion engines—cars, trucks, powerboats, ATVs, snow mobiles, snow blowers, lawn mowers, portable generators; and gas-powered garden and construction tools. Electrical appliances are generally safe, unless through careless or faulty wiring, they start a fire.

The critical point is that CO poisoning is almost entirely preventable. The first line of defense against CO is to make sure that all fuel-burning appliances are correctly installed, operated properly, and cleaned and maintained regularly. Annually, before cold weather sets in, home heating systems, including chimneys and flues, should be inspected and cleaned by a qualified technician. Make sure vents aren't blocked or leaking. All appliances that burn fuel and their mechanical and electrical components and thermostat controls should be checked, too. Never run internal combustion engines or fuel-burning space heaters, generators, or barbecue grills indoors or in enclosed areas. And still, appliances deteriorate with time and problems can occur anytime, anywhere, and without your knowledge.

The surest safety measure is to put a CO detector in your home and take one with you when you travel. Unlike odorized propane, smoke, or fire, you cannot smell, see, or taste CO, and it doesn't cause skin or eye irritation. Without the aid of a CO detector, it's nearly impossible to know if CO is present at harmful levels until you start to feel sick or worse. CO detectors measure CO in the air and sound an alarm before dangerous levels of CO accumulate. In small amounts, CO can hurt you slowly over time; at higher amounts it can have deadly effects within hours or minutes. Some people never experience symptoms, they just go to sleep and never wake up.

Often, people mistakenly think that smoke detectors are also CO detectors. They are not. People need to equip their homes with both smoke detectors and CO detectors. Specialized units that are dual smoke/CO detectors are available.

At a minimum, install a CO detector in or near sleeping areas. Better still, put one on each floor or end of your home. Electric CO detectors can be hardwired or plugged in and have a battery back-up that kicks in if the electricity goes out. I recommend having at least one CO detector that runs solely on battery power. Mine fits nicely on my nightstand and I never take a trip without putting my CO detector in my bag.

Congress mandated smoke detectors in every guest room across the U.S. in 1990. The distressing fact is that only a few states have a law requiring CO detectors in hotels and motels, and not a single state has a law requiring

CO detectors in all guest rooms. So I carry my own. Extra cautious is part of who I am now.

A CO detector costs between $20 and $50 and should usually be replaced every five years or according to the instructions.

Don't think it can't happen to you; a carbon monoxide detector can save lives and beings.

About the Author

Lyrysa Smith is a nonfiction writer because she has always written down her observations and feelings in an effort to understand them. She writes to explore, discover, accept all truths, and share what she's learning with the hope of helping others. She greatly admires artists and fiction writers because of their fantastic imaginations. Her next book will be another true life story.

To challenge and train her brain, she enjoys exercising, and reads about human health, music, film, the environment, national and world news, and cats, and studies nature, birds, and dance, and plans to learn to speak Spanish well.

http://www.lyrysasmith.com

Made in the USA
Charleston, SC
19 June 2014